The complete paintings of

Canaletto

Introduction by **David Bindman**

Notes and catalogue by **Lionello Puppi**

Harry N. Abrams, Inc. *Publishers* New York

Classics of the World's Great Art

Editor
Paolo Lecaldano

International Advisory Board
Gian Alberto dell 'Acqua
André Chastel
Douglas Cooper
Lorenz Eitner
Enrique Lafuente Ferrari
Bruno Molajoli
Carlo L. Ragghianti
Xavier de Salas
David Talbot Rice
Jacques Thuillier
Rudolf Wittkower

This series of books is published in Italy by Rizzoli Editore, in France by Flammarion, in the United Kingdom by Weidenfeld and Nicolson, in the United States by Harry N. Abrams, Inc., in Spain by Editorial Noguer and in Switzerland by Kunstkreis

Standard Book Number
8109-5504-0
Library of Congress Catalogue
Card Number 71-95195
©Copyright in Italy by
Rizzoli Editore, 1968
Printed and bound in Italy

Table of contents

David Bindman	Introduction	5
Lionello Puppi	An outline of the artist's critical history	8
	The paintings in colour	15
	List of plates	16
	Bibliography	82
	Outline biography	83
	Catalogue of works	86
Appendix	Other works attributed to Canaletto	123
Indexes	Subjects and titles	124
	Topographical index	125

Photographic sources   Colour plates: Fogg Art Museum, Cambridge (Mass.); Lord Chamberlain's Office, London; Marzari, Milan; Nimatallah, Milan.
Black and white illustrations: Alinari, Florence; Rizzoli Archives, Milan; Art Gallery of Ontario, Toronto; Courtauld Institute of Art, London; Feruzzi, Venice; Gabinetto Fotografico Nazionale, Rome; National Gallery of Art, Washington D.C.; Parke-Bernet Galleries, New York; Philadelphia Museum of Art, Philadelphia, Pa.; Photo Flammarion, Paris.

Introduction

Canaletto was rarely short of enthusiastic patrons, but academicians and serious thinkers about art held him in little esteem in his own time and for at least a century after his death. Sir Joshua Reynolds must have been familiar with Canaletto's work, but did not consider him worthy of mention in the *Discourses to the Royal Academy*, while Ruskin saved some of his bitterest invective for Canaletto, comparing him in imbecility to Dutch animal painters. Only late in the nineteenth century did he become academically respectable, and regarded as worthy of scholarly study. The opprobrium that surrounded his name came from the very qualities that we now prize in him. Canaletto's painstaking precision and sensitivity to the nuances of light were suspect to eighteenth-century connoisseurs, because they were applied to the external appearance of nature rather than its ideal structure. Landscape that incorporated recognisable views or buildings was considered to be merely imitative, and, therefore, could appeal only to the senses and not to the intellectual powers.

It is no coincidence that France, which had the most powerful Academy and the most active debate on matters of taste, should have shown no interest in Canaletto, while England, to the despair of artists who had been trained abroad, provided his most avid patrons. Despite the efforts of many foreign artists and some native ones, England was not to have a regular system of artistic education until the founding of the Royal Academy in 1768. The writings of Shaftesbury and Richardson had earlier been influential in associating the contemplation of "History" painting and the remains of Antiquity with virtue and high-mindedness, but many noblemen who took the Grand Tour were cheerfully unconcerned about the educational purpose of their visit to Italy, and became captivated by the colour and pageantry of Venice.

Venetian painting had, from as early as the fifteenth century, been intimately bound up with the public ceremonies that so dazzled the rest of Europe. The Bellini family had been engaged on large paintings of processions in which the city of Venice was lovingly depicted, while familiar landmarks like the Doge's Palace are often to be seen in the background of paintings by the great Venetian masters of the sixteenth century. In no sense, however, could these masters be called *vedute* painters, and only in the seventeenth century, as the ceremonial became more nostalgic with Venice's economic decline, did the picturesque qualities of Venice and its way of life become a pictorial subject in its own right.

The first fully identifiable painter of *vedute* was the northern artist Joseph Heinz, who was born *c.* 1600. Heinz made a number of paintings of festivals within the familiar setting of the canals, but it was with Luca Carlevaris (1663–1730) that *vedute* painting became a genre in its own right, so that one could talk about a school of *vedute* painters in Venice who were quite distinct in manner from those who recorded other towns. Carlevaris virtually created the conditions that allowed Canaletto to flourish, and the latter's rise was initially at the former's expense. Carlevaris opened up the market to English patrons and, like Canaletto, and Francesco Guardi after him, he offered not only views of the principal landmarks of Venice, *vedute prese da i luoghi* but also *vedute ideate* in the form of purely imaginative landscapes, or, more distinctively, compositions made up of the fanciful juxtaposition of familiar and unfamiliar buildings. It is difficult to be certain of the extent of Carlevaris' influence on Canaletto, but it is clear that Canaletto was regarded as the older painter's principal challenger, and in 1725, it was noted by a commentator that the younger artist had surpassed Carlevaris on his own ground, because of the superior luminosity of his paintings.

Canaletto's early reputation for truth and freshness based on direct observation has not been challenged to this day. In the *Stonebreaker's Yard* (Plate XXIII), a masterpiece of the 1720s, topographical accuracy is tempered by a warm, luminous atmosphere, while the figures are painted with a good-humoured vitality that would not be out of place in a Dutch painting of the previous century. The stonebreaker's yard in the foreground is almost symbolic of the organic relationship between the activity of the figures and the buildings that arise out of it. By the second half of the decade he had been discovered by the English, initially in the person of Owen McSwiney, an impresario of the arts, and later by his friend Joseph Smith, who was to be British consul in Venice.

The relationship between Canaletto and Joseph Smith remains rather shadowy, but it was clearly based on mutual self-interest. English aristocrats had already shown a notable enthusiasm for Canaletto's work, and there is little doubt that Smith was the middleman in a number of major transactions in the 1730s. Despite his erratic personality, Canaletto succeeded admirably in keeping both the supply and the demand at full pitch, but with unfortunate artistic consequences, for there is a notable decline in quality in the later 1730s. The figures are often reduced to calligraphic squiggles, and the buildings seem to owe more to a study of earlier Canalettos than to fresh contemplation. It is likely that at this time he used the *camera ottica* as an aid, but in a strictly limited way, and that he employed a number of assistants, although at present virtually nothing is known of Canaletto's studio organisation. Yet, for all the over-production in the 1730s, and the demand for the most obvious landmarks, the standard was sometimes remarkably high, even through a series of twenty-two paintings for the Duke of Bedford.

In 1740, the War of the Austrian Succession cut down the number of tourists from England and Germany, and possibly under the advice of Joseph Smith, Canaletto began to diversify his production in order to open up new markets for his work by producing more *vedute ideate*. He even painted a series of Roman views, probably derived from his own youthful drawings and engravings of Rome available in Venice rather than from a visit to Rome. Most of the Roman views remained in Joseph Smith's collection, which he eventually sold to George III, and it is possible that their lack of commercial success led Canaletto to seek fresh pastures in England.

He arrived in London in May 1746 amid a certain enthusiasm, but almost immediately the scurrilous suggestion was put about that he was an impostor, partly because of confusion with his own nephew, Bernardo Bellotto, who had adopted the name Canaletto himself, but also because of an initial and not altogether unjustified disappointment with his first English views. Even so, he quickly found important clients, and until about 1750 he was occupied on views of London, and country houses as far afield as Alnwick Castle in Northumberland. His English works are always incisive and often strikingly composed, but he showed little sensitivity to the special atmosphere of London, and some English connoisseurs felt that there were English *vedute* painters who could paint just as well and certainly more cheaply. To some extent, Canaletto's reputation was submerged by the rising tide of chauvinism and the growing resentment, fomented by Hogarth, against the domination of foreign artists. After 1750, his career in England becomes harder to trace, and it is not known exactly when he returned to Venice, although it was probably about 1756.

In Venice, he remained a respected figure, but the English, who had been drawn to Venice by the Palladian revival in the earlier part of the century, were now more likely to see Rome as the culmination of the Grand Tour. They spent their money on dubious antiquities, that conveyed more the aura of learning than view paintings, and they are perhaps commemorated better in portraits by Pompeo Batoni showing them standing against the background of the Colosseum or discussing the merits of the Apollo Belvedere, than they are by their own purchases. Canaletto continued to paint *vedute* either for himself or for a dwindling clientèle. His last works are seldom dated, but scholars have recently become more confident in identifying Canaletto's late syle, which is more likely to be confused with his early work than that of the intervening period. In the two small paintings of *St Mark's Square towards the Basilica from the South-west Corner*, and *from the North-west Corner* (*Catalogue*, 318–9) in the National Gallery, London,

Venice is no longer seen in the unchanging sunlight of the middle period, but in terms of strong light and shade. The calligraphic highlighting of the figures, which appears mannered in the English views, now adds an element of mordant humour, and their realistic gestures contrast with their seemingly arbitrary method of construction.

Canaletto's death in 1768 did not mark the end of *vedute* painting, which flourished well into the nineteenth century, but only the end of the classical phase. Just as Tiepolo brought a lighter and more informal construction to "History" painting in Venice, Francesco Guardi softened Canaletto's ruled edges by a painterly handling that anticipates the freer and more natural landscape of the nineteenth century.

DAVID BINDMAN

An outline of the artist's critical history

Canaletto's favour with critics is witnessed by early expressions of general approval and even, at times during the artist's life, by professions of reverent admiration. These early judgments may be understood to be based on ready perception of his skill in "painting views of Venice" [De Brosses, 1739] and of his "understanding and mastery ... in the art of so perfectly rendering and imitating the real" [Guarienti in Orlandi, 1753]. They are also connected with, and to some extent even influenced by, current tendencies in the art market, especially the Anglo-Saxon, [McSwiney; Vertue; etc.] which was concerned with the painting of views as a faithful representation of particular places, either the goals and stages of the common touring routes, or of familiar spots dear to those wealthy classes which naturally constituted the principal clientèle of the master. But there was, at the same time, a continual movement to redeem Canaletto from his position as a "virtuoso" [Tessin, 1736] in a minor genre, the only excellence of which was to render a given reality with rigorous attention to exact copying – and to exalt his work to the highest levels of originality and painterly grandeur. Burney's words [1771] are the first sign, but Zanetti immediately emphasises the "great art" employed by the master in his choice of even positional scenes and in his "handling of light and shade". At the same time, Lanzi contrasts the judgment of "the common viewers" who are able to distinguish only "nature" in the master's works, with that of the experts who perceive "art therein". From this time, too, there was a continual struggle to explain in useful terms Canaletto's employment of the *camera ottica* and his ability to transform its data into expressive and original features. The purist rigours of neo-classical culture did not halt Canaletto's fortunes although it tended to underline, and at the same time deplore, his irregularity, which payed less than dutiful respect to the holy "laws of perspective" in the organisation of images [Ticozzi, 1818]. If anything, it was the romantic movement – on historical grounds that contested too great a brilliance of illumination, of a kind that must have been noted as vividly realised in the best views of Canaletto – that openly revealed disagreement, and found an aggressively resolute leader in Ruskin [1843]. On the other hand, we know that Turner never concealed his admiration for the Venetian master whom Whistler did not hesitate to compare with Velázquez; while Le Blanc [1854] did not scruple to express his own enchantment, especially in front of certain etchings by Canaletto which were "steeped in light". Not even critical reception by the impressionists (we know that Manet was an admirer of Canaletto) which effected a startling reaction in the fortunes of Francesco Guardi, caused a real eclipse of Canaletto's favour. Damerini's attempt [1912] to relegate him did not find any followers: it happened, in fact, about the same time as the first tentative monographs appeared, those by A. Moureau [1894] and O. Uzanne [1906]. This century has witnessed an intensification of enquiries, at every level, and a movement to establish a corpus of documents and definite ascriptions which has been enlarged and reinforced by the important reassessment of Canaletto's graphic work, previously rather neglected. There has been a similar movement in studies aimed at the clearest possible scrutiny of the painter's art, at a real understanding of all its richness and difficulties, its historical significance and values. This has been achieved above all by disentangling the processes of composition and its developments in a context which is rich and bursting with stimuli. In this way much light has been thrown on the late work, which was discarded earlier or misunderstood, and much discovered about the early works which are much more important and original in linguistic complexity and stylistic quality than was formerly believed. Considerable attention has also been given to the imaginative character of Canaletto's art, amply revealed by his taste for "ideal" views. His creative processes have also been examined (the use and real function of optic instruments, etc.) with important results. The exhibitions in Toronto (1964) and Venice (1967), although incomplete have revealed the *terminus ad quem* of long intensive criticism. They have also served as a balance sheet from which, thanks to the ready assemblage of an important, evolving complex of works, we can assess Canaletto in his true historical role. He must indeed be counted as one of the most outstanding figures in European art in the eighteenth century.

... Mr Ant. Canale who astounds all in this country who behold his works, which follow the tradition of Carlevaris except that we can see the sun shine within them ...

A. MARCHESINI, Letter to Stefano Conti, July 1725

I hope you will like them [some pictures by Canaletto] when they are finished. Perhaps I am rather too demanding in my choice as out of twenty I have rejected eighteen; I have moreover seen several sent to London for which I should neither find room at home nor give two pistols. He's a covetous, greedy fellow and since he is famous, people are content to pay as much as he demands.

O. MCSWINEY, Letter to John Conduitt, 27 September 1730

A painter of views with whom, in intelligence, taste and truth, few recent and no contemporary artists may be compared.

A. M. ZANETTI, *Descrizione di tutte le pubbliche pitture ...* 1733

...The Venetian School is apparently doing very well, and prices in Italy are high; but there are few or none among all those "virtuosi" who carry conviction. We will review these gentlemen if you wish. 1st Canaletti, Painter of Views, whimsical, intractable, "Baptistise" [sic?] who sells collectors' pictures (since he paints no other kind) at up to 120 pieces and who has engaged himself to paint for four years for an English merchant called Smith. To be discarded.

C. G. TESSIN, Letter to C. Horleman, 16 June 1736

As for Canaletto, his speciality is painting views of Venice: a genre in which he far surpasses any other artist ever. His manner is gay, lively, clear and wonderfully detailed. The English have so spoiled him by offering three times as much for his pictures as he himself asks, that one can no longer afford to buy anything from him ...

CH. DE BROSSES, *Lettres familières ...* 1739

Latter end of May came to London from Venice the Famous Painter of Views Cannalletti ... of Venice. The Multitude of his works done abroad for English Noblemen & Gentlemen has procured him great reputation & his great merrit & excellence in that way, he is much esteemed and no doubt but what Views and works He doth here, will give the same satisfaction ...

G. VERTUE, *Notebooks,* 1746

After studying for a spell with his father, a painter, he went while still a young man, to Rome. There in a few years, by unwearying application to exact drawing and through his wonderful taste in depicting the fine, old buildings, he achieved such understanding and mastery in painting on canvas that few earlier artists and none of our moderns could equal him in the art of so perfectly rendering and imitating the real.

P. GUARIENTI in P. A. ORLANDI, *Abecedario pittorico,* 1753

This building [the Rialto bridge, as it was designed, not executed, by Palladio] rightly praised by its designer, painted and sun-washed by Canaletto's brush, which I myself used – I can hardly describe the wonderful impact it makes, massively reflected in the water below ...You may be sure that there is a goodly number of boats and gondolas, at which Canaletto excels, and everything else that enables the viewer to imagine himself in Venice; and I can tell you that many a Venetian has asked what part of the city it was that he had not yet seen.

F. ALGAROTTI, *Works* (Collection of letters) 1765

We form such romantic ideas of this city from its singular situation about which we read and hear so much that it did not at all answer my expectation as I approached it, particularly after seeing Canaletti's view all of one colour: for I find it like other

famous cities composed of houses of different magnitude, orders of architecture, ages and materials.

CH. BURNEY, *The Present State of Music,* 1771

Canaletto united pictorial liberty and nature with such economy that his true works are obvious to those who have no more than common sense to judge with; while the connoisseur all the more finds great art in them in the choice of sites, the distribution of figures, the handling of light and shade; and in addition, a lucidity and piquant facility of colour and of brushwork, the effects of a calm mind and happy genius.

A. M. ZANETTI, *Della pittura veneziana,* 1771

...became renowned for his skill in painting views and for a long time practised painting of this genre. The finesse of his touch, the truth he gave it and the singularity of his viewpoints made them objects of quest for many foreigners, the English above all, for whom he worked a good deal. He went twice to London where he filled his pockets with guineas. He worked in the style of van Wittel, but I deem him superior.

P. J. MARIETTE, *Abecedario* [before 1774] 1851–3

He loves a grand effect, and in achieving it he retains something of Tiepolo who at times gives him his figures and wherever he uses his brushes, be it buildings, water, clouds or figures, he bestows a vigour which is manifested by drawing objects from their most imposing viewpoint. He employs a certain pictorial licence, although with restraint, and in such a way that the common viewer finds nature, the connoisseur art therein. This he possessed in an outstanding degree.

L. LANZI, *Storia pittorica della Italia* [4th ed.] vol. III, 1818

Nobody could portray objects so vividly, nor with greater effect, although not always within the limits laid down by the laws of perspective.

S. TICOZZI, *Dizionario dei pittori ...* 1818

The mannerism of Canaletto is the most degraded that I know in the whole range of art. Professing the most servile and mindless imitation, it imitates nothing but the blackness of the shadows; it gives no single architectural ornament, however near, so much form as might enable us even to guess its actual one ... neither I nor anyone else should have dared to say a word against him; but he is a little and a bad painter, and so continues everywhere multiplying and magnifying mistakes ...

J. RUSKIN, *Modern Painters,* 1843–60

Canaletti's painterly qualities can be found almost entire in his graceful etchings, steeped in light ...The figures of Canaletti – and this is where we can easily see that he was quite capable himself, without having recourse to the help of Tiepolo – are engraved with incisions that follow their shapes, that follow them, perhaps, too slavishly ...On the other hand, Canaletti is a true exemplar of the way to engrave architecture and to render the movement of waves ...

CH. LE BLANC, *Manuel de l'amateur d'estampes,* 1854

The ascendance of the painting of Francesco Guardi over that of Canaletto and Longhi is not a consequence of fashion but the result of an artistic accident. Guardi, in fact, conquers our spirit just when this spirit of ours already finds Canaletto anti-quated and excessively stiff, Pietro Longhi often infantile rather than innocently limpid... In other words, while sympathy with Canaletto and Longhi diminishes and we discover more than a little inherited love for them and submission to what has been the general consensus for over a century and a half, appreciation of Francesco Guardi increases daily.

G. DAMERINI, *L'arte di Francesco Guardi,* 1912

Canaletto [the engraver] does not look for intense blacks: he is the master of silver greys within which the light expands in wide waves. Everywhere the paper can be seen. Curved down like little waves, the objects seem to sway in rhythm, they move about, receive and reflect the sun, give the very essence of the atmosphere which undulates around the shapes and permits us to conceive them not as dry figures defined by planes, but as volumes hanging in a changeable dimension...Mariette reproaches Canaletto "too uniform and too delicate a touch", and he is unjust.

H. FOCILLON, *Piranesi,* 1918

There is no scene painting in Canaletto: he entirely submerges himself in the country, and there between water, stones and skies, he rediscovers his painting as fresh as things born at that moment. Bound to the tradition of his elders, restricted to "the view", which the enchanted traveller wishes to carry away with him, the basis of his conception indisputably lies in linear perspective ... All around him Venice sparkled too brilliantly: while over and above that exact, linear perspective, not moulded as in scene painting, he distilled and poured out the atmosphere of the lagoon. Here was to flow the triumph of colour. He found in the atmosphere a softening for the edges and a sweeter fusion for the conjunction of too rigid parallel lines, and he found in it the vehicle for light which at times hangs in the air, imprisoned by humid vapours, like a veil drawn between us and our vision of the objects. The life of pale stones, in the light, along the stretches of water, between the salt spray of the sea and the breezes of the lagoon, was the subject of his painting. As refined as an epidermis, as porous and full of puckers as it, silky like it, even in the wrinkles so finely drawn by his brush, his textures clothed like living garments the forms of his preliminary drawings. As for the minute details which perspective does not include in its discipline, a flashing gondola, a beggar on a step, a leaning pole, a limp sail, a crumbling bridge – for these he finds touches of careless brio which may amaze the man who has not noticed how vivid and compact is the smoothing and flattening of his scenes of houses.

L. DAMI, *La pittura italiana del Seicento e Settecento,* 1924

While there was a rebirth in Venice...of the art of landscape, the art of painting views reached one of its highest peaks with Giannantonio Canale, called Canaletto. Learning theatrical painting, he deliberately dedicated himself to a programme which only a mature mind could have conceived. A programme which is both the strength and weakness of his art. He was at once convinced of the worthiness of his plans by the somewhat cold, but financially rewarding example, of Luca Carlevaris. He was encouraged too by that of Giampaolo Pannini – not much warmer but more expert – whom he got to know in Rome, whither he immediately set out. The latter was the greatest

exponent of the style of view painting followed by the Bibbienas and of the paintings of Roberti, Ghisolfi and Locatelli. This painting, which excluded the use of dabs of colour, and had more in common with draughtsmanship than with free art was rendered even more systematic by Canaletto with his use of the *camera oscura* ... Fortunately for him, the painter was also blessed with a rich sense of colour, a taste for the airy and picturesque which in the early works leads us to expect him to accomplish the finest expressions of the picturesque...His "documentary" vision is enlivened by the richness of his touch, splendid contrasts of light and shade, fine variety in his skies, and a wealth of human elements. No trace of the "porcelain" quality until the great Roman view of the Colosseum, and the one of Hampton Court, dated 1743. But after his journeys to England, Canaletto stiffens, becomes increasingly precise and meticulous in line, mechanical in dabs of impasto, which are reduced to spherical balls of pigment, to commas, no longer the stylised, but vital figures of the early paintings...

G. FIOCCO, *La pittura veneziana del Seicento e Settecento,* 1929

A drawer above all, Canaletto found etching a direct means of expression especially suitable to his vision of light and shade; and we might go so far as to assert that in this respect his paintings are inferior to his prints. In fact, the master lines of his architecture remain rather inflexible even under the colour of his paintings, but blend in a perfectly natural manner among the engraved lines of his prints.

A. CALABI, *L'incisione italiana,* 1931

...I prefer to see him not so much as the precursor of modern landscape, the kind copied from nature, but rather as the originator of his own brand of monumental landscape. The plainness of the realist, with which he sets out, is only the begin-ning: but in giving meaning to views and in his choice of view-point and perspective he is a builder, a poet of light who tries to catch all the clarity of sunlight in his distances. Sometimes he smooths his paint like a Dutchman; sometimes he impetuously heaps up layers and even clots of colour, especially in his fore-ground figures. I have heard him bracketed by recent inter-preters, whose exaggeration I admit not without sharing it a little, with the monumental masters of the Italian classical art, like Masaccio...But if most people do not yet know his real form and power, it is because his views are so agreeable that one is distracted from considering his real artistic worth and because too many canvasses pass as his which are not by him at all.

G. FOGOLARI, *Il Settecento italiano,* 1932

Of the Venetian views, some are not free from artificiality in the waves and buildings: but most of them astonish, by the freedom of their brushwork, the well-judged finesse of their tones and the immensity of their atmosphere in which the sun's light is filtered through a silvery haze.

U. OJETTI & L. DAMI, *Atlante di storia dell'arte italiana,* 1933

It seems to me that one can perceive in the paintings as well as in the engravings the bold anticipation of impressionism, not only because of the special attention Canaletto gives to light and shade, but also in the way that the objects – which are viewed from much closer than was customary – react upon each other.

M. PITTALUGA, "Le acqueforti del Canaletto" in *L'Arte,* 1934

...[he] reveals a calm spirit, gently ecstatic, a slight touch of elegiac melancholy: a spirit which yields to things and at the same time places them in strange and, in a manner of speaking, unnatural proximities.

D. VALERI, "La mostra degli incisori del '700", in *Le tre Venezie*, 1941

...he builds by dreaming on the visions of his imagination. Canaletto contemplates the different aspects of reality on which he reposes his calm joy. With him particularly there begins a new manner of seeing, or rather of beholding and rendering. To distinguish Canaletto from the real view painters who were his contemporaries, it has been generally remarked that his essential novelty was in finding an arbitary viewpoint, frequently chosen for personal caprice, unlike the formalised vantage points of perspective taken up by the mannerists. But the real distinction is something quite other than such practical resources: it is his moral state of mind which permits him a lyrical transposition of the subject viewed. It is just the effectiveness of his dealing with the subject which most often maintains him in that state of grace. All the silvery wash of reflections in sky and water are a vehicle by means of which he conveys to us the sweetened, contented state of his mind.

A. DE WITT, *L'incisione italiana*, 1941

We get the strong impression that Venice was really the kindly muse of Canaletto's painting. Here is no molecular atmospheric vibration such as we find in Francesco Guardi by whom the city is transformed into an imaginative, whimsical vision. Instead there is a calm delight in the exact depiction of certain monumental and scenografic views, a delight expressed according to the strictest cannons of perspective, and refreshed with a warm, harmonious, almost sensual limpidity.

R. PALLUCCHINI, *Canaletto e Guardi*, 1941

We must, while considering the etchings of Canaletto, bear in mind the quality and character of his artistic personality. It is the very fullness of feeling for figures allied to calm contemplation of the view points afforded by man and nature which in Canaletto assumes a shape, becomes substantial, defines itself and recreates itself with the same sense of poetry, in the paintings as in the etchings, in colour as in black and white ... They ... make no explosion, they do not, in other words, exhaust themselves in one moment of isolated creation, but are the expression, graphically executed, of the poetic feeling of Canaletto.

R. PALLUCCHINI, *Le acqueforti del Canaletto*, 1945

The great Antonio Canal...set out from the dry Roman "view" in the style of van Wittel and Pannini. Then, to acquire greater truth, he made use of the optic camera, and at once transformed everything, miraculously, into poetry. When one thinks that sixty years earlier the landscapes of Monsù Cussin were in vogue, while in Holland Vermeer was painting his views of Delft, one begins to understand the level to which Canaletto had now raised Venetian painting. That sureness and absolute truth in illumination which he turned on the golden light, with its oblique bars of shade, of the useless afternoons in a Venice which crumbles and cracks like the wrinkles of his marvellous engravings, are filled with the far-sighted sadness of views of the "new world".

R. LONGHI, *Viatico per cinque secoli di pittura veneziana*, 1946

Canaletto's etchings, which as specimens of Venetian art may be compared in quality only with those of G. B. Tiepolo and Piranesi owe their astonishingly new character to the function of light, on which everything in them depends: their effects of volume, space, line and feeling. This function is revealed in various ways, even if the contrary has generally seemed true. Whereas sometimes the light coincides with a wide, golden spaciousness which contains no shadows, at other times it creates chiaroscuri. These, however, are without contrasts since the shadows themselves contain light by the various interplay of planes. At other times still, it exerts a dissolvent power over objects, in a distinctly modern manner. According to the various instances, which as listed here do not amount to much, light becomes the absolute disposer of these compositions, and intensifies their spaciousness sometimes to the point of destroying every veil of the atmosphere. Or else it attenuates the sense of space precisely by means of the atmosphere; or it merely suggests it by evocation. It gives feeling to the objects and, on the other hand, crystallises the movement of figures in the immediacy of a moment, to intensify their feeling. In every instance, moreover, through his patient, careful, highly-skilled work, the contained emotion, equilibrium and moral seriousness of the artist are felt as he applies himself to every detail of the work.

M. PITTALUGA, *Acquafortisti veneziani del Settecento*, 1952

Prevailing taste once again asks for the lively detailed little canvasses of the Venetian view painters, above whom Canaletto rises just as he dominated his own times. The Canaletto view of Venice is a happy vision filled with sunlight, to which he gives expression by combining the play of actual light with an imaginative vitality which is constantly repeated yet always new. This is the secret of all the artist's graphic work, including the engravings and all the many drawings. Of the latter there are examples of every possible kind: from rapid pencil jottings to perspective sketches, from dotted studies to finished drawings, which fetch a very high price. For Canaletto the graphic image is not merely a means towards attaining poetic expression, it is often pure poetic expression itself...In our belief there are few other drawings (apart from those of his contemporary Tiepolo) which can convey such intense fields of brightness and white sunlight.

T. PIGNATTI, *Il quaderno di disegni del Canaletto alle Gallerie di Venezia*, 1958

...Canaletto is more than this. He is not only the poet of the abstract poetry of pictorial material, or of the graphic "gesture" for its own sake. He has sufficient breadth of vision to take as a motif the "photographic" datum (which he then inserts afresh into the vivid play of his imagination), even in those instances where he appears to have been passively influenced by it. On the contrary: if one wanted to separate this very photographic element mentally and give it a separate value, that is, to abstract it – by reversing the procedure followed before – from the quality of the material and from the character of the sign, we would have to recognise the presence in his work of almost all those requisite qualities we look for in a photograph when we wish to consider it "a work of art". Thus we may well believe that Antonio Canal would have been most eloquent with a Leica camera (or cinematograph), for he knew in so far that he was able to relate them eloquently within the economy of his finished work how to make those images speak that he had previously taken bodily from reality or at any rate derived by mechanical means. His choice of subject, time, atmospheric condition, his prepared angle of view, sagacious cutting, incidental use of distance and wide angles, and carefully selective recourse to "photomontage" are sufficient evidence of his real originality: they are the marks and emblems of the artist's imaginative freedom. They are (in his case) the originality of the photographer of genius; of one who builds his argument by using view points and fragments of visible reality like words (or of the director who mounts his own show and assigns different parts to a particular skill according to his own judgment). And this originality is the greater in so far that others had taken only a few steps, and those uncertain, along this path. So he merits the title of innovator even more, since it is only with Canaletto that the paradigm of photographic truth really begins to play a part in the history of painting, by employing every means in its power to come to terms with it.

"Graphic" and "photographic" originality. Although separable as ideas, the language of "the true" and "the sign" appear totally integrated in Canaletto's work, although in a vision which achieved unity only after long periods of alternating phases. And the medium that resolved its contraries and enabled them to become one whole, can be found in the ever fresh vitality of the European tradition of painting; upon the course of which his art acts historically and follows without any visible breaks or interruptions.

Nonetheless, Canaletto also represents the first clear skirmish, the first disturbing premonitory symptom of the instrumental crisis which was openly declared only a century later. In another century of wearing out tradition and perfecting mechanical methods the result of this vision was the separation, in our own day, both materially and visually, of the two terms that had previously only been considered separate in thought. And its final fruit were informalism on the one hand and, on the other, technicolor.

D. GIOSEFFI, *Canaletto. Il quaderno delle Gallerie veneziane e l'impiego della camera ottica*, 1959

... Together with the views of diagonal or telescopic composition, all of them [compositions that are constructed and arranged according to a large, simple compass with a lateral climax, and views looking forward or towards a background] are more or less personal solutions of a historical preoccupation, whether Italian, Venetian (view painting) or Dutch. The presence of a formal discussion of such severity, so rich in inflexion and invention should cause no surprise since the development of "view" themes, such as were founded and elaborated in the Renaissance, is accomplished via an extensive theoretical and artistic argument in Dutch painting of the seventeenth century: in its landscapes, exteriors and interiors. But it is worked out in tones very different from those of the heroic, historical landscape of traditional sixteenth century, Venetian composition, such as that elaborated above all by Annibale Carracci and Poussin. If we do not take this line of culture, on which Canaletto based his work, into consideration we are less able to understand, or run the risk of misunderstanding an essential quality of his art, a much deeper and more complex art than is allowed by those who consider him in terms only of "petit-maître". But whoever looks at his works

with this in mind is bound to realise that an analysis of this aspect which is almost self evident, of Canaletto's art reveals that the artist was fully aware in his manipulation of a composition. That is why the other modes of painting should also be separated out and studied, modes which fulfil different aesthetic requirements and which eventually, when combined with the complexities and suppleness of the preceding ones, give Canaletto a less tranquil, contemplative look than is generally attributed to him. He emerges, in fact, all the more intensely dramatic precisely in consideration of the relatively small number of his themes and views.

C. L. RAGGHIANTI, "Procedimento del Canaletto", in *Sele Arte*, 1959

The wonderful precision and glowing purity of the smallest area or shortest line will remain, in these divine paintings, amongst the greatest achievements of a civilization at the height of its powers. Only a painter who was the rightful heir to all Italian painting could succeed in fusing Italian view painting and the genius of Vermeer in a formal conception of such daring perfection. It will be immediately clear that the simplest interpretation, namely that Canaletto's unique ellipse of light and colour is derived wholly from his incomparable virtuosity in drawing and etching, must be discarded. It is clear that, in the continuous evolution of Canaletto's style towards maturity, drawing and painting are but phases of a single vision: nor may one deduce that his painting derives from the fact that a drawing precedes the corresponding finished painting chronologically. The one was the work of the artist, the other of the formal intention. His particular stenographic ellipse is not the fruit of some drawing formula, of entrusting, that is, the whole burden of the image to the line, but of incontrovertible spatial necessity... according to which light and shade, to determine the stereoscopic view, must continually be advancing or retreating in relation to the object they refer to: they must be detached from it and retreat into the depths whence every modulation of chiaroscuro or form has to be resolved by juxtapositions, echelons, and sharp overlappings. It is in accordance with the degree to which the smallest white dot (a nose, maybe, or a button) emerges more than it ought – so to say – that he succeeds in establishing the spatial nexus of the whole image and the density of an object, without recourse to any intermediate terms. Whoever criticises Canaletto for that has failed to understand the depth of the formal, not imitative, search which is always the guiding power of his painting. Without that special ellipse and refined technique akin to that of marquetry neither Vermeer nor Canaletto would have succeeded in achieving their matchless sense of space which reverberates like the sea. This is no superficial spatiality, it does not claim its existence through the effects of light: rather, it makes use of the light as a defining agent. It is in those points of light which sparkle like chaff that we find proof of the success of his method ... This is anything but naturalism, manual objectivity, or passive optic virtuosity. As for those "ideal views", as he himself called them, which were sometimes mere compositional caprices and sometimes followed Pannini – they have always caused his critics considerable ill-concealed anguish. For they have always wished to see the real Canaletto only in the man who seemed to be copying nature exactly... what a stroke of luck for those who long to see in him the conscientious forerunner of impressionism, ever "en plein air".

C. BRANDI, *Canaletto*, 1960

...After visiting Rome in 1719 and again in 1740 he imitated Pannini and embarked on exercises in perspectives with a rigorous, unyielding perception of light and dense volumes. The series of etchings he made reproduced these qualities even more emphatically. He may be considered the master of traditional topography...Subsequently he turned to artifice, composing ideal views for Algarotti, on the theme of famous monuments. They are extremely cold.

A. CHASTEL, *Il Settecento veneziano nelle arti*, 1960

The usual conception of Canaletto as primarily a painter, and more particularly a topographical painter is, on the whole justified; but it needs some modification to obtain a just view of his position as an artist. Many of his drawings, among them some of his finest, were made as ends in themselves quite independently of his paintings; and as an etcher he was highly accomplished. So, had he never put brush to canvas, he would still have ranked as a considerable master of the graphic arts ....

Opinion concerning his topographic work has varied widely. Once he was regarded as little more than a photographer; today, there is a tendency to accuse him of frequent inaccuracies. In most of his paintings he was astonishingly close to the facts in detail. His concern with these is witnessed by the many diagrammatic drawings he made, notably those in the sketchbook in the Accademia, in which not only are details carefully indicated, but frequent notes are added to identify buildings and to record colour ....

Canaletto did not wholly confine himself to topography. In the inscription on the frontispiece to his etchings, he himself makes a distinction, between *vedute prese da i luoghi* and *vedute ideate*, emphasized by occasional notes on his drawings such as *veduta esatta* and *veduta dal naturale*. In his hands, the *veduta ideata* took two main forms: the imaginary view proper, and the capriccio, a collection of identifiable motives from different buildings or localities, arranged into a composition. The difference between the two is easy to recognize in extreme cases ... Usually, however, imaginary and identifiable elements were mixed ...

W. G. CONSTABLE, *Canaletto*, 1962

In the basic group of drawings, now in Windsor, which Canaletto passed to the Consul Smith and which were mostly done at his commission, although the relevant documents and definitive preliminary sketches are missing, there is a notable difference in the character and extent of finish. This must be related to various moments in the thirty years of an artist's working life. This difference extends from artificial, repeated subjects sketched with pointiliste vigour to others cross-hatched in the usual way with something of the manner of an etching, and yet others with linear contours and watercolour shadows. But this is not all, since Canaletto sometimes practiced faithfully copying the very subject he had already done in the second manner, with different instrumentation in the third. Thus we have cause to reflect on the dominant part which, to him at the time, might have been the stylistic intention.

Perhaps the various styles of Canaletto's drawings ought to be judged each for itself. This might result in a preference, on traditional critical lines, for the rapid sketches which throw off instantaneous impressions and ideas in a few essential strokes. But if we progress however implicitly from this attitude, which may be entirely reasonable, to that of setting aside certain finished drawings just because they are so, we run the risk of inverted academism and of misunderstanding not only Canaletto's historical position, but the results that he achieved in those drawings. It is useless to contrast lyrical impetus with deliberate planning: far more important to recognise just where, even in the most finished drawings there are unmistakable vibrations of poetic feeling, even when all the instruments and calculation that Canaletto used in other pictures and engravings have been employed in them.

V. MOSCHINI, *Canaletto*, 1963

Canaletto's was a warm, calm genius similar to Tiepolo's, whom he also resembles in colour and in the sunlit brightness in which he visualises everything. There is no agony in his pictures: exact, sure, almost mathematical craftsmanship, but one pervaded by a purifying and limpid sensibility, makes it all astonishingly humane. It is precisely in this antithesis, this function of opposites, that the originality of his painting is to be found. This it is that raises him even above many fine Dutch painters, this transcendence of the object in view, the greater feeling and more intense spirituality which inform his depictions of a view, a landscape and even a perspective. Historically his case, if we except that of his nephew Bernardo, is unique. Canaletto is certainly not a typical representative of the rococo: he is not like the Guardis nor does his painting foreshadow the imminent romantic mood. If this... happened occasionally (as in some extraordinarily free caprices) it seems to have resulted from external suggestion and not from the depths of his own spirit. Because of that guise of almost mathematical precision in which he presented himself to his contemporaries, he was as acceptable to the followers of "luministic" painting as to the disciples of the recent neoclassical aesthetic. For us, today, Canaletto is still the greatest master of "real views". Nobody could paint the objective reality of that strange composition of water and stone which is the city of Venice as pictorially as he: nobody could paint its tense, bright sky with greater purity. So it is with the glow of the sun on its red stucco and white marble; thus with the silence of its squares and motionless boats ... And so again is it with the vast skylines over the Thames and the parks of England: a sun, a light, a transparent almost tangible atmosphere, which can never be seen.

E. MARTINI, *La pittura veneziana del Settecento*, 1964

In the act of displaying Venice in its more humble as well as its grandiose aspects, Canaletto discovers a new concept of reality, a poetically optimistic one, free from all the decoration of scene painting and the baroque. And from the artist's new attitude towards reality, one no longer *mitizzata* but in harmony with the contemporary concern for light, there bursts forth a new power of poetic expression. It should not be forgotten that in the middle of the eighteenth century Diderot, in the preface to his Encyclopedia, inclined "to bestow the name of art upon any system of recognition that could be reduced to positive, invariable rules unaffected by caprice or opinion". Canaletto even used the *camera ottica* to determine the vanishing point of a predetermined view. In his hands a canvas with a view became a malleable means of creating spatial relations which vibrate with pictorial counterpoint. As has been noted, in the middle of this spatial dimension, accomplished by stages and gradations of colour, figures and objects acquire a three dimensional look. Shade in Canaletto is always limpidly transparent, it never falls in dots but seems to exist as a break in the exalting effects of light...By his constant interpretation of views Canaletto becomes the poet and historian of Venice. Behind the monuments and localities, reproduced with such visual clairty, we discern the pride of a man who understands the miracle of that city, mistress for so many centuries of her fate. A few decades later Francesco Guardi will not show the same faith: the fall of the Republic is at hand.

R. PALLUCCHINI, *I vedutisti veneziani del Settecento*, 1967

Canaletto may possibly have known either directly or indirectly the great Dutch painters; but he may have begun from van Wittel, without recourse to any more elevated source. The forerunners of Venetian painting are not so much the works of Titian and Savoldo...but the view of Carpaccio, which are so related to the viewer as to give him the illusion that he is right there, in the middle...Thus Canaletto succeeded by degrees in the mastery of light and space; gradually he effected those strokes of colour which give body to the tiny images inserted in his views and shine like bright pearls.

Brandi's recent arguments [1960] on the difference between Venetian painting of the sixteenth century and that of Canaletto are certainly just. But it seems to me that the precedents are in fact to be found further back, even if certain of the artist's achievements are entirely new; and I accept his observations on Canaletto's space just as a guide towards an understanding of those more spectacular works (because more recent); "the actual spatiality of the image is intensified in a third dimension not in relation to the illusion of depth, but as an abrupt thrust forward which is impelled to crash the barrier of our living space, to burst out at us, and not lead us towards the background... Canaletto's perspective does not build a retreating image, but an advancing one. The vanishing point of the horizon does not draw the architectural shapes and landscapes, to swallow them up in the haze of distance, it rather makes them emerge from the indistinct towards the spectator." [id.]

In this way, by continually seeking out and reviewing the truth of Canaletto, we exalt and exploit his poetry. In his much discussed English period he reached the highest attainment of his aspirations, his most genuine triumphs. Here we should state that Canaletto was, in his own way, a classical artist (I do not mean neo-classical): because that detachment and contemplation which he achieved after going through the various well-known formative phases testify to his desire to reduce reality, in a manner of speaking, to its essentials; to transform it, in other words, from a phenomenon of the moment into an everlasting and changeless event of consciousness.

P. ZAMPETTI, *I vedutisti veneziani del Settecento*, 1967

The paintings in colour

List of plates

CLASSICAL RUINS: A
CAPRICCIO [15]
PLATE I
Whole
PLATE II
Detail, right

THE GRAND CANAL FROM
CAMPO SAN VIO NEAR THE
RIALTO BRIDGE [13]
PLATE III
Whole
PLATE IV
Details: A and B, gondolas, left
centre; C and D, the boat in the
centre foreground

RIO DEI MENDICANTI [14A]
PLATE V
Whole
PLATE VI
Detail, right

CHURCH OF SANTI GIOVANNI
E PAOLO WITH THE SCUOLA
DI SAN MARCO [18]
PLATE VII
Whole
PLATE VIII
Detail of the canal, left

CAMPO SAN GIACOMETTO
[62]
PLATE IX
Whole
PLATE X
Detail of the house, left

THE PIAZZETTA TOWARDS
THE TORRE DELL'OROLOGIO
[52]
PLATE XI
Whole

THE OLD CUSTOMS HOUSE
AND THE GIUDECCA CANAL
[37]
PLATES XII-XIII
Whole
PLATE XIV
Detail of foreground, right

THE HARBOUR OF ST MARK'S
AND THE ISLAND OF SAN
GIORGIO FROM THE
PIAZZETTA [34A]
PLATE XV
Whole

CUSTOMS HOUSE POINT [38]
PLATE XVI
Whole

THE IMPERIAL AMBASSADOR
BEING RECEIVED AT THE
DOGE'S PALACE [61]
PLATE XVII
Whole
PLATE XVIII
Detail, centre
PLATE XIX
Detail, extreme right, below

THE DOLO LOCKS [60A]
PLATES XX-XXI
Whole

THE RIVA DEGLI SCHIAVONI
TOWARDS ST MARK'S [39A]
PLATE XXII
Whole

THE CHURCH AND SCHOOL OF
THE CARITÀ FROM THE
MARBLE WORKSHOP OF SAN
VITALE (The Stonebreaker's
Yard) [33]
PLATE XXIII
Whole
PLATE XXIV
Detail, centre left
PLATE XXV
Detail, centre right

THE QUAY AND THE RIVA
DEGLI SCHIAVONI FROM THE
HARBOUR OF ST MARK'S [35]
PLATE XXVI
Whole

THE ENTRANCE TO THE
GRAND CANAL WITH THE
CUSTOMS HOUSE AND THE
CHURCH OF THE SALUTE
[70B]
PLATE XXVII
Whole

THE BUCINTORO RETURNING
TO THE QUAY ON ASCENSION
DAY [67B]
PLATES XXVIII-XXIX
Whole
PLATE XXX
Detail, centre foreground

THE HARBOUR OF ST MARK'S
WITH THE CUSTOMS HOUSE
FROM THE GIUDECCA
POINT [36A]
PLATE XXXI
Whole
PLATE XXXII
Detail, centre foreground

THE HARBOUR OF ST MARK'S
TOWARDS THE EAST [161A]
PLATE XXXIII
Whole
PLATE XXXIV
Detail, below centre

THE ARSENAL BRIDGE [100]
PLATE XXXV
Whole

CAMPO SANTA MARIA
FORMOSA [101 A]
PLATES XXXVI-XXXVII
Whole

THE GRAND CANAL FROM
PALAZZO BEMBO TO
PALAZZO VENDRAMIN
CALERGI [97]
PLATE XXXVIII
Whole

THE SCUOLA DI SAN ROCCO
[105A]
PLATE XXXIX
Whole
PLATE XL
Detail, above left

THE CHURCH OF SAN NICOLÒ
DI CASTELLO [131]
PLATE XLI
Whole
PLATE XLII
Detail, centre

THE GRAND CANAL FROM
THE RIALTO BRIDGE
TOWARDS CA' FOSCARI [138]
PLATE XLIII
Whole

REGATTA ON THE GRAND
CANAL [68A]
PLATES XLIV-XLV
Whole

ST MARK'S SQUARE
TOWARDS THE BASILICA
[165A]
PLATE XLVI
Whole

THE FONTEGHETTO DELLA
FARINA [162A]
PLATE XLVII
Whole
PLATE XLVIII
Detail, left

CAMPO SANTI APOSTOLI
[128]
PLATE XLIX
Whole
PLATE L
Detail, left, with bridge
PLATE LI
Detail, right

THE THAMES FROM THE
TERRACE OF SOMERSET
HOUSE WITH WESTMINSTER
BRIDGE IN THE BACKGROUND
[286B]
PLATES LII-LIII
Whole

THE DOGE VISITING
THE CHURCH OF SAN ROCCO
[146]
PLATE LIV
Whole

THE QUAY WITH THE LIBRERIA
AND THE SAN TEODORO
COLUMN TOWARDS THE
WEST [144A]
PLATE LV
Whole
PLATE LVI
Detail, right

SOUTH FRONT OF WARWICK
CASTLE [290A]
PLATE LVII
Whole
PLATE LVIII
Detail, right

WESTMINSTER ABBEY WITH
THE PROCESSION OF THE
KNIGHTS OF THE ORDER OF
THE BATH [283]
PLATE LIX
Whole

THE RANELAGH ROTUNDA:
INTERIOR [303A]
PLATES LX-LXI
Whole

THE OLD HORSE GUARDS
FROM ST JAMES'S PARK
[281]
PLATE LXII
Detail, right

A COLONNADE AND A
COURTYARD: A CAPRICCIO
[355A]
PLATE LXIII
Whole

THE SCALA DEI GIGANTI IN
THE DOGE'S PALACE [323A]
PLATE LXIV
Whole

(JACKET ILLUSTRATION)
Detail of *The Bucintoro Returning to
the Quay on Ascension Day.*

*In the captions to the plates the actual
width of the original or of the section
of the work illustrated is given in
in centimetres.*

PLATE I   CLASSICAL RUINS: A CAPRICCIO Milan, Private collection
Whole (323 cm.)

PLATE II   CLASSICAL RUINS: A CAPRICCIO Milan, Private collection
Detail (117 cm.)

PLATE III   THE GRAND CANAL FROM CAMPO SAN VIO NEAR THE RIALTO BRIDGE   Milan, Mario Crespi Collection
Whole (207 cm.)

PLATE IV   THE GRAND CANAL FROM CAMPO SAN VIO NEAR THE RIALTO BRIDGE   Milan, Mario Crespi Collection
Details (12.5 cm. each)

PLATE V   RIO DEI MENDICANTI Milan, Mario Crespi Collection
Whole (200 cm.)

PLATE VI   RIO DEI MENDICANTI Milan, Mario Crespi Collection
Detail (70 cm.)

PLATE VII   CHURCH OF SANTI GIOVANNI E PAOLO WITH THE SCUOLA DI SAN MARCO Dresden, Gemäldegalerie
Whole (165 cm.)

PLATE VIII   CHURCH OF SANTI GIOVANNI E PAOLO WITH THE SCUOLA DI SAN MARCO Dresden, Gemäldegalerie
Detail (70 cm.)

PLATE IX   CAMPO SAN GIACOMETTO Dresden, Gemäldegalerie
Whole (117 cm.)

PLATE X CAMPO SAN GIACOMETTO Dresden, Gemäldegalerie
Detail (actual size)

PLATE XI THE PIAZZETTA TOWARDS THE TORRE DELL'OROLOGIO Windsor Castle, Royal Collections
Whole (129.5 cm.)

THE OLD CUSTOMS HOUSE AND THE GIUDECCA CANAL   Milan, Mario Crespi Collection
Whole (61 cm.)

PLATE XIV   THE OLD CUSTOMS HOUSE AND THE GIUDECCA CANAL   Milan, Mario Crespi Collection
Detail (actual size)

\.ATE XV   THE HARBOUR OF ST MARK'S AND THE ISLAND OF SAN GIORGIO FROM THE PIAZZETTA   Milan, Mario Crespi Collection
Whole (63 cm.)

PLATE XVI CUSTOMS HOUSE POINT Vienna, Kunsthistorisches Museum
Whole (62.5 cm.)

PLATE XVII THE IMPERIAL AMBASSADOR BEING RECEIVED AT THE DOGE'S PALACE Milan, Aldo Crespi Collection
Whole (265 cm.)

PLATE XVIII   THE IMPERIAL AMBASSADOR BEING RECEIVED AT THE DOGE'S PALACE   Milan, Aldo Crespi Collection
Detail (55 cm.)

PLATE XIX   THE IMPERIAL AMBASSADOR BEING RECEIVED AT THE DOGE'S PALACE   Milan, Aldo Crespi Collection
Detail (55 cm.)

THE DOLO LOCKS Oxford, Ashmolean Museum
Whole (94.6 cm.)

PLATE XXII   THE RIVA DEGLI SCHIAVONI TOWARDS ST MARK'S Vienna, Kunsthistorisches Museum
Whole (62.5 cm.)

PLATE XXVII THE ENTRANCE TO THE GRAND CANAL WITH THE CUSTOMS HOUSE AND THE CHURCH OF THE SALUTE Houston (Texas), Museum of Fine Arts
Whole (72.5 cm.)

THE BUCINTORO RETURNING TO THE QUAY ON ASCENSION DAY   Milan, Aldo Crespi Collection
Whole (259 cm.)

PLATE XXX   THE BUCINTORO RETURNING TO THE QUAY ON ASCENSION DAY   Milan, Aldo Crespi Collection
Detail (26 cm.)

PLATE XXXI   THE HARBOUR OF ST MARK'S WITH THE CUSTOMS HOUSE FROM THE GIUDECCA POINT   Cardiff, National Museum of Wales
Whole (152.5 cm.)

PLATE XXXVIII   THE GRAND CANAL FROM PALAZZO BEMBO TO PALAZZO VENDRAMIN CALERGI   Woburn Abbey, Duke of Bedford Collection
Whole (80 cm.)

PLATE XXXIX   THE SCUOLA DI SAN ROCCO   Woburn Abbey, Duke of Bedford Collection
Whole (80 cm.)

PLATE XL   THE SCUOLA DI SAN ROCCO Woburn Abbey, Duke of Bedford Collection
Detail (larger than actual size)

PLATE XLI   THE CHURCH OF SAN NICOLÒ DI CASTELLO   Milan, Private collection
Whole (77.5 cm.)

PLATE XLII   THE CHURCH OF SAN NICOLÒ DI CASTELLO   Milan, Private collection
Detail (actual size)

PLATE XLIII   THE GRAND CANAL FROM THE RIALTO BRIDGE TOWARDS CA' FOSCARI   Rome, Galleria Nazionale
Whole (93.9 cm.)

PLATES XLIV-XLV   REGATTA ON THE GRAND CANAL Windsor Castle, Royal Collections
Whole (126 cm.)

PLATE XLVI   ST MARK'S SQUARE TOWARDS THE BASILICA   Cambridge (Massachusetts), Fogg Art Museum
Whole (114.5 cm.)

PLATE XLVII THE FONTEGHETTO DELLA FARINA Venice, Giustiniani Collection
Whole (112 cm.)

PLATE XLVIII   THE FONTEGHETTO DELLA FARINA Venice, Giustiniani Collection
Detail (33 cm.)

PLATE XLIX   CAMPO SANTI APOSTOLI Milan, Private collection
Whole (77.5 cm.)

PLATE L   CAMPO SANTI APOSTOLI Milan, Private collection
Detail (33 cm.)

PLATE LI   CAMPO SANTI APOSTOLI   Milan, Private collection
Detail (33 cm.)

PLATES LII-LIII   THE THAMES FROM THE TERRACE OF SOMERSET HOUSE WITH WESTMINSTER BRIDGE IN THE BACKGROUND   Haddington, Duke of Hamilton and Brandon
Whole (185.5 cm.)

PLATE LIV   THE DOGE VISITING THE CHURCH OF SAN ROCCO London, National Gallery
Whole (199 cm.)

PLATE LV   THE QUAY WITH THE LIBRERIA AND THE SAN TEODORO COLUMN TOWARDS THE WEST   Rome, Albertini Collection
Whole (185.5 cm.)

PLATE LXIII   A COLONNADE AND A COURTYARD: A CAPRICCIO Venice, Gallerie dell'Accademia
Whole (93 cm.)

PLATE LXIV   THE SCALA DEI GIGANTI IN THE DOGE'S PALACE Mexico City, Pagliai Collection
Whole (29 cm.)

The Works

Key to symbols used

So that the essential elements in each work may be immediately apparent, each commentary is headed first by a number (following the most reliable chronological sequence) which is given every time that the work is quoted throughout the book, and then by a series of symbols. These refer to: its execution, that is, to the degree to which it is autograph, its technique, its support, its present whereabouts. The following additional data: whether the work is signed, dated; if its present-day form is complete; if it is a finished work. Of the other two numbers in each heading, the upper numbers refer to the picture's measurements in centimeters (height and width); the lower numbers to its date. When the date itself cannot be given with certainty, and is therefore only approximate, it is followed or preceded by an asterisk, according to whether the uncertainty relates to the period before the date given, the subsequent period, or both. All the information given corresponds to the current opinion of modern art historians; any seriously different opinions and any further clarification is mentioned in the text.

Execution

⊞ Autograph

▨ With assistance

⊞ With collaboration

⊞ With extensive collaboration

⊞ From the workshop

⊞ Generally attributed

⊞ Generally not attributed

▨ Traditionally attributed

▨ Recently attributed

Technique

⊕ Oil

Base

⊕ Panel

⊕ Canvas

⊕ Metal

⊕ Paper or cardboard

Location

⋮ Open to the public

○ Private collection

○ Whereabouts unknown

○ Lost work

Additional data

⊟ Signed work

⊟ Dated work

⊟ Part or fragment

⊟ Unfinished work

Information supplied in the text

Bibliography

There is no complete bibliography of writings on Canaletto, but Moschini's volume (*Canaletto*, Milan, 1954) contains a fairly exhaustive bibliography of 218 entries up to 1953. Particularly useful for later publications are P. Zampetti's exhibition catalogue, *I vedutisti veneziani del Settecento* (Venice, 1967) and the bibliographical appendices to *AV* (for this and other abbreviations, see below) for the years 1953–66. For biographical information, the most valuable works are Constable's (vol. I), listed below, and the works of H. F. Finberg (*WS*. 1920–1 and 1922), T. Ashby and W. G. Constable (*BM*, 1925), F. Haskell (*BM*, 1956), and R. Gallo (*AIV*, 1956–7).

The most important work is the two-volume study by W. G. Constable (*Canaletto*, Oxford, 1962). Important reviews of it include those by M. Levey (*BM*, 1962), F. Haskell (*AB*, 1962), and V. Moschini (*AV*, 1962). The following works that were important when they first appeared have therefore been superseded: R. Mayer (*Die beiden Canaletto*, Dresden, 1878), A. Moureau (*Antonio Canal dit le Canaletto*, Paris, 1906, 2d ed., 1925), G. Ferrari (*I due Canaletto*, Turin, 1914), and M. Stübel (*Canaletto*, Berlin, 1923). The monographs written by F. J. B. Watson (*Canaletto*, London and New York, 1949, 2d ed., 1954) and C. Brandi (*Canaletto*, Milan, 1960) are still important, as are the accounts by R. Pallucchini (*Canaletto*, Milan, 1958;

La pittura veneziana del Settecento, Venice and Rome, 1960), E. Martini (*La pittura veneziana del Settecento*, Venice, 1964) and G. M. Pilo (*Canaletto*, Deventer, 1961, and Rome, 1966).

The fundamental texts on Canaletto's drawing and work in engraving are by D. von Hadeln (*Die Zeichnungen von Antonio Canal genannt Canaletto*, Vienna, 1930), M. Pittaluga (*A*, 1934), R. Pallucchini and G. F. Guarnati (*Le acqueforti del Canaletto*, Venice, 1945), O. Benesch (*Venetian Drawings of the Eighteenth Century in America*, New York 1947), K. T. Parker (*Drawings of Antonio Canaletto at Windsor Castle*, Oxford and London, 1948), V. Moschini (*AV*, 1950; *Canaletto*, Milan, 1963), and T. Pignatti (*Il quaderno di disegni del Canaletto alle Gallerie di Venezia*, Milan, 1958). For information on Canaletto's use of the *camera ottica* and on other questions of technique, see the work by Pignatti mentioned above (1958) and studies by A. Morassi (*BM*, 1955), D. Gioseffi (*Canaletto. Il quaderno delle Gallerie veneziane e l'impiego della camera ottica*, Trieste, 1959), and C. L. Ragghianti (*SA*, 1959). For Canaletto's place in the artistic market of his time, a particularly useful study is that of F. Haskell (*Painters and Patrons*, London, 1963). For Canaletto's position among the *vedutisti* (view painters), see the studies by H. Voss (*RKW*, 1926), F. J. B. Watson (*GM*, 1954), and R. Pallucchini (*AIV*, 1966–7).

Other works of critical or historical

note are those by L. Cust (*BM*, 1913 1914); G. A. Simonson (*AA*, 1914; *BM*, 1922); W. G. Constable (*BM*, 1921, 1923, 1927, and 1954; *OMD* 1929 and 1938; *BMFAB*, 1939 and 1949; *SLV*, 1956; *BWA*, 1963; Catalogue of the Toronto show, Ottawa, Montreal, 1964; *AP*, 1964); T. Borenius (*P*, 1929), P. G. Konody (*AP*, 1929), H. A. Fritzsche (*GK*, 19 and 1930), W. Arslan (*RA*, 1932, A 1948), H. F. Finberg (*BM*, 1938), A Mongan (*OMD*, 1938), G. Fiocco (*KR*, 1940), R. Pallucchini (*P*, 1943 *AV*, 1949), E. P. Richardson (*BDIA* 1943–4), J. L. Allen (*MMAB*, 1946 A. F. Blunt (*AV*, 1948), A. C. Swete (*BM*, 1949), F. J. B. Watson (*BM*, 1950, 1951, and 1955), M. Levey (1953 and 1962), C. L. Ragghianti (*ASNSP*, 1953), J. Hayes (*BM*, 19 Vari (*JRIBA*, 1958–9), E. Skrivanko (*U*, 1960), E. Safarik (*Canaletto's V of London*, London, 1961), H. S. Fra (*BCMA*, 1962), J. Byam Shaw (*AP* 1962), and A. Morassi (*AV*, 1963 a 1966). For information concerning museum, private collection, and exhibition catalogues, see the bibliography by Zampetti (1966). Special mention should be made, in connection, of the catalogues by K. Parker and J. Byam Shaw (*Canalett and Guardi, Catalogue of the Drawi Exhibition*, 1962) and by M. Levey (*National Gallery ... Catalogue*, Lon 1956; *Canaletto. Paintings in the R Collection*, London, 1964).

Abbreviations
A: *L'Arte*
AA: *Art in America*
AB: *The Art Bulletin*
AC: *Acropolis*
AIV: *Atti dell'Instituto veneto di scienze, lettere e arti*
AJ: *The Art Journal*
AP: *Apollo*
ASNSP: *Annali della Scuola normale superiore di Pisa*
AV: *Arte veneta*
AVE: *Archivio veneto*
BA: *Bollettino d'arte*
BCMA: *Bulletin of the Cleveland Museum of Art*
BDIA: *Bulletin of the Detroit Institute of Art*
BJRL: *Bulletin of the John Roland Library*
BM: *The Burlington Magazine*
BMFAB: *Bulletin of the Museum of*

Fine-Arts – Boston
BWA: *Bulletin of the Wadsworth Atheneum*
CA: *Connaissance des Arts*
CMV: *Catalogo della mostra I vedutisti veneziani del Settecento (Venice 1967)*
D: *Dedalo*
DBI: *Dizionario biografico degli italiani (Rome)*
ES: *Enciclopedia dello spettacolo (Rome)*
GK: *Die Graphischen Künste*
GM: *The Geographical Magazine*
IS: *Italian Studies*
JPK: *Jahrbuch der preussischen Kunstsammlungen*
JRIBA: *Journal of the Royal Institute of the British Architects*
KR: *Kunst-Rundschau*
MA: *Magazine of Art (London)*
MF: *Middeldorf Festschrift (London 1966)*

MMAB: *Metropolitan Museum of A Bulletin (New York)*
OMD: *Old Master Drawings*
P: *Pantheon*
RA: *Rivista d'arte*
RKW: *Repertorium für Kunstwissen schaft*
SA: *SeleArte*
SLV: *Scritti di storia dell'arte in ono Lionello Venturi (Rome 1956)*
TBKL: *Allgemeines Lexikon der bildenden Künstler*
U: *Umeni (Prague)*
VE: *Venezia e l'Europa. Atti del Congresso internazionale di storia dell'arte (Venice 1956)*
VP: *Venezia e la Polonia (Rome 19 WS: *The Walpole Society*
ZKW: *Zeitschrift für Kunstwissensc*

Outline biography

1697 28 October Giovanni Antonio Canal was born in Venice. This is confirmed by the certificate of his baptism, which took place two days later in the parish of San Lio: "30 October 1697. Zuane [Giovanni] Antonio son of Sig. Bernardo [son of] Cesare Canal, painter, and of Signora Artemesia, daughter of Sig. Carlo Barbieri, husband and wife, born on the 28th of this month. Godfather Signor Paolo, son of Vendramin Giambattista of this quarter. Godmother Rucchi." This document corrects the slight inexactitude of Mariette, who gave the birth date as 18 October 1697. This date was accepted by all later scholars until Constable [1962] published the baptismal certificate. Constable also used documents to correct the painter's genealogy. There is therefore reason to doubt the assertion of Mariette, who claims to have had the information from the painter himself, and Zanetti, that the Canals were members of the Venetian aristocracy. It seems, rather, that they were an old and quite wealthy Venetian family who owned some buildings. We know that the artist's father, Bernardo, usually referred to as a painter in archive documents, was actually a theatrical painter, i.e. a set designer, and it was for this career, in which the father had acquired a certain reputation [Povoledo, *ES*], that Antonio and another son, Cristoforo, were trained.

1716–18 Antonio and Cristoforo helped their father to design several sets; backdrops for Vivaldi's *Arsilda regina di Ponto* and *L'incoronazione di Dario* and for Chelleri's *Penelope la casta* at the Sant'Angelo Theatre (1716); for Pollarolo's *L'innocenza riconosciuta* and the anonymous *Il vinto trionfante del vincitore*, given in the same theatre; for Porta's *Argippo* at the San Cassiano Theatre (1717); for Pollarolo's *Farnace* and Orlandini's *Antigone*, also at the San Cassiano Theatre (1718) [*Ibid.*]. No graphic or pictorial documents of Antonio's theatrical work have survived, but it is probable that in the work he did for the theatre he

(Left to right) Probably a self-portrait (detail; see Catalogue, *259). – Detail of portrait of Canaletto in an engraving by A. Visentini (after Piazzetta's drawing) for* Prospectus Magni Canalis Venetiarum *(1735).*

Detail of a portrait of Canaletto (ANTONIO CANAL NOB. VEN. ACCAD. DEGLI ARGONAUTI D'ETÀ D'AN. [The age was left blank; as for the assertion of nobility, see **1697**]*). probably imaginary, in an engraving in Moureau's book (1894).*

began to paint "scenes from life," under the dominant influence of Marco Ricci and Carlevaris.

1719 *c.* Antonio went to Rome with his father. According to Zanetti [1771], on the occasion of this journey Antonio "solemnly excommunicated, so he said, the theatre" to give himself over entirely to "painting scenes from life ... especially in the genre of antiquities", and in short – as Orlandi correctly observe [1753] – to paint "with admirable taste ... beautiful old structures". In fact recently discovered documents show that the Canals went to Rome for work connected with the theatre [Constable, 1962], and Antonio and his father seem to have painted the sets for Scarlatti's *Tito Sempronio Greco* and *Turno Aricino*, which were performed at the Capranica Theatre during Carnival, 1720. Nevertheless the young Venetian artist certainly came to maturity in Rome and there decided to give up set design for painting, and view painting in particular. The Roman milieu must have stimulated him a great deal, particularly the work of G. P. Pannini, who had been engaged in decorating the Villa Patrizi since 1718, and secondarily that of the Dutchman van Wittel. He may

also have been slightly influenced by V. Codazzi and the so-called "Bambroccianti". We do not know exactly how long Antonio stayed in Rome, but he was probably there for two years, on the evidence of the extent of his theatrical commissions and the number of "views of the antiquities of Rome" that he painted. The work of this period has been reconstructed by recent scholars (in particular Morassi [*AV*, 1966]). There is a set of drawings in the British Museum and a series of "views" engraved by G. B. Brustolon with the following caption: "Anto. Canal Pinx. Romae".

1720 He seems to have returned to Venice, since his name appeared for the first time among those of the "*Fraglia dei Pittori*", the professional guild of painters. Some scholars argue that he returned only briefly to Venice at this time and that his Roman stay lasted until 1721 or 1722. It is worth noting that on 30 January 1720, Antonio's sister Fiorenza and Lorenzo Bellotto (or Belotto) had a son called Bernardo, who was to follow in the footsteps of his uncle.

1722 8 March Antonio Canal and Cimaroli were employed by McSwiney to paint the

perspectives and landscape in a *capriccio* depicting the tomb of Lord Somers (*Catalogue*, 9), on which Piazzetta also collaborated. This was the first occasion on which Antonio was referred to as Canaletto. Owen McSwiney, an Irishman who had tried his fortune with little success as an actor, author, and manager in England, had been living on the continent since 1711 and dealt in paintings [Haskell, 1966]. About 1722 he was commissioned by Lord March (who became the second Duke of Richmond in 1723) for the ambitious project of having the most famous Italian painters execute a series of paintings of the allegorical funerary monuments of the most illustrious figures of English history between the seventeenth and early eighteenth centuries. (Concerning the fate of this project, see – among others – Constable [*BM*, 1954] and Haskell [1966], as well as the volume *Tombeaux des Princes* [1741], which documents the undertaking and its partial failure.) Canaletto's name figures in a letter that McSwiney sent to his patron, Lord March, at this time, and confirms the fame that the young painter must already have won as a master of perspective and view painting.

1725 By July of this year his superiority over Carlevaris had been explicitly proclaimed [Haskell, *BM*, 1956]. On 2 August Canaletto gave the painter Alessandro Marchesini of Verona, agent for the collector Stefano Conti of Lucca (erroneously believed to be the builder of the new Bucintoro), a receipt for ten sequins paid to him on account for "two pictures of views" which he had agreed to paint for the sum of twenty sequins, after Antonio's initial request for twenty-five sequins. On 25 November the painter announced that the pictures were ready and mentions that the subjects were a *View of the Rialto Bridge* (*Catalogue*, 20) and a *Grand Canal* (19 A). He acknowledged receipt of the final payment and agreed to paint two other pictures at the same price. (He tried to have the price increased to thirty sequins.) By 25 December he was already at work on these pictures and had received an advance of ten sequins.

1726 15 June The two paintings mentioned above, and *Church of Santi Giovanni e Paolo* (*Catalogue*, 22 A) and the *Church of the Carità* (*Catalogue*, 21), were completed and paid for. Canaletto prepared a receipt for the payment and for a

83

"supplementary gift" of ten sequins. From these documents emerges a very important piece of information: that Antonio "always goes to the place and does everything from life". (For detailed information concerning his relations with Conti and Marchesini, see Haskell [*BM*, 1956]).

1725–6 The increasing success of the artist in the marketplace is confirmed by other events. In August 1725 Canaletto showed his works in public and had "astonished everyone", On 25 November 1725, Canaletto was employed by the French Ambassador, Count de Gergi (see *Catalogue*, 31), and on 3 March of the following year he was engaged in painting a *View of Corfu* for "Marshal Salenburg", the well-known Marshal Johann Mathias Schulenburg. Schulenburg had led several important military campaigns for Venice and was now retired with a handsome pension from the Venetian government. He was a fervent collector [Haskell, *BM*, 1956, and 1966, on Schulenburg].

1727 From 28 November until October 1729 there was a correspondence between McSwiney and the Duke of Richmond about four paintings that Canaletto was preparing for the latter, for which the artist was paid a total of eighty-eight sequins [Finberg, *WS*, 1921–2; Constable, 1962]. Already on 8 March 1726, McSwiney had told the Duke about the *capriccio* of the tomb of Lord Somers, commissioned in 1722, and a new one of the tomb of Archbishop Tillotson [Arslan, *RA*, 1932; Watson, *BM*, 1953].

1728 24 July A. M. Zanetti sent Canaletto's receipt for the final payment of a small painting to Niccolò Gaburri [Moschini, 1954].

1729 Canaletto's drawing of the Doge's Palace, now in the collection at Darmstadt [Hadeln, 1930], and of the Piazzetta now in the De Burlet Collection, Basle [*Ibid*; Constable, 1962] one dated this year.

1730 17 July A letter to Samuel Hill from Joseph Smith [Chaloner, *BJRL*, 1940–50] confirms that Canaletto had already been working for Smith for some time. Smith was to play an important role in Canaletto's future, and he became both a patron and an intermediary between Canaletto and the world of collectors, particularly British ones. Smith had settled in Venice at the beginning of the century, where he was engaged (not altogether honestly, according to some sources) as an importer of meat and fish. He became rich enough to be able to retire and devote himself to art, publishing and collecting. His salon in a sumptuous palace near the Church of Santi Apostoli on the Grand Canal was famous. In 1744 he became the British consul to Venice, and he died there in 1770 [Parker, 1948;

Possible portrait of Canaletto, attributed to the Venetian Pietro Longhi. The work was sold at the Parke-Bernet Galleries, New York (13 November 1958; no. 33).

F. Vivian, *BM*, 1962 and 1963; *IS*, 1963]. From the very beginning his relationship with Canaletto was stormy. In the letter mentioned above, Smith complained that more than once he had been obliged on behalf of his friends to bow to the painter's impertinence. This complaint casts some light on Canaletto's rather difficult character and prima donna temperament. This side of his character is also documented by other contemporaries of his (for instance by McSwiney in a letter to J. Conduitt, of 27 September 1730, reprinted here in the *Critical outline*). In addition to doing work directly for Smith, Canaletto was engaged in painting works which Smith could pass on to British collectors. There is a document in the Wicklow family archives which mentions, for the date 22 August 1730, two paintings (see 80 and 81) by Canaletti [*sic*] procured by "Mr Smith", probably for Hugh Howard, who later became the Earl of Wicklow [Constable, 1962]. Meanwhile, since the preceding June, John Conduitt had been wanting Mr S[mith] to procure three paintings by Canaletto for him [Haskell, 1966].

1732 July Canaletto was totally engaged in works for English customers. On a drawing of the Piazzetta now in the Darmstadt collection, he wrote "Year 1732, the month of July for England". He was probably completing a series of views for the Duke of Bedford at this time.

1733 Canaletto was publicly proclaimed to be the best "view painter" of the time (see *Critical outline*).

1734 16 July This is the date on a drawing of the Santa Chiara Canal, now in Windsor Castle (no. 7469), formerly in the J. Smith Collection. Canaletto was still working for Smith at this time. This is confirmed by a letter of Smith's to the Earl of Essex, dated 18 September 1734, [Watson, 1949] about four paintings.

1735 On 15 January Canaletto was a candidate with Domenico Claverin for the post of "prior" of the Venetian painters' *fraglia*, but the members decided not to vote for him because he was a "son at home", (he was probably ineligible because he was not demonstrably independent economically), [Constable, 1962], as he lived with relatives without clear distinction of individual property. In 1735

there appeared an album of fourteen views by Canaletto etched by Antonio Visentini: *Prospectus / Magni Canalis Venetiarum. / addito Certamine Nautico et Nundinis Venetis /. Pictis ab Antonio Canale, / in Aedibus Josephi Smith Angli, / Delineante atque Incidente, / Antonio Visentini, / Anno MDCCXXXV*. These were reproductions of works that Canaletto had painted for the English market. This album which was prepared in the house of Joseph Smith was intended as a kind of illustrated catalogue of the skills of Canaletto, compiled by his agent [Haskell, 1966].

1736 On 16 June, the Swedish Count Charles Gustave Tessin, who had gone to Venice to find a painter for the decoration of the Royal Palace in Stockholm, noted that Canaletto was bound by an exclusive contract to Smith for four years (see *Critical outline*). Tessin also provides us with important information about Canaletto's very high prices. On 22 June there appeared a series of six views of Venice copied from Canaletto and engraved by Louis-Philippe Boitard the Elder [Constable, 1962].

1739 A series was published on 26 June of six views of Venice engraved after Canaletto by Henry Fletcher [Finberg, *BM*, 1932; Watson, *BM*, 1955]. On 24 November President de Brosses, writing from Rome to de Neuilly, mentioned Canaletto as the only important painter living in Venice (see *Critical outline*).

1740 Canaletto may have made another trip to Rome. [Voss, *RKW*, 1926], since there is no documentary evidence that the trip was made, there is disagreement among scholars. It has been suggested that such a trip might instead have been made in 1742.

1741 Canaletto gives this date to an etching [Pallucchini and Guarnati, no. 9] from a series that was to appear three years later (see **1744** below); the drawing for the etching is in the British Museum. This is evidence that at least by this year Canaletto had not only planned but had begun to execute his set of etchings, without interrupting his work for the English market.

1742 A second edition of

Visentini's engravings appeared, with two new sections and twenty-four new plates from views by Canaletto. The title was unchanged from that of the 1735 edition, but with the addition: *Elegantius recusi*, together with the date *MDCCXLII*. These were still not altogether successful reproductions of works done for Smith or his clients. Some Roman views, now in Windsor Castle, were dated that year by Canaletto (see *Catalogue*, 203–7).

1743 24 October This date was given by Canaletto to views of the Piazzetta and of the Doge's Palace, now in Windsor Castle (220, 219).

1744 The album of thirty *Vedute Altre prese da i Luoghi altre ideate* appeared. Drawn and etched by Canaletto, the work was dedicated to J. Smith as a "mark of esteem and devotion", on the occasion of Smith's appointment as British consul to the Republic of Venice. It seems, therefore, that relations between the painter and the patron were still good. Smith was still a controversial figure and he was often sharply criticised. On 18 June 1744 Walpole described Smith in a letter to Horace Mann as "the merchant of Venise". He was to use much stronger language on other occasions. Canaletto signed and dated some views and *capricci* (238–41) this year.

1745 23 April Canaletto wrote the following on a drawing of the Piazzetta, now in Windsor Castle (no. 7426): "23 April 1745, Knight St George's Day, the Campanile of St Mark's has been struck by lightning". So Canaletto must still have been working full stint in Venice at this time.

1746 At the end of May, G. Vertue recorded in his *Notebooks* [*WS*, 1930] the arrival in London of the "famous view painter" Cannalletti [*sic*], who was distinguished in his field and particularly esteemed by the English collectors. From other sources we know that Canaletto arrived in Great Britain with a letter of recommendation from Smith to McSwiney. Smith asked McSwiney to introduce the painter to the Duke of Richmond, who, through McSwiney, had commissioned the funerary *capricci* from Canaletto (see

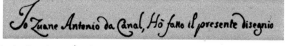

(Above, left to right) Two rare signatures by Canaletto on paintings nos. 203 (note that the D in the year has been omitted, making it read 1242) and 206 in this book.
(Below, left to right) A signature of Canaletto in the series of engravings published in 1744 (see p. 88); and a detail of the inscription he wrote in a 1766 drawing (of the Cantoria of the Basilica of St. Mark's), now in the Kunsthalle, Hamburg.

1722). On 20 May Thomas Hill wrote to the Duke that it would be a great boon to Canaletto if he were allowed to paint the Thames from the dining room window of Whitehall Palace [Finberg, WS, 1920–1]; the view was painted (*Catalogue*, 260). In October Vertue recorded that Canaletto had decided to come to England at the suggestion of "Signor Amiconi" (Jacopo Amigoni, a "History" painter), on his return from a stay in England, and that Canaletto was already at work on some views of the Thames. Vertue suggests that Canaletto had been obliged to make the journey because of the scarcity of tourists in Italy, particularly in Venice, as a result of the War of the Austrian Succession.

1747 Canaletto completed a view (see 273) for Sir Hugh Smithson, later first Duke of Northumberland [Morassi, 1954], for whom the artist did other work, including two splendid views of Westminster Bridge (*Catalogue*, 265–6). It is likely that Canaletto did two other views of this bridge in this year for Prince Lobkowicz – probably an unexpected customer – who wanted to take back some prestigious souvenirs of his London visit [Constable, 1962]. It can be assumed, then, that Canaletto's circle of patrons was growing and that there were an increasing number of invitations to other cities. An invitation to Dresden came, perhaps through Lobkowicz, from the King of Poland and Elector of Saxony. Canaletto declined, and it may have been at his suggestion that the King invited his nephew, Bernardo Bellotto, instead [Mariette, 1851–3].

1749 An entry for June in Vertue's *Notebooks* mentions that Canaletto had already painted pictures of the Badminton countryside for the Duke of Beaufort, as well as London views. There was, however, a notable decline in quality compared with work done in Venice and, in view of the great privacy with which Canaletto worked, it would have been tempting to wonder whether the artist that landed in England was not a different person from the "genuine Canaletto of Venice", or whether Canaletto did not use assistants when he was in England, particularly in painting figures. This suspicion may have been entertained by some of his English patrons, for Canaletto published an announcement on 25 July in an English newspaper – probably in the *Daily Advertiser* or the *London Journal* [Finberg, WS, 1920–1]. Vertue copied out this notice, in which Canaletto invited anyone who wanted to see the view of St James's Park he had painted to visit his lodgings at the house of Richard Wiggan in Silver Street, Golden Square, between the hours of 9 and 3 or between 4 and 7 in the afternoon. Silver Street, off Regent Street, has been called Beak Street since 1883, and Wiggan's house has been

identified as no. 41 [*Ibid.*]. The view of St James's, which has given rise to some problems of identification, must have been painted for promotional purposes, to give the lie to any doubts about his skill, and to attract new clients [Constable, 1962]. This clever enterprise probably achieved its aims. Vertue himself suggests that doubts about the "reality" of Canaletto must have resulted from the fact that there was another painter known as Canalletti [*sic*] whose real name was Bellotto. This was Canaletto's nephew, Bernardo. It is interesting that an absurd hypothesis was advanced at the end of the last century. [Home, *MA*, 1899] that Canaletto never went to England, and that an impostor painted under the name of the Venetian master.

1750 Canaletto returned to Venice on business perhaps towards the end of September and remained there for eight months.

(Above) Drawing (ca. 1740), landscape with terrace and rustic courtyard, with an autograph inscription (Berlin, Kupferstichkabinett) (Below) The frontispiece of the autograph engravings published in 1744 (VEDUTE/Altre prese da i Luoghi altre ideate/DA/ANTONIO CANAL/e da esso intagliate in prospetiva) with a dedication to J. Smith (umiliate/All' Ill. mo Signor/GIUSEPPE SMITH/Console di S. M. Britanica appresso la Ser. ma/Repubblica di Venezia/In segno di stima ed ossequio).

1751 On 8 March "Signor Zuanne Antonio Canal, son of Bernardo, in my presence" drew up a real estate contract in Venice for the notable sum of 2,500 ducats to be paid to the School of Luganegheri for property purchase. On 24 May he was already back in London, for he depicted "exactly" a garden party held at Ranelagh to celebrate the birthday of Prince George of Wales [Finberg, WS, 1920–1], who was to become King George III in 1760 and later purchased from Smith (see **1763**) an impressive group of works by Canaletto. On 30 July the *Daily Advertiser* published a notice in which "Signior" Canaletto announced that he had painted a picture of Chelsea, Ranelagh House and the Thames and invited connoisseurs to see it at his apartment in Silver Street, where it was on view for fifteen days, from 8 to 1 and from 3 to 6 in the afternoon [Finberg, WS, 1920–1; Constable, 1962] (*Catalogue*, 289). On 2 December a licence was issued

for the publication of two engravings by E. Rooker and two by J. S. Müller from drawings by Canaletto, with views of Vauxhall Gardens [Finberg, WS, 1920–1; Morassi, 1954].

1752–3 Individual prints executed by English engravers after works by Canaletto appeared in these years [Constable, 1962]. On 28 July Pietro Gradenigo noted in his *Notatori* [1942]: "Antonio Canaletto, celebrated Venetian painter of views, is returning home from England". This must have been a very short visit, since Zanetti explicitly mentions only two visits that Canaletto made to England ("He sojourned twice in London …"). There is either a misunderstanding here or the Venetian diarist made an error [Constable, 1962].

1754 The following inscription appears on the back of a view of Walton Bridge, now in the Dulwich Gallery, London (302): "Done in 1754 in London for the first and last time with every care for the Rt Hon. Mr Hollis, my very esteemed patron. Antonio Canal, known as Canaletto". An almost identical inscription appears on the back of his view of the *Interior of the Ranelagh Rotunda*, now in the National Gallery, London (*Catalogue*, 303). As far as one can tell the fragmentary inscription on the back of the *capriccio* showing the Capitol and the Cordonata, in the Gavito Collection, Mexico City (299), must have been the same, although the date of the painting has disappeared. The artist, then, had found an influential new patron in Thomas Hollis, a man vitally engaged in political life, full of republican passions, bound to the cause of the American colonies, a writer, bibliophile and collector. It is interesting to note that Hollis met Consul Smith in Venice during a stay between 8 December 1750 and 28 February 1751 and remained in correspondence with him [Constable, 1962].

1755 On a drawing of Walton Bridge, in the Mellon Collection, Washington, appears an autograph inscription: "Done by me, Antonio Canal, known as Canaletto, for my picture painted in London for Rt Hon. di Kers [*sic*]". This inscription can be compared with the one on the back of the painting (315) he did for the same man, who has been identified as Samuel Dickers, MP, the financier responsible for the bridge.

1756 Canaletto returned permanently to Venice probably in this year, if not as early as the end of the preceding year.

1759 28 September In a letter to the Bolognese painter Prospero Pesci, Algarotti describes a *capriccio* of the Rialto bridge as it had originally been designed by Palladio [Algarotti, 1784], which Canaletto had done for him.

1760 John Hinchliffe (later Bishop of Peterborough) was

tutor to John Crewe during a visit to Venice. There he saw "a little man" intent on sketching the campanile of St Mark's and, on a hunch, called out "Canaletti". The man replied, "Do you know me?" and invited Hinchliffe and his pupil to his studio. They struck up a friendship: Hinchliffe asked Canaletto to do a painting of the sketch he had been working on, and the painter made a gift of the drawing to Hinchliffe.

1763 On 11 September, after the death of Nogari, the Academy elected Canaletto (10 votes against 4) as a "skilled and celebrated Professor, Painter of the highest honesty and virtue". [*Ibid.*] Canaletto took an active part in the life of the Academy until 23 August 1767. Negotiations – begun in 1756 – were finally completed for George III's purchase of Smith's collection of Canalettos. This included fifty-three paintings and about one hundred drawings. Most of these have remained in the British royal collections [Parker, 1948].

1765 In accordance with the Academy practice that each new member should present the association with an example of his work, Canaletto gave a *capriccio* (335 A), which is still in the Gallerie dell'Accademia in Venice.

1766 Canaletto was still working. He wrote on a drawing of this year, now in the Kunsthalle, Hamburg, "I, Zuane Antonio da Canal, did the present drawing of singers in the Ducal Church of St Mark's in Venice at the age of sixty-eight, without glasses. 1766".

1768 On 20 April we find the official entry in the Venetian health authority's offices of the death of "Antonio … Canal, 71, of fever and inflammation of the bladder, 5 days. Doctor Musolo, death at 7 o'clock". The death list of the Parish Church of San Lio (now in Santa Maria Formosa), in whose precincts Canaletto had lived (at no. 5484 of what is now Corte Perini [Tassini, *Curiosità veneziane*, 1965]) confirms the death report and that death occurred at seven in the evening [Moschini, 1954; Constable, 1962 (q.v. for the correct transcript of the documents)]. In his entry in the *Notatori* [1942] for this date, Gradenigo confirmed that "after a long and pitiful illness we have lost a fine brush in the death in the San Leone parish of the painter Antonio Canale, known as Canaletto, who was famous for his view paintings". Canaletto's tomb has not been identified. On 14 May an inventory of Canaletto's possessions was drawn up, for he had died intestate. Among his possessions were "Pictures, Medium and Small, 28". His heirs were his sisters, Fiorenza, a widow, and Viena and Francesca, unmarried. On 20 May the bill was prepared for expenses involved in his funeral, as well as for his medical and pharmaceutical expenses [Constable, 1962].

Catalogue of works

Artistic development

Recent studies, particularly Morassi's [AV, 1966], have shed light on the problems of the rather enigmatic beginnings of Canaletto's artistic career. Careful study of his few surviving early works and the identification of some of the novelties of his style, have enabled scholars to recognise the original contributions he made to the tradition of view painting as practised by van Wittel and, more especially, by Carlevaris. Pallucchini properly emphasised [1960; to AIV, 1966–7] the baroque sensibility which was in harmony with the contemporary taste in painting as it was expressed by Piazzetta, Bencovich, and the very young Tiepolo and it is also now possible to assess the great influence that Marco Ricci's treatment of landscape had on the development of the young Canaletto. The same may be said of the influence of Canaletto's early experience in the theatre, which probably gave him a feeling for highly dramatic effects, in the manner established and popularised for instance by the Bibbienas, particularly Ferdinando Bibbiena. There is little doubt that Canaletto began to paint very early, and at the same time that he began his work for the theatre, to which family tradition had dedicated him. This obviously would be before the famous "excommunication" of the theatre from his life. Thus Morassi is probably correct in thinking that Canaletto's trip to Rome in 1719 was not the vital turning point that other scholars have considered it. Nevertheless the milieu of Roman figure painting must have had a profound influence on the young artist, particularly the arrangements of figures that were being introduced by Pannini especially. This is even more evident when one realises that Pannini came from Piacenza, which was well known to the Bibbienas, whose scenographic innovations had already influenced the young Canaletto's imagination. The northern painters influenced by Rome, together with the "Bamboccianti" (who were firmly bound to Dutch tradition),

must also have engaged his attention, particularly in their straightforward sense of realism and local colour in handling details of everyday life [Morassi, AV, 1960]. In any case, the first known works by Canaletto are marked by a feeling for scenography [Pallucchini, 1960] comprehending all these components and assimilating them in a highly personal and individual form. "Ideal" views based on classical remains figure notably in Canaletto's production in these years, until about 1725–6. But he was gradually making more views "from nature", and this marks a decided change in his choice of subjects probably caused by the demands of the market. In the early 1730s Canaletto began to temper his agitated and dramatic manner of composition. At the same time he placed less emphasis on *chiaroscuro* effects, giving his pictures a peaceful and spacious luminosity and he confined his work almost exclusively to views of Venice and its environs. This change again parallelled the change in Venetian taste in painting. Canaletto used optical instruments, strictly for expressive purposes, in his search for new compositional motifs that could also be used in fantastic compositions, and he explored every corner of Venice, from the most famous – St Mark's Square, the Piazzetta, the Harbour, the Quay, the Grand Canal, etc. – to the least known smallest squares and canals. He achieved a remarkable series of images and created "a spatial dimension obtained through passages and gradations of colour", charged with a light that created a heightened "sunlit secularisation" of reality [Pallucchini, AIV, 1966–7]. All the baroque accents were dissolved in a counterpoint so that the Venetian topography was not treated with the documentary exactitude of Carlevaris, but raised to the level of imaginative transformation and historical representation. Canaletto's formal methods – walking around and making jottings in his sketchbooks, to be used for his paintings, were most varied; he handed perspective with increasing daring and

gradually moved back the focal point of the view, thereby "increasing the picture's capacity to retain the atmosphere of the scene" [Ibid, AV, 1964]. But he controlled his methods in a way that respected the objective character of reality whilst being rendered poetically. During this felicitous phase of Canaletto's career, he achieved on a European level of style and quality "the enlightened certainty of absolute truth" [Longhi, 1946] that was typical of contemporary culture, within the style and idiom of his own particular situation, namely the Venetian tradition [Ragghianti, SA, 1959]. From about 1740 Canaletto enlarged his repertory to include views of the Venetian mainland as well as "ideal" subjects depicted in hard sunlit colours but within the framework of the rational world of the Enlightenment. Classical elements returned too, as a result of his second Roman visit (if we accept the opinions of those who admit that this journey might have happened). Aside from these classical elements, this second Roman stay would seem to have had no formative influence on him. But compared with his youthful work the material appears radically different. In connection with the *capricci* Canaletto painted between 1742 and 1744, it might be worth examining a possible relationship (hitherto unconsidered) that may have existed, perhaps through Algarotti, with northern European circles, where architectural concepts were being rethought and the whole question of city planning was being considered. One has only to think of Etienne-Louis Boullé and even Diderot's theories.

The English visit did not, as some scholars have said, mark a change in the artist's work. However he may at first have been somewhat disoriented by the differences in British towns and landscape and the different quality of light, crystalline and cold. Also he must have been affected by the relationships he established with an artistic circle of a different kind, which had connections with contemporary Dutch painting, particularly that of J. van der Heyden, a reflection

of whose work some scholars have found in Canaletto's painting. But Canaletto was soon to impose his own warm sense of light onto the English landscape, as Pallucchini observed [AV, 1964]. According to him, Canaletto's two stays in London did not alter his style. Canaletto ended by revealing to the English "a London bathed in southern light", treating the new landscape "with an expansive sense of luminous space" [AIV, 1966–7]. This may well explain the initial perplexities of the British dilettanti.

The last period of Canaletto's activity, beginning in 1755, when he returned to Venice, has not been sufficiently studied. Morassi has pointed this out [AV, 1966], and recommends the merits of such study, noting a distinct increase in vitality in the later work coupled with a deep feeling of romantic nostalgia. These qualities are expressed by a greater dramatic tension with an occasional unexpected cropping of the view, the unreality of which is accentuated by a cold light. Canaletto's isolation from the local artistic world (which admission to the Academy did not alter), his declining popularity on the art market, and the profound crisis of Venetian society (which has its effects on the sturdy conscience of the Enlightenment) must have had their influence on him. Other aspects are also worth studying in the later development of Canaletto, who continued to go

around to paint "on the spot", proud of the fact that he could work without glasses. He may have worked primarily for himself, because of his own innate and urgent need for self-expression.

This catalogue includes all the paintings – among the immense number that have been attributed to Canaletto – that can be considered autograph works because of documentation or because of stylistic qualities unanimously recognised by scholars. (Very few works of Canaletto are signed.) Also listed are pictures attributed to Canaletto by a majority of scholars. In addition to originals, contemporary other versions of the same subjects are also listed. If these versions are notably later in time, they are recorded separately. The best source and reference remains the formidable *corpus* established by Constable [1962], and the present author expresses his debt to that scholar at the outset. The immense number of works in the manner of Canaletto makes it impossible to discuss details and models here. Nevertheless an exception has been made for a group of paintings that were considered, until recently, major works of Canaletto, but which recent scholarship has assigned to other artists. The section below should be consulted on the question of imitations, of which there are countless numbers, and collaborations. Great care has been taken to check the locations of pictures, to locate

(Left) A small eighteenth-century camera ottica *(strictly speaking a* camera oscura*) in use out of doors (from a print by G. F. Costa). (Right) Reflex viewer (open for use), which is traditionally believed to have been Canaletto's; (Venice, Museo Correr).*

those that may have escaped Constable's diligent research and to locate those which have changed hands since that scholar's book was published. The extraordinary activity of the art market makes it impossible to be absolutely certain of the present location of works in private collections. In some cases the collectors have preferred anonymity. As to illustrations, although the greatest possible number have been used, qualitatively inferior versions of subjects that Canaletto frequently painted have not been used. And there are some works that could not be shown because the works could not be traced or the owners declined to allow reproduction.

The Camera Ottica

Some contemporary and near contemporary sources record Canaletto's use of a *camera ottica*. Zanetti [1771] says that Canaletto "taught the proper use of the *camera ottica*, and showed what defects can be introduced into a painting when its whole perspective arrangement is taken from what can be seen in the *camera*, particularly the colours of the atmosphere, and when one does not eliminate things offensive to the senses". Mariette confirms [1851–3] this report. It was repeated again until Sagredo's time [in E. De Tipaldo, *Biografia degli italiani illustri*, 1834]. We also know that such devices were very commonly employed by view painters. It is interesting that this is confirmed by Algarotti, for example: "The most celebrated view painters that we have today make much use of it" [1762]. Zais also on 28 March 1770 wrote to a patron in Bergamo who had invited him there "to copy" views of that city: "I will bring my optical box with me", [in Camesasca, *Artisti in bottega*, 1966]. Recent scholars have not denied that Canaletto used this device, but they have disagreed on just what particular use he made of it. Opinion is divided between those who think that he made very limited use of the device, and those who think that he used it extensively. Some believe that he did not use it in executing his view paintings ("taken from nature" or "ideally imagined") or in the preparation of "finished" drawings, and they consider it only in relation to his *ex tempore* drawings from life intended for later elaboration (see *Graphic work* below). For example Pignatti (1958) thought Canaletto did not use the device very much, whilst Gioseffi [1959] thought the artist used it a great deal. In any case both scholars were really concerned with showing the expressive originality of Canaletto and the formal dignity of his results. Ragghianti [*SA*, 1959] finally established a balanced view of the situation achieving a formulation universally acceptable (see *Critical outline*).

The instrument most commonly used by eighteenth-century view painters because of its practicality, and almost certainly used by Canaletto, was a reflecting device constructed on the principle (already well known to optical science) of the *camera oscura*. A hole was made in one side of a closed dark box and external images were projected on the opposite side of the box. These images were perspectively faithful but reversed, upside down, and out of focus. These images could be straightened out and made sharp enough by the use of mirrors and lenses and could then be easily copied. All the work of the adjustment of the images obviously had to be carried out inside the box, and this was inconvenient, notwithstanding various modifications (fabric on the sides, etc.); also the box itself had to be extremely large. The reflex viewer, adapted from the *camera oscura*, was a small box that enabled the images (collected as it were in a tube with a lens and reflected by a mirror set at an angle within the box) to be projected on to a glass screen. Though with some difficulty, one could place a sheet of tracing paper on the uneven surface of the glass and trace the outlines of the images, or one could simply make a rough copy of this reflected inverted image to be transferred later to paper. Since copying was difficult, it may be assumed that the device was used merely to establish the colour arrangement of the view, that is, of the principal masses of colour For perspective lines and the individual elements of a picture, one would need a real *camera oscura*, even though a much smaller one. In this way one could remain outside the box and look into it, taking care to cover one's head with a dark cloth and resting the sheet of paper on a surface of smooth glass.) This smaller *camera oscura* was transportable. In the storage rooms of the Museo Correr, Venice, a reflecting device has been found with a large angle lens, bearing an old inscription "A. CANAL". Although there is no documentary evidence to prove that this device actually belonged to Canaletto (in the *post mortem* inventory of his possessions, which is extremely detailed, no mention is made of such a device), it may well be one of the many and various kinds that he used. It should be pointed out, as Gioseffi [1959] has shown in his extremely thorough discussion of the problem, that view painters must have used various kinds of optical devices and *camere*, depending on the particular problem to be solved; the observer could be either on the outside or inside. J. Meder [*Die Handzeichnung*, 1919], H. Fritzsche [*Bernardo Bellotto*, 1936], and Camesasca [1966] have also examined the problem. Gioseffi notes that there were fixed and portable models of both types of devices, the lenses were of three sorts, normal, wide-angle, and telescopic, and that a painter could make use of each kind of device. But only the devices where the observer was

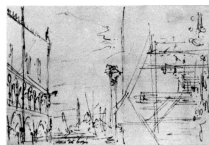

(Top, left to right) Two sketches made perhaps with the camera ottica (the shaky line is typical of the technique) and not elaborated: the Lido (Cambridge, Mass., Fogg Art Museum) and the Piazzetta (sketchbook, Venice Gallerie dell'Accademia).
(Centre, left to right) Drawing of the Piazzetta, with the column and the lion of St Mark, and a corner of the Libreria (Windsor Castle, Royal Collections); probably a pencil drawing made with the camera ottica and then gone over in pen and ink. Two similar drawings, more finished, with the Grand Canal and the Church of the Salute (above) and the Grand Canal from Ca' Rezzonico to Palazzo Balbi (below).
(Below, left) Finished drawing of the Island of Sant'Elena and the Lido (Windsor Castle), and (below) two sketches of figures (London, Witt Collection). (Right) Finished drawing of the Campanile of St Mark's (Windsor Castle).

inside were really useful for copying images; the others were more suitable for observation and study. As far as one can determine today, and as Gioseffi's experiments have shown, Canaletto must have been extremely skilled in the use of the *camera*, particularly in the selection of lenses, apertures, etc., for he managed to correct the images (by slight alterations) and harmonise them with the demands of composition. This must have been the source of what is usually defined as his "independence". He did not make slavish use of the devices, but employed them as instruments of scientifically controlled work and subordinated their use to aesthetic ends.

The problem of the workshop

Reference has frequently been

made to a Canaletto workshop because of the existence of "strictly Canaletto-like" views. Although there is no historical evidence to prove that such a workshop existed, these works do suggest that there was indeed an atelier, one that was both efficient and very productive. This hypothesis would resolve the question of classifying paintings that cannot be attributed to Canaletto himself. It is not based on specific research that might have suggested a different view of the artist's development from that usually accepted. Furthermore, in our present state of knowledge, one cannot even suggest what this workshop would have been like, because we have no certain knowledge of the organisation and operating methods of the workshops, despite the extent and intensity of present studies of the Venetian eighteenth century, and in particular the view painting "factory" of the Guardi brothers.

It has been justly remarked [Constable, 1962] that the existence of a great number of Canaletto-like paintings which cannot be attributed to Canaletto because of their inferior quality, may largely be explained by the "imitability" of view painting in general and that of Canaletto in particular. Furthermore there were many engravings of Canaletto's paintings, so that one could easily and quickly produce works that resembled Canaletto's without ever having seen the original paintings. Outside the group of students and followers who might have worked in his putative workshop, it would have been harder to consult the originals. And Canaletto's popularity in the art market must have invited extensive and indiscriminate imitation. It seems therefore unlikely that Canaletto had any sort of large workshop. The stylistic characteristics of his paintings are so rigorous and organically uniform that it is hard to imagine that collaborators ever took a hand, and the extensive contemporary sources of our knowledge of Canaletto give no indication of the existence of a workshop. Watson's hypothesis [1949] that Canaletto's many sketches with notes about the paintings to be made from them were prepared for assistants who would execute the paintings is contradicted by the artist's known procedure from the sketch to the final execution which has been established by the analyses of Pallucchini [1945], Pignatti [1958], Gioseffi [1959], Ragghianti [1959], Moschini [1963], and others. (See *Graphic work*, below.) However, it is certain that he made use of assistants occasionally. First of all, there was his nephew Bernardo Bellotto, who, Orlandi [1753] says, saw his uncle regularly. In fact Bernardo enrolled in the *Fraglia* in 1738 alongside his uncle [Nicoletti, *AVE*, 1890]. He worked with his uncle until about 1742, when he began a series of journeys (first to Rome

(Top to bottom) Two of the splendid autograph engravings published in 1744, one imaginative and the other taken from nature: a capriccio with a classical portico, Roman ruins and "modern" Venetian houses; View of the Marghera Tower. Drawing (detail) for one of the 1744 engravings, showing a river town (Cambridge, Mass., Fogg Art Museum); its firm dating to 1742 established the chronology of the whole series of engravings.

and then to Lombardy and elsewhere), but must have worked quite independently, as recent studies would indicate [Kosakiewicz, *AV*, 1964, and *DBI*, 1965; Pallucchini, *VP*, 1965; Pignatti, *AV*, 1966]. Michele Marieschi may have worked in Canaletto's studio for a short period between 1730 and 1735 [Morassi, *MF*]. There is evidence (see *Outline biography*), which includes the engravings after drawings in the British Museum and the Museo Correr, Venice, executed between 1735 and 1742, suggesting that Antonio Visentini was an active collaborator of Canaletto at least during those years. This collaboration is indirectly confirmed by the fact that Visentini was in touch with Consul Smith, for whom (among other things), he designed a palace that the Englishman built in Campo Santi Apostoli [Pallucchini, 1960; Levey, *BM*, 1962]. It has also been suggested that the mediocre

view painter Giuseppe Moretti also collaborated with Canaletto [Voss, *RFW*], though doubts have been advanced [Constable, 1962] and some have rejected the theory outright [Pallucchini, 1960]. The inscription "Giuseppe Guerra" may be seen at the bottom of an "ideal" view (the present location of which is not known), alongside the abbreviation "A.C.", and this has made some scholars think that this mysterious person, known from a drawing with a self-portrait, signed and dated 1760, now in Windsor Castle [Constable], may be a collaborator of Canaletto, perhaps during his English stay. The theory that Francesco Guardi worked in Canaletto's atelier seems less tenable and, is in fact, unacceptable. This was suggested by an uncertain entry in Gradenigo dated 25 April 1764 ("a good student of the famous Canaletto"). A more interesting theory, and one that would be worth pursuing, has been advanced by Watson

[1949], suggesting that there was collaboration between Canaletto and Giambattista Cimaroli, who had been involved as early as 1722 (see *Outline biography*) with Canaletto in the "funerary" undertaking promoted by Owen McSwiney and whom Tessin linked with Canaletto in 1736 [Siren, 1902]. Watson has, in fact, identified a painting of St Mark's Square with a bull fight, formerly in the Jones Collection, Chester, and now in Italy, that Dodsley considered as early as 1761 to be a joint work of Canaletto and Cimaroli, datable to the period before Canaletto's departure for England.

Graphic work

The immense quantity of Canaletto's graphic work – both drawings and etchings – constitutes an absolutely fundamental element (as recent studies have shown), of any understanding of the artist's development. The drawings have chiefly been identified by their provenance, by stylistic evidence, and by inscriptions in Canaletto's hand. Few of the drawings are signed. (Few of the paintings are signed either.) Two major groups of drawings, sketches from life or imaginary, are related to his paintings. There are rapid sketches that suggest that they were used as documentary notes. They were made on the spot, perhaps with the aid of optical devices, were frequently marked with notes about colour, topographical location, etc., and were intended as preparatory for paintings or engravings, or for series of drawings. There were also "finished" drawings.

A large number of quick sketches have been preserved in a big album donated by Guido Cagnola to the Accademia, Venice, in 1949. It is a large album (228 × *ca.* 170mm.) originally used as a note and sketch book. The drawings in black pencil were taken from life, and most of them were inked later in Canaletto's studio. There are 148 pages (74 numbered leaves) with 138 sketches and ten blank pages. The sketches are numbered from 1 to 74, verso and recto. The present binding, which must have been made in the nineteenth century, is probably a copy of the original binding [Moschini, *AV*, 1950; Pignatti, 1958]. We know that the album was in Venice in 1844 and was authenticated by the painters G. Borsato and T. Orsi under the supervision of the scholar E. Cicogna. But we do not know where the album was before that, nor do we know how it came into the possession of Guido Cagnola. Pignatti [1958] wrote in the introduction to a facsimile edition of the album that "a great many of the sketches ... were used ... for paintings in the group of works preserved at Windsor, by the Duke of Bedford at Woburn Abbey, and in the Harvey Collection, formerly at Langley Park" and later broken up. He also said that some of these sketches are directly related to

"at least eight engravings by Visentini in the famous collection of [views of] the Grand Canal" and to "finished" drawings at Windsor Castle [Moschini, *AV*, 1950]. The sketchbook can be dated with some certainty, for many reasons but chiefly because of the uniformity of the drawing style, to a fairly precise period, between 1728 and 1730 at the latest. Pignatti considers this to be the correct dating. He has also found other drawings with similar characteristics in various public and private collections. Among these, fifteen sketches formerly in the Viggiano Collection, Venice, now divided between the Accademia, Venice, and the Miotti Collection, Udine, should be mentioned. Although the sheets are a different size and the drawings date from various periods, they formed a single unit with another twenty sketches, and they all belonged to the Corniani Algarotti Gallery, Venice. Part of this collection later belonged to Italico Brass, Venice, and is now dispersed. The location of only a few of the drawings is now known [Constable, 1962]. Some of them went to the Cini Foundation and some to the Janos Scholz Collection, New York [Miotti, *AV*, 1966].

The most substantial corpus of "finished" graphic work is in Windsor Castle, where it went after George III's purchase (*Outline biography*, 1763) from the English Consul Smith. Most of the works are derived, though admirable in their independence of style and treatment, from paintings that Canaletto did for Smith, which the latter kept in his houses in Venice and his villa at Moggiano or sold to English collectors. Some of the drawings, however, are independent works or related to etchings executed by Canaletto or others. The Windsor Collection can be dated over a long period of time, from 1726–7 to about 1750 [Parker, 1948]. Many other drawings, of similar quality and in various places can be dated to different periods throughout Canaletto's career. (See the careful inventory in Constable's catalogue [1962] and Hadeln's important study [1930].) Another group of twenty-two works deserves special mention. Twenty-one are in the British Museum and one is in the Landesmuseum, Darmstadt. They consist of Roman views and were engraved by G. B. Brustolon [Watson, *BM*, 1950; Constable, 1962]. Many scholars date this group to Canaletto's youth, but some reject the attribution to Canaletto. One other group should be mentioned. It consists almost exclusively of scenes "from life" or imaginary scenes, with some ten sheets of figures. It is thanks to Constable, once again, that this group has been studied and dated.

Canaletto's graphic technique and his use of materials was fairly simple and uniform. He worked in pencil, mostly black though occasionally red, and strictly from life. Later he would ink these drawings with a pen,

1

2

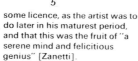

3

4

5

8

usually goose quill or metal of some kind. He rarely worked in brush and wash. It is, of course, difficult to analyse the inks he used. Most of the works are now sepia in colour, but it is possible that they were originally black and have lost their original colour through oxidation. If this is the case, Canaletto used very ordinary inks that brown with age. The very few drawings which have remained black are those which one assumes were done in Indian ink, which does not brown. Sometimes Canaletto used a compass and devices for drawing lines. He also used a technique, peculiar to him, described by Parker as pin-pointing, which joined the principal points and distances in his architectural compositions.

Canaletto's engraved work consists of thirty-one aquaforte etchings collected in the volume that appeared in 1744, with a warm dedication to his friend and patron J. Smith on the very beautiful frontispiece (there is a drawing for another version, never etched, in the Kupferstichkabinett, Berlin [Spranger, JPK, 1904]. There are also three other etchings in aquaforte. Two of these are known from a single copy at Windsor Castle [Fritzsche, GK, 1930], and the other from two copies, one in the Kupferstichkabinett, Berlin; the other in Windsor [Spranger]. Guarnati and Pallucchini, in their fundamental work on Canaletto's etchings [1945], established the date of these works. They related the single work at Windsor to an imaginary view from the album (no. 13 in their book) and the other two (nos. 28 and 30) were restored to their original chronological order, which was firmly established after the attempts of Meyer [1878] and De Vesme [Le peintre-graveur italien, 1906]. The dating has given rise to much debate, for only one etching (no. 12) is dated, 1741, while the drawing (now in the Fogg Art Museum, Cambridge) for another (no. 9) was done in 1742. Generally, the more convincing studies suggest that the plates were begun in 1741 [Goering, GK, 1941] or a year earlier [Pittaluga, A, 1934]. The most persuasive thesis of all [Pallucchini and Guarnati] dates the execution of the etchings between 1740 and 1743. Ragghianti has pointed out their great importance, noting that the cutting of the etchings seem to be inspired by the same sense of form and feeling that led Canaletto, in painting as well, to upset patterns of composition that were more balanced and closed.

During his life, Canaletto provided paintings and drawings for engravings without executing the actual etchings. These are works of varying quality (see Outline biography).

6

7

9

10

1 ⬛️ 🔘 105 × 130 *1719*

The Arch of Septimius Severus Bergamo, Private collection
Morassi [AV, 1966] ascribed this painting to Canaletto as one of the artist's very first works. He identified it as one of the paintings of antique subjects mentioned by Zanetti [1771]. The preparatory drawing is in the British Museum and belongs to the series that Brustolon used for his series of etchings, now in the Museo Correr [Constable, 1962, no. 713/223]. (Constable relates this sheet to imaginary views of the Arch of Septimius now in Windsor Castle – signed and dated 1742 [no. 205] – and the Cincinnati Art Museum [no. 213].) Morassi notes that this painting, like the later imaginary views painted during Canaletto's stay in Rome, reveals a tendency to alter compositions from life with

some licence, as the artist was to do later in his maturest period, and that this was the fruit of "a serene mind and felicitious genius" [Zanetti].

2 ⬛️ 🔘 113 × 148,5 *1719*

The Arch of Constantine New York, Bracaglia Collection (?)
Formerly ascribed to the brothers Antonio and Giovanni Paolo Gaspari [A, 1913], it has been published by Constable [BM, 1964], who considers it to be one of Canaletto's youthful works painted during or immediately after Canaletto's stay in Rome, about 1719–20. Constable's view was accepted by Pallucchini [AV, 1964] and Morassi [AV, 1966]. The latter relates the painting to a drawing of the same subject in the British Museum which was, engraved by Brustolon [Constable, 1962, no. 713/222].

3 ⬛️ 🔘 *1719*

Imaginary View of Rome
Pallucchini published this work [AV, 1964] and dates it near the views in the Cini Collection (nos. 4 and 5, below). The attribution was confirmed by Morassi [AV, 1966], who dates it to the first trip to Rome.

4 ⬛️ 🔘 113 × 149 1720-21

Classical Ruins: a Capriccio Venice, Cini Collection
This work, like the following one, has been attributed to Canaletto's youth – about 1723 – by Morassi [VE, 1956] and Constable [1962], who paid no acknowledgment to the former. Morassi discussed the picture again [AV, 1963] and later [AV, 1966] dated the painting to 1721. (See also Valcanover in Great Private Collections, 1963, and Zampetti [CMV, 1967].) The two paintings reveal close attention to the style of Marco Ricci.

5 ⬛️ 🔘 113 × 149 1720-21

Classical Ruins: a Capriccio Venice, Cini Collection
See no. 4, above, for attribution. The elements of Ricci's style appear "composed and regenerated by an artistic personality that was already sure of itself, with great vibration of light and an almost dramatic rhythm of composition so rich in details, episodes, and visual wonders", [Zampetti, CMV, 1967].

6 ⬛️ 🔘 73 × 55,5 *1722*

Landscape with Ruins and a Renaissance Building Hartford, Conn., Wadsworth Atheneum
This was traditionally ascribed to Marco Ricci, and has only recently been attributed to Canaletto by Morassi [AV, 1966]. This attribution was confirmed by the Venice exhibition of the vedutisti (view painters) [Zampetti, CMV, 1967]. The picture is nevertheless marked, though the transfiguration is very personal and unmistakable, by

the use of a very rich red background, strong contrasts of light and shade, and free impasto brushwork, characteristics of the proto-Romantic imaginary view painting of Ricci [Constable, 1962].

7 ⬛️ 🔘 82 × 63,5 *1722*

View of Rome
Formerly in the Agosti Collection, Belluno. Ascribed to Canaletto by Morassi [AV, 1966], who rejected the traditional attribution to Marco Ricci (cf. Valcanover, Catalogo della Mostra di pitture del Settecento nel Bellunese [1954]). It has correctly been dated to the Roman period or, rather, just after it, for it has been shown to be connected with the canvas of the "funerary" painting commissioned by McSwiney (see p. 84) on the basis of similarities with an engraving in the Tombeaux des Princes (1741) [Ibid.].

8 ⬛️ 🔘 *1722*

Imaginary View of Rome
Formerly in the Agosti Collection, Belluno (see no. 7, above). It was also attributed to Marco Ricci and then by Morassi [AV, 1966] to Canaletto's youth, at a time when he was much influenced by both Marco Ricci's style and his own experience in the theatre.

9 ⬛️ 🔘 279,4 × 142 1722

Imaginary Funerary Monument for Lord Somers Oakly Park, Shropshire, Earl of Plymouth Collection
This work was commissioned by McSwiney (see Outline biography, 1772), who mentioned it as finished in a letter of 8 March 1722 [Constable, 1962]. According to this letter the landscape was painted by Canaletto and Cimaroli and the figures by Piazzetta. Canaletto probably painted the architectural elements as well. The work was not engraved in the Tombeaux des Princes (1741).

11A

13 (Plates III–IV)

12A

12B

14A (Plates V–VI)

17

10 ⊞ ◐ 21b × 138,5 / 1722 目 ⁝

Imaginary Funerary Monument for Archbishop Tillotson Great Britain, Private collection
Executed in the same way as no. 9 above and also mentioned in the letter of 8 March 1722, which says that only the landscape, painted by Canaletto and Cimaroli was finished; Pittoni was still at work on the figures, which he completed between October and November 1726. The engraving is in the *Tombeaux des Princes* (1741, III).
A later version (not autographed) is mentioned, after Watson, by Constable [1962] as the property of Cecil Gosling at Barrington Hall (Bishop's Stortford)

11 ⊞ ◐ 145 × 205 / *1723 目 ⁝

St Mark's Square with the Basilica Castagnola, Lugano, Thyssen Foundation
A. This scene was painted several times with only minor variations. It was identified, together with the next three canvases, with paintings in the 1767 *Description* of the collection of Prince Josef Wenzel. It came to its present owner, along with the other three works, from the Liechtenstein Collection.
Universally dated to shortly before 1723, the year in which Andrea Tirali did the new pavement of the square [Watson, 1949; Moschini, 1954; Pallucchini, 1960; Brandi, 1960, etc.]. Pallucchini observed that, despite the influence of

Carlevaris in the details, Canaletto has achieved "a theatre-like perspective", an occasion for an interplay of *chiaroscuro* effects of great style and force. He noted a "totally new sense of light and colour", as compared to the view painting of Carlevaris and that certain traces still remained of Marco Ricci's style.
B. An autograph replica, slightly later and slightly smaller in size (137 × 200 cm.), was published by Constable [1962]. It is in the Bayerische Staatsgemäldesammlungen, Munich (no. 5914).

12 ⊞ ◐ 142 × 214 / *1723 目 ⁝

The Grand Canal from Campo San Vio Castagnola, Lugano, Thyssen Foundation
A. See no. 11 A, above, for provenance. The subject was frequently painted by Canaletto.
B. A beautiful version in the Gemäldegalerie, Dresden (65,5 × 97,5 cm.), formerly in the collection of the King of Saxony (1741). It was painted no later than 1725, and is a companion piece to no. 23 A, also in Dresden.
Constable [1962] tends to attribute two other versions, one lost and one in Munich, to Canaletto as well.

13 ⊞ ◐ 144 × 207 / *1723 目 ⁝

The Grand Canal from Campo San Vio near the Rialto Bridge Milan, Mario Crespi Collection
See no. 11 A, above.

14 ⊞ ◐ 143 × 200 / *1723 目 ⁝

Rio Dei Mendicanti Milan, Mario Crespi Collection
A. See no. 11 A, above.

B. A small view (40,7 × 61 cm.), initialled and dated ("A.C. 1731"), was in a private collection in Venice until 1937 [Constable, 1962]. It is not certain that the work is by Canaletto.
C. A view painting (114 × 74 cm.) of this subject that appeared on the New York market could not be traced by Constable, who places it in the school of Canaletto.
A small view that also included the Scuola di San Marco (39 × 69 cm.) building, now in the Accademia, Venice (no. 494), is more likely to be by Bellotto.

15 ⊞ ◐ 180 × 323 / 1723 目 ⁝

Classical Ruins: a Capriccio Milan, Private collection
This is the first absolutely certain work by the young Canaletto, because it is signed and dated: "I, Antonio Canal 1723". It was published by Morassi [*AV*, 1963], who remarked: "The scene is treated like a large-scale sketch, without accentuation of perspective lines or fixed contours, but with a skill … with a sense of perspective that surely captures the essence of every form".

16 ⊞ ◐ 71 × 135 / *1723* ? 目 ⁝

View of Rome with the Venetian Monument to Colleoni: a Capriccio
Signed "Antonio Canale[tto]". Its provenance is not known [Ashby and Constable, *BM*, 1925], and the work has been lost from sight since its appearance on the Paris art market in 1938. It seems to have

been an imaginary subject of the artist's youth, similar in its theatrical composition to no. 15 above.

17 ⊞ ◐ 146 × 234 / 1724-25 目 ⁝

The Grand Canal with the Rialto Bridge from Palazzo Corner Spinelli Dresden, Gemäldegalerie
Mentioned in the 1754 inventories of the Dresden gallery. It is generally attributed to the artist's youth, and considered slightly later than the group executed for Stefano Conti between 1725 and 1726 [Brandi, 1960; Constable, 1962 etc.] or slightly earlier [Pallucchini, 1960]. The predilection for diagonal composition, still theatrical, and the colour relations, aimed at creating an imaginary atmosphere, would tend to support Pallucchini's dating. Pallucchini says that it is a "view of noble proportions, a bold and serious attempt … fundamental to the beginnings of Canaletto's art; and that transcended the influence of Carlevaris and Marco Ricci."

18 ⊞ ◐ 125 × 165 / 1725 目 ⁝

Church of Santi Giovanni e Paolo with the Scuola di San Marco Dresden, Gemäldegalerie
It is mentioned in the inventories of the royal collections of Saxony as early as 1754. This is almost certainly the work that Marchesini mentions in a letter of 18 August 1725, in which he informs Stefano Conti of the purchase by the imperial ambassador of a view of the

15 (Plates I–II)

16

19A

20

18 (Plates VII–VIII)

22A

90

Church of Santi Giovanni e Paolo at the painting exhibition at San Rocco [Haskell, *BM*, 1956]. It is on stylistic grounds as well a larger version of the same subject painted at the same time for Stefano Conti of Lucca (see no. 19, below).

21

25

19  90 × 132 1725

The Grand Canal with the Fabbriche Nuove from near the Rialto Bridge Montreal, Pillow Collection
A. Painted for Stefano Conti of Lucca, between 2 August and 25 November 1725 [Haskell, *BM*, 1956]. Canaletto made the following three views (20–2) for him as well. See also no. 21.
B. Another version, simpler in details but of almost the same size (92 × 135 cm.) is in the I. J. Lyons Collection, London. Constable [1962] suggests it might have been a replica painted after the success of the first commission, for another member of the Conti family.
C. Another beautiful version, close in date to the prototype in the Pillow Collection (*ca.* 1726, according to Constable) but different in size (150 × 192 cm.) is in Pillnitz Castle, near Dresden, together with a companion piece (no. 42 A).

20 91,5 × 134,5 1725

The Rialto Bridge with Palazzo dei Camerlenghi Montreal, Pillow Collection
Executed as no. 19 above. A drawing in the Ashmolean Museum, Oxford, [Moschini, 1954] is believed to be the preparatory sketch.

21 90 × 132 1725-26

The Grand Canal with the Church of the Carità towards the Harbour of St Mark's Montreal, Pillow Collection
See no. 19 above for its origin. According to Pallucchini [1960], in the Pillow views "Canaletto carefully studied the composition of the scene at a particular time of day in order to extract a host of effects from the sunlit and shady areas from the play of masses, which were mostly reflected in the Grand Canal. He accepted the view "motif" of Carlevaris but with a much deeper feeling for *chiaroscuro*, which naturally makes harmonies more intense. Thus he achieves a variety of colour changes from this alteration of light and shade". [Pallucchini, 1960].

22 91,5 × 136 1725-26

Church of Santi Giovanni e Paolo with the Scuola di San Marco Montreal, Pillow Collection
A. Painted for Stefano Conti, as were nos. 19–21 (*q.v.*); derived from the Dresden painting (no. 18).
B. A replica (92,5 × 135 cm.), companion piece of 19 B, probably painted for the same client; it is in the I. J. Lyons

23A

23B

24

27

26A

26B

Collection, London [Constable, 1962].

23 65 × 98 1725*

Entrance to the Grand Canal with the Church of Santa Maria della Salute Dresden, Gemäldegalerie
A. Companion piece to the view of the Grand Canal from the Campo San Vio (no. 12 B), similar in style to the paintings done for Stefano Conti (nos. 19–22). Both paintings were in the collections of the King of

Saxony as early as 1741. Constable [1962] dates the companion piece to 1725–6 and this view to 1726–8, though agreeing that the works were intended as companion pieces.
B. A variation (124 × 213 cm.) with the angle of vision to the church altered. It is of high quality and very close in date (1725–6, according to Constable). It is now in the Louvre, Paris. Although considered by Morassi as well to be an autograph work by Canaletto, recent criticism has taken up an old suggestion of

Fogolari and attributed it to Marieschi [Pallucchini, *AV*, 1966; Zampetti, *CMV*, 1967].

24 43 × 58,5 1725*

The Quay and the Right Side of the Doge's Palace
This is close in date to the views, also painted on copper, that were done for the Duke of Richmond. This view is the prototype of a frequently repeated composition. It is a companion piece to no. 25. Its ownership, as recorded by Horace Walpole, is known as

early as 1760, when it was in the possession of the second Earl of Ashburnham, together with its companion view [Constable, 1962].

25 43 × 58,5 1725*

The Riva degli Schiavoni Companion piece to no. 24, above (*q.v.*).

26 187 × 200 1726

The Harbour of St Mark's with the Island of San Giorgio from the Piazzetta The Hague, Thurkow Collection
A. Constable [1962] dates it before 1726–8, on the basis of external evidence, that the top of the Campanile of San Giorgio was modified after 1728. In this painting it seems flattened. It was probably done around 1726, for it shows some of the sense of the imaginary evident in the views painted for Stefano Conti in 1725–6 (nos. 19–22).
B. A fairly faithful copy, of very fine quality, but seen from a point slightly farther away. It belongs to the Rasini Collection, Milan (68,5 × 96,5 cm.).

27 65 × 86 1725*

The Quay with the Doge's Palace and the Paglia Bridge Turin, Galleria Sabauda
Another work (see also no. 26) characterised by a dramatic treatment of light and shade [Constable, 1962]. It marks a highpoint in the paintings executed in the style of these in the Pillow Collection, to which it is very close in date. It was once ascribed to Bellotto [Ferrari, 1914], but this now seems untenable.

28 40,3 × 57 1726?

Study of Figures London, Private collection (1961)
This picture can be considered together with the following two (nos. 29 and 30). The techniques were the same and they were done at the same time. Constable attributes the work to Canaletto [*AP*, 1964] and believes it was used for the painting of the figures in the views of Windsor Castle dated 1742 (nos. 204 and 205). There is no evidence of figure painting by Canaletto before this, not even in connection with his view painting. However, Constable's arguments, despite their shrewdness, are not altogether convincing. The technique has notable precedents, however, in the work of Carlevaris.

28

29

30

31

33 (Plates XXIII–XXV)

35 (Plate XXVI)

29 🎴 ⊕ 39,6 × 57 / 1726? 📊 ⦂

Study of Figures London, Private collection (1961)
See no. 28, above.

30 🎴 ⊕ 40,3 × 58,4 / 1726? 📊 ⦂

Study of Figures London, Private collection (1961)
See no. 28, above.

31 ⊞ ⊕ 181 × 259 / 1726-27 📊 ⦂

The French Ambassador Being Received at the Doge's Palace Leningrad, Hermitage
This is the final episode of the solemn entry of Jacques-Vincent Languet, Count de Gergi, into Venice, on 4 November 1726. Hence the picture must have been painted at that time or shortly after [Haskell, *BH*, 1956; Brandi, 1960; etc.].

Constable dates it as late as 1730, considering it stylistically different from the Pillow pictures (nos. 19–22). The picture once belonged to Catherine II of Russia and is now in the Hermitage, Leningrad [*CMV*, 1967], but in 1939 it was recorded as being in Berlin, in the Tziracopoulo Collection [Constable, 1962].

32 ⊞ ⊕ 187 × 259 / 1726-27 📊 ⦂

The Bucintoro Returning to the Quay on Ascension Day
Moscow, Pushkin Museum
The companion piece to no. 31, above, and was also once the property of Catherine II, and then the Hermitage. It should be contemporaneous with the painting above. Constable [1962] agrees and points out that the Bucintoro shown here is the one built in 1728–9. On Ascension Day each year a ritual ceremony was performed uniting Venice and the sea, during which the Doge threw a golden ring into the sea from the sumptuous barge known as the "Bucintoro".

33 ⊞ ⊕ 124 × 163 / 1726-27 📊 ⦂

The Church and School of The Carità from the Marble Workshop of San Vitale
(The Stonebreaker's Yard)
London, National Gallery
This was certainly painted before 1741 (or 1744?), when the campanile of the Church of the Carità collapsed, but scholars are unanimous in dating it much earlier, between 1726 and 1730 [Watson, *AV*, 1955; Levey, 1956; Constable, 1962]. Pallucchini's dating to 1726–7 seems most convincing [1960], because, as he says, the "great panoramic breadth of the superbly theatrical shape of the composition" and the "remarkable control of the warm light" are characteristic of those years and here they are achieved in a way that makes this painting one of Canaletto's masterpieces.

34 ⊞ ⊕ 47 × 63 / 1726-28? 📊 ⦂

The Harbour of St Mark's with the Island of San Giorgio from the Piazzetta
Milan, Mario Crespi Collection
A. Formerly in the Liechtenstein Collection, where it was considered to be by Bellotto. It was ascribed to Canaletto by Seidlitz [*TBKL*, 1911]. Constable dates it after 1726–8, when the flattened form of the campanile of San Giorgio was altered. Zampetti agrees with this dating [*CMV*, 1967].
B. A variant, close to it in date, in the Toronto Art Gallery (48,5 × 81 cm.), convincingly ascribed to Canaletto by Constable.
Constable has doubts about the authorship of a replica of the Crespi painting in the Darmstadt Landesmuseum (no. 136) and dates it to the 1730s [1964].

35 ⊞ ⊕ 46,5 × 63 / 1726-28? 📊 ⦂

The Quay and the Riva degli Schiavoni from the Harbour of St Mark's Toledo, Ohio, Museum of Art
Companion piece of no. 34 A (*q.v.*), with the same provenance. The date (which Zampetti gives as 1729–30 [*CMV*, 1967]) seems the same, despite the two scrolls painted on the back: "Anton Canale M. ... zu Venedig / a. 1740" and "No. 191 Tablau [*sic*] Apartenant au Prince Joseph Wenceslau de Liechtenstein". (1740 clearly refers to the year the painting entered the Liechtenstein Collection.)
A doubtful version exists in the Landesmuseum, Darmstadt, (48,5 × 81 cm.), convincingly [*TBKL*, 1911] considers it autograph, but the museum catalogue of 1914 ascribes it to Bellotto.

36 ⊞ ⊕ 141 × 152,5 / 1726-28? 📊 ⦂

The Harbour of St Mark's with the Customs House from the Giudecca Point
Cardiff, National Museum of Wales
A. An extraordinary youthful achievement, both in the originality of the composition and in the fine quality of the painting. Constable's general dating [1962] of shortly before 1730 has been clarified to about 1726 [*CMV*, 1967].
B. A wider view of the same scene (144,4 × 235 cm.), taken from the Church of San Giorgio. Its date is close to the original. It is in Upton House, Warwickshire.
C. A version of 36 B (92 × 178 cm.), inferior in quality and not certainly by Canaletto, belongs to the Earl of Malmesbury, Heron Court [Constable, 1962].

37 ⊞ ⊕ 46 × 61 / 1726-28? 📊 ⦂

The Old Customs House and the Giudecca Canal Milan, Mario Crespi Collection
Formerly in the Liechtenstein Collection. Zampetti [*CMV*, 1967], for "external" reasons (former ownership, size, etc.) and for reasons of style, connects this work with the two preceding and the five following works. Constable [1962] saw some relationship between these paintings (see also Moschini [1954]).

38 ⊞ ⊕ 46 × 62,5 / 1726-28? 📊 ⦂

Customs House Point
Vienna, Kunsthistorisches

34A (Plate XV)

34B

36A (Plate XXXI)

36B

37 (Plates XII–XIII)

38 (Plate XVI)

39A (Plate XXII)

39B

41A

41B

Museum
A fine work, which may be related to the group of paintings formerly in the Liechtenstein Collection (see no. 37 above), marked by a freedom in composition and clear arrangement of a variety of motifs.

39 ⊞ ◐ 46×62.5 1726-28? ▤ ⋮

The Riva degli Schiavoni towards St Mark's Vienna, Kunsthistorisches Museum
A. Constable [1962] points out that this is a companion piece to no. 38, but simply dates it before 1745, the year the façade of the Church of the Pietà was given its new appearance. See no. 37, above.
B. A variant (122 × 201 cm.) with a different angle of vision, certainly executed by Canaletto, is in the Soane Museum, London. It is close in date to, though not part of, the homogeneous group of works formerly in the Liechtenstein Collection (see no. 37). It is related to two drawings at Windsor Castle, one of which can be dated to 1729 [Watson, 1949]. Constable [1962] as well dates it c. 1726–8.
Constable mentions some eight variations of this view, none by Canaletto.

40 ⊞ ◐ 47×63 1726-28? ▤ ⋮

The Church of San Giorgio from the Giudecca Canal
Originally part of the former Liechtenstein group (see no. 37). Constable [1962] refers it to a period just after 1726–8.

41 ⊞ ◐ 46×63.5 1726-28? ▤ ⋮

The Grand Canal with the Church of the Carità towards the Harbour of St Mark's
USA, Private collection
A. Formerly in the Liechtenstein group (see no. 37, above). It varies slightly from the view painted in 1726, now in the

45

Pillow Collection, Montreal (no. 21). However it was certainly painted before 1730 [Constable, 1962].
B. A replica is in Windsor Castle (47,5 × 79 cm.). It was painted for Consul Smith and sold to George III (1763). It was drawn and engraved by Visentini, who included it in the 1735 album [Moschini, 1954]. This suggests that the work was painted before 1730 and probably about 1729, the date of the whole series by Visentini (see no. 67, below). But it might have been painted as early as 1728.
Constable [1962] lists seven other variants, not autograph and attributable to the school of Canaletto. They are in various collections.

42 ⊞ ◐ 150×198 1726-28? ▤ ⋮

The Grand Canal from Palazzo Balbi Dresden, Pillnitz Castle
A. Variation on a theme painted earlier (Crespi Collection, see no. 13 above) and frequently painted again. This one, the companion to another work at Pillnitz (no. 19 C), is dated c. 1726 [Constable, 1962].
B. A derivation rather similar to the Crespi painting but stylistically akin to no. 42 A is in the Accademia Carrara, Bergamo (61 × 99 cm.). A preparatory sketch is in the Courtauld Institute, London [Hadeln, 1930].
C. This painting, in the Uffizi (45 × 73 cm.), is related to no. 42 A. The present author considers it to be by Canaletto (see also Moschini [1954]).
D. A fine variant, containing the compositional elements of nos. 42 A and B, has been re-attributed to Canaletto by Constable [1962] and dated c. 1728. It is in the Warde Collection, London (65 × 96 cm.).

43 ⊞ ◐ 47×79 1726-28? ▤ ⋮

The Island of San Giorgio with the Customs House from the Entrance to the Grand Canal Windsor Castle, Royal Collections
The form of the Campanile of San Giorgio provides a *terminus post quem* (see no. 26 A), which therefore gives an approximate date for this view, painted for Smith and sold to George III.
Other versions noted by Constable [1962] are not by Canaletto.

42C

42D

43

44A

46A

46B

44 ⊞ ◐ 191×203 1726-28? ▤ ⋮

The entrance to the Grand Canal with the Customs House and the Church of the Salute Grenoble, Musée de Peinture et de Sculpture
A. Linked stylistically with the large views painted in his youth and now in Windsor Castle (nos. 47–52), a group whose homogeneity was identified by Watson [1954]. The dating is influenced by this. The selection of a view from above gives the painting a vivid theatrical effect.
B. A version in the Kauffman Collection, Strasbourg (44,5 × 59,5 cm.), is similar in angle of view. It is also similar in style and executed in a technique (oil on copper) typical of the years before 1730. The *terminus ante quem* is established by the

engraving that Boitard made with only slight variations, published by Bandin in 1736.

45 ⊞ ◐ 29×28 1726-28? ▤ ⋮

The Piazzetta towards the Island of San Giorgio
Van Wulften Palthe, Oldenzaal, Ten Cate Collection
Companion piece of another view (no. 49 B) in the same collection. Both were formerly attributed to Bellotto but are certainly by Canaletto. For dating, see no. 49 B, below.

46 ⊞ ◐ 62×100 *1727-29 ▤ ⋮

The Grand Canal from Palazzo Vendramin Calergi to Palazzo Michiel dalle Colonne Birmingham,

(Alabama), Museum of Art, Kress Collection
A. A beautiful work of his youth, perhaps slightly earlier than the six large views at Windsor Castle (nos. 47 and ff.) [Constable, 1964].
B. A fine, slightly different version, perhaps only a little later, is in the Borletti Collection, Milan (61 × 100 cm.). Its authenticity is confirmed by its mention in Dodsley's *Guide* as early as 1761.

47 ⊞ ◐ 170×133,5 1726-29? ▤ ⋮

The Entrance to the Grand Canal from the Piazzetta Windsor Castle, Royal Collections
A. Part of the Smith collection sold to George III (1763). A late dating, between 1735 and 1740, was rejected by Watson [1949], who dated it, together with five other works at Windsor, to 1726–8. Other scholars [Pallucchini, 1960; Constable, 1962; etc.] are in substantial agreement about this splendid painting. (See also nos. 48–52, below, and no. 52 in particular). Levey [1964] has justly extended the period of execution to 1726/7–1729. A drawing at Windsor Castle (no. 7445) is a free variation rather than a preparatory sketch [Parker, 1948, considered it a sketch].
B. There is another version

47A   47B   47C

48

51

52 (Plate XI)

49A

49B

50

53

(known also as the *Fish Market*) that is certainly by Canaletto and very fine, and is close in date [Pallucchini, 1960] to 47 A. It is in the Metropolitan Museum, New York (131,5 × 130 cm.). C. Another autograph version, similar in composition to the New York view and painted about the same time, belongs to the Trustees of the Chatsworth Settlement and the Devonshire Collection (46 × 61 cm.). It is a companion piece to no. 59.

48 ⊞ ◑ 170×132 1726-29? ▤ ⁝

The Piazzetta towards the Island of San Giorgio Windsor Castle, Royal Collections
Also painted for Smith and part of the group mentioned under no. 47 A, above. There are four drawings which are certainly related to this painting: two at Windsor Castle (nos. 7442, 7446), the first of which is "finished"; one in the Ashmolean Museum, Oxford; and one in the album in the Accademia, Venice (fol. 2 v.).

49 ⊞ ◑ 133,3×170,7 1726-29? ▤ ⁝

St Mark's Square towards the Basilica from the Procuratie Nuove Windsor Castle, Royal Collections
A. Another very fine piece from

the series reconstructed by Watson [1949] (see no. 47). A closely related drawing is also preserved at Windsor Castle (no. 7429).
B. Derivation from the above-mentioned drawing suggests that a small view of the Square (Van Wulften Palthe, Ten Cate Collection; 29 × 28 cm.) is related to the Windsor paintings. This small view, like its companion piece in the same collection (no. 45), is certainly the work of Canaletto, although it was formerly ascribed to Bellotto.

50 ⊞ ◑ 170×129,5 1726-29? ▤

St Mark's Square towards the Church of San Geminiano from the Piazzetta Windsor Castle, Royal Collections
One of the most remarkable works in the series grouped together by Watson [1949] (see no. 47). Related to a drawing at Windsor Castle (no. 7434) [Parker, 1948] and to a preparatory sketch of two figures in the album in the Accademia, Venice (fol. 58 r.) [Constable, 1962].

51 ⊞ ◑ 170×133,5 1726-29? ▤ ⁝

St Mark's Square towards the Procuratie Vecchie from the Basilica Windsor

Castle, Royal Collections
See nos. 47-50, above. A drawing at Windsor Castle (no. 7444) may have been a preliminary version [Parker, 1948].

52 ⊞ ◑ 170,2×129,5 1726-29? ▤ ⁝

The Piazzetta towards the Torre dell'Orologio Windsor Castle, Royal Collections
Formerly dated 1735-40.

Watson places it in the group discussed under no. 47 [1949]. A related drawing is at Windsor Castle (no. 7443) [Parker, 1948]. Pallucchini [1960] wrote that these six paintings present "an easier and surer sense of perspective, with a slightly lighter [colour] … although warm tones still predominate; the figures acquire a new importance in the overall economy of the view, painted as they are with solid, thick brushwork and clearly delineated within a complex of surprising vitality. Canaletto depicts a monumental Venice in robust, slightly gloomy tones, a Venice experienced in a dense and humid summer air"

53 ⊞ ◑ 131×196 1726-30? ▤ ⁝

The Rialto Bridge from the the Fondamenta del Vin Leningrad, Hermitage
Incorrectly ascribed to Bellotto in the 1899 catalogue of the Hermitage. It is in fact an early work of Canaletto, certainly painted before 1730, perhaps inspired by an engraving by Carlevaris (no. 57 in the *Fabbricche*) [Constable, 1962].

54 ⊞ ◑ 44×89 1726-30? ▤ ⁝

The Church of the Salute and the Customs House from the Vicinity of Palazzo Cornaro Berlin, Staatliche Museen-Gemäldegalerie
It has the stylistic features of paintings of this period, though with a certain stiffness and harshness that have puzzled some scholars. Constable [1962] ascribes it, with some caution, to Canaletto, and dates it roughly to the period of the Pillow pictures (nos. 19-22). A drawing, with a more "open" view, that seems to be related to it, is at Windsor Castle (no. 7461) [Parker, 1948].

55 ⊞ ◑ 46×58,5 1727 ▤ ○

The Grand Canal from near the Rialto Bridge towards the North Goodwood, Duke of Richmond and Gordon's

Collection
This painting, like no. 56, below, is mentioned in the correspondence of McSwiney and the Duke of Richmond. In the letter of 28 November 1727, it is described as finished [Finberg, WS, 1920-1]. It is a variation on the view painted in 1725 and now in the Pillow Collection (no. 19). It is unusual, being painted on copper, a technique Canaletto only used in his youth, before 1730 [Constable, 1962].

56 ⊞ ◑ 46×58,5 1727 ▤ ⁝

The Grand Canal with the Rialto Bridge from the North Goodwood, Duke of Richmond and Gordon's Collection
See no. 55, above.

57 ⊞ ◑ 46×62,5 1727* ▤ ○

The Grand Canal from Campo San Vio towards the East Holkham Hall, Earl of Leicester's Collection
Companion piece of no. 58 (*q.v.*).

58 ⊞ ◑ 45,5×62,5 1727* ▤ ⁝

The Rialto Bridge from the South Holkham Hall, Earl of Leicester's Collection
The technique and style suggest a date in the artist's youth, about the time of the works for the Duke of Richmond (nos. 55 and 56). Companion piece of no. 57, in the same collection. Both works were acquired by 1759 [Constable, 1962]. They were mentioned as early as 1773 [Brettigham, *The Plans … of Holkham … 1773*]. Engraved by Fletcher and published by Baudin (1739).

59 ⊞ ◑ 46,5×62 1728? ▤ ⁝

The Riva degli Schiavoni towards the West Trustees of the Chatsworth Settlement and the Devonshire Collection
Companion piece to no. 47 C. It came from the Duke of Devonshire's Collection (although the 1792 inventory

54

55

56

58

57

59

60A (Plates XX–XXI)

61 (Plates XVII–XIX)

62 (Plates IX–X)

64C

65

66

does not list it). Constable [1962] argues that the use of copper as a support makes it datable to the artist's youth, and that this is confirmed by the stylistic qualities of the painting. He also suggests that these two pictures may be the ones mentioned in the 1727 correspondence between McSwiney and the Duke of Richmond about the other two still in the Richmond Collection (nos. 55 and 56).

60 ▦ ◔ 61 × 94,6 / 1728?
The Dolo Locks Oxford, Ashmolean Museum
A. It was Watson [AV, 1950] who identified the subject and dated the work before 1729 (or better, 1728), the year in which the new Dolo church, not shown here, was dedicated.
B. Among other versions discussed by scholars, only one — and that one doubtful and certainly late (80 × 95,3 cm.) —

might be by Canaletto, the one in the Dunkels Collection, Sussex [Constable, 1962].

61 ▦ ◔ 184 × 265 / 1729
The Imperial Ambassador Being Received at the Doge's Palace Milan, Aldo Crespi Collection
Usually dated to shortly after 16 May 1729, the day the Emperor's envoy, Count Joseph

of Bolagno, arrived in Venice [see also Zampetti, CMV, 1967]. Constable [1962] rejected tradition that Tiepolo painted the figures in this view and dated the work somewhat later, about 1730. Pallucchini [1960] pointed out connections between this treatment by Canaletto of similar themes by Carlevaris and paintings in the Birmingham (1707) and Dresden (1726) galleries. (See no. 67 B, below.)

62 ▦ ◔ 95,5 × 117 / 1729?
Campo San Giacometto Dresden, Gemäldegalerie
This celebrated view was inventoried among the possessions of the King of Saxony in 1754. The dating of this work and no. 63 to just before 1730 has been confirmed Constable [1962] and generally accepted [Zampetti, CMV, 1967]. There is a drawing in the Seilern Collection, London, whose authenticity is guaranteed by a handwritten inscription by Canaletto. Hadeln [1930] considered it a preparatory drawing, but Constable judges it to be later than the painting.

63 ▦ ◔ 96 × 117 / 1729?
St Mark's Square towards the Basilica
This is one of the first versions of a subject Canaletto frequently painted. Formerly in the Dresden Gemäldegalerie, along with its companion piece (no. 62), but it was no longer to be found after World War II.

64 ▦ ◔ 134,5 × 126 / 1729-30
The Church of San Geremia and the Entrance to Cannaregio Tissington Hall, Derbyshire, Fitzherbert Collection
A. Version of the subject depicted in the view in Windsor Castle (no. 79) but without the balustrade and statue. Hence it is earlier than 1742 — and by several years, judging by the style. Constable [1962] sees some assistance in the execution.
B. Another version (46,5 × 78,5 cm.) without balustrade or statue is in a private collection in England. Constable dates it to just after 1730. The work seems fairly similar to the Windsor Castle version (no. 79).
C. A version in an Italian private collection (46 × 73 cm.) is also datable to 1729–30. It is similar in style to the Quay with the

Doge's Palace (no. 66) and the Piazzetta (no. 65) in a private collection in the United States.

65 ▦ ◔ 46 × 63 / 1729-30
The Piazzetta towards the Island of San Giorgio with a View of the Basilica and the Doge's Palace USA, Private collection
Constable [1962] connects the work — which certainly dates after 1728, because of the new form of the campanile of San Giorgio — to the views showing the Church of San Geremia and the entrance to Cannaregio (no. 64) and to that of the Grand Canal from Ca' Foscari (no. 71 C), all of which can be firmly dated between 1729 and 1730.

66 ▦ ◔ 46 × 63 / 1729-30
The Quay with the Right Side of the Doge's Palace
USA, Private collection
This forms a set [Constable, 1962] with the preceding work and with no. 64 C. All three were formerly in the Liechtenstein Collection.

67 ▦ ◔ 77 × 126 / 1729-34?
The Bucintoro Returning to the Quay on Ascension Day Windsor Castle, Royal Collections
A. One of Canaletto's favourite subjects. The first version (no. 32) is in Moscow. This version was in the collection of Consul Smith. It is reproduced in Visentini's album of 1735 (pl. XIV). In view of this fact, which affects all fourteen of the reproduced paintings, Watson [1949], Pallucchini [1960], Constable [1962] and others date the works to just before 1730, because of Smith's letter to Samuel Hill (17 July 1730), in which Smith says that the Visentini prints are almost ready [Chaloner, BJRL, 1950]. Consequently they reject Levey's dating [BM, 1953] (see no. 68, below). Levey discussed the matter again [1964] and his view that the fourteen pictures which Visentini engraved should be dated between 1729 and 1734, seems the most likely. A drawing related to the following two versions of the subject is in Windsor Castle (no. 7451).
B. A fine version in the Aldo Crespi Collection, Milan, (182 × 259 cm.) is a companion piece to no. 61 and hence datable shortly after May 1729 [Zampetti, CMV, 1967].
C. Another good version,

67A

67B (Plates XXVIII–XXX)

68A (Plates XLIV–XLV)

70A

70B (Plate XXVII)

70C

contemporary or slightly later, in an English private collection (150 × 218 cm.) is a companion piece to no. 68 B [Constable, 1962].

D. Another version, of doubtful attribution, is in a private collection in Milan (100,5 × 108 cm.) [Constable, 1962].

68  77 × 126 1729-34?

Regatta on the Grand Canal Windsor Castle, Royal Collections

A. Visentini's engraving of this painting was in the 1735 album (pl. XIII). Constable therefore dates the painting to just before 1730 [1962], together with all the pictures reproduced in that album, in particular no. 67 A.

Levey [BM, 1953] argues that the work must date no earlier than 1732, because the insignia of Carlo Ruzzini, Doge from June 1732 to January 1735, appear on the Bucintoro (and this is also shown in the Visentini engraving). Constable rejects this theory, arguing that the coat-of-arms could have been added some time later. Levey [1964] disagreed with Constable, who observed that this is the first regatta by Canaletto. He indicated the source as Carlevaris' painting in Frederiksborg Castle of the regatta in honour of Frederick IV of Denmark in 1709.

Five derivations in various places are mentioned by Constable but not considered autograph.

B. One version, close in date, is in an English private collection (150 × 218 cm.). It is the companion piece of no. 67 C.

69 ⊞ ◐ 47 × 78 1729-34?

The Grand Canal from the Rialto Bridge to Ca' Foscari Windsor Castle, Royal Collections

A. Visentini's engraving of this painting appeared in the 1735 album (pl. I). Thus the work can be dated as nos. 67 A and 68 A and as the next ten paintings, below.

Constable [1962] lists three versions, including one in the Alvan Fuller Collection, Boston. Its authorship is highly questionable, and it should not

be considered autograph.

B. An autograph version in the Museum of Fine Arts, Houston, (49,5 × 72,5 cm.), the companion piece to no. 70 B. Documents indicate that it was painted about 1730 or a little earlier [Constable, 1964].

C. An autograph version of no. 69 B (54, × 91,5 cm.), of uncertain date, is in the Mills Collection, Hillborough (Thetford) [Constable, 1962].

D. A version that anticipates the treatment in the latest version (no. 117) is in an English private collection (45 × 75,5 cm.) together with a companion piece (no. 72 B). It dates from about 1730.

70 ⊞ ◐ 47,5 × 79,5 1729-34?

The Entrance to the Grand Canal with the Customs House and the Church of the Salute Windsor Castle, Royal Collections

A. The engraving of this painting is plate VI in Visentini's album of 1735. For dating, see nos. 67 A and 68 A.

B. A fine variation (49,5 × 72,5 cm.) in the Houston Museum of Fine Arts has been dated closely to the Windsor version, because of a document found and published by Constable [1962]. This document, of 22 August 1730, contained Hugh Howard's announcement of the arrival of the painting, which he had purchased together with a companion piece (no. 69 B) from Smith. (See Zampetti [CMV, 1967]).

C. Another fine version, dated to just after 1730, is in the Poss Collection, Novara (58 × 91,5 cm.); it is the companion piece to no. 75 C.

D. Another version, very close in style to the Houston painting but weaker and of uncertain attribution (it was once even ascribed to Bellotto) is in the Rocchetti Collection, Rome (84 × 133 cm.).

Constable [1962] mentions many other versions, some of uncertain authorship and some certainly not by Canaletto.

71 ⊞ ◐ 47,5 × 80,5 1729-34?

The Grand Canal from Ca' Foscari towards the Church of the Carità Windsor Castle, Royal Collections

A. For Visentini's engraving (pl. II) and other matters, see nos. 67 and 68, above.

B. Another version, with a different angle of view, is in the Wallace Collection, London (44,5 × 75,5 cm.). The authorship is much debated.

Some ascribe it to Bellotto, though Constable [1962] assigns it, with its companion piece (no. 83 A), to Canaletto. Its dating remains an open question (see no. 83 A).

C. A good version (101 × 162 cm.), in the National Museum, Stockholm. The fact that it may have been purchased in Venice in 1736 by Tessin [Siren, 1902], suggests a dating before 1736. In any case it is close to the Windsor Castle version in style. Constable [1962] would date it about 1735.

72 ⊞ ◐ 46 × 77,5 1729-34?

The Grand Canal from Campo San Vio towards the Church of the Salute Windsor Castle, Royal Collections

A. For Visentini's engraving (pl. IV) and other information, see nos. 67 and 68, above.

B. Another version, contemporary or slightly later, is in an English private collection (45 × 75,5 cm.) and is a companion piece to no. 69 D. According to Constable [1962], who published them, they are two works mentioned in an unpublished letter from the Venetian merchant Sasso to Sir Abraham Hume (11 February 1789): "two small views by Canaletti [sic] ... among his most beautiful ones".

C. Another version, also mentioned by Constable [1962], who dates it before 1730, belonged to the Whatman Collection, Kent (now in an English private collection). It is bigger (129,5 × 165 cm.) and the view is larger.

D. Probably of the same period and certainly autograph is the version in the Brooks Memorial Art Gallery (Kress Collection), Memphis, Tennessee (113 × 167,5 cm.); the companion piece to no. 82 B.

For another version, see no. 57, above.

73 ⊞ ◐ 47,5 × 79,5 1729-34?

The Entrance to the Grand Canal with the Church of the Salute Windsor Castle, Royal Collections

For Visentini's engraving of this picture and for other information, see nos. 67 and 68, above. The first treatment of this subject by Canaletto dates from some years earlier (see no. 23, above).

74 ⊞ ◐ 47 × 80 1729-34?

The Grand Canal with the Rialto Bridge from the North Windsor Castle, Royal

69A

69B

71A

71B

72A

72D

73

74

Collections
For Visentini's engraving of this picture and for other information, see nos. 67 and 68, above

75 ▦ ◑ 47,5×78 / 1729-34? 目 ⋮

The Grand Canal from near the Rialto Bridge towards the North Windsor Castle, Royal Collections
A. Earlier treatments of the subject are nos. 19 A and 55, above. For Visentini's engraving of this picture and for other information, see nos. 67 and 68, above.
B. A very cold version, considered autograph despite some doubts, and of uncertain date, is in the Musée Cognacq-Jay, Paris (48,5 × 79 cm.); companion piece to no. 99 C.
C. Another autograph version is in the Poss Collection, Novara (58 × 92 cm.); companion piece to no. 70 C.

76 ▦ ◑ 47×80 / 1729-34? 目 ⋮

The Grand Canal from Palazzo Vendramin Calergi towards San Geremia Windsor Castle, Royal Collections
For Visentini's engravings of this picture and for other information, see nos. 67 and 68, above.

77 ▦ ◑ 47×79,5 / 1729-34? 目 ⋮

The Grand Canal with the Church of San Simeone Piccolo towards the Fondamenta della Croce Windsor Castle, Royal Collections
For Visentini's engraving of this picture and for dating, see nos. 67 and 68, above. The date is certain because of the incomplete state of the parapet of the staircase of San Simeone, which was only completed by 1738 [Constable, 1962].

78 ▦ ◑ 46,5×77,5 / 1729-34? 目 ⋮

The Grand Canal at Santa Chiara towards the Lagoon Windsor Castle, Royal Collections

A. For Visentini's engraving of this and for dating, see nos. 67 and 68, above. For this picture, Constable [1964] confirms the date (before 1730) which he had already advanced for all the paintings in the Windsor Castle series [1962].
B. A splendid version in the Mario Crespi Collection, Milan, (58 × 80 cm.) was engraved by Fletcher and printed by Baudin in 1739 [Finberg and Watson, BM, 1955]. An eighteenth-century inscription on the back says that it was painted "about 1730". This suggests that the person who commissioned it may have been Colonel E. Burgess, an Englishman who lived in Venice from October 1719 until March 1722, and again from December 1728 until his death in November 1736 [Morassi, BM, 1955; Constable, 1962].

79 ▦ ◑ 46,5×78,5 / 1729 or 1742? 目 ⋮

The Entrance to Cannaregio and the Church of San Geremia Windsor Castle, Royal Collections
Visentini did an engraving of this for his 1735 album (see nos. 67 and 68, above). But the engraving, the preparatory drawings in the Museo Correr and the British Museum and the sheet itself (at Windsor Castle, no. 7475, whose attribution to Canaletto is controversial, do not show the balustrade and the statue of St John Nepomuk. These were put up at the entrance in 1742 or 1743 [Arslan, BA, 1926-7]. The statue does appear in the 1742 edition of Visentini. This raises a difficulty in dating the painting, in which the statue is shown. The style of the painting is like that of the other works in this group (see nos. 67 and 68). Constable [1962] advances the rather difficult hypothesis that Canaletto retouched and "up-dated" his painting after the new balustrade was set up.

80 ▦ ◑ 58,5×102 / 1730 目 ⋮

The Quay with the Libreria on the Right and the Church

75A

76

78A

78B

82A

82B

of the Salute towards the **Left** London (?), the late Lord Egerton of Tatton's Collection
Two letters of 1730 to S. Hill [Chaloner, BJRL, 1950], one from Smith (17 July) and the other from a nephew (15 December) make the dating of this picture and its companion piece (no. 81) certain. A drawing at Windsor Castle (no. 7460) and another in the Pennsylvania Academy of Fine Arts, Philadelphia [Parker, 1948] are related to the picture. The latter is also connected with an important sketch, now in the De Burlet Collection, Basle [Constable, 1962], which bears the autograph inscription "1729, view of the square toward the sea" [Hadeln, BM, 1926].

81 ▦ ◑ 58,5×102 / 1730 目 ⋮

The Riva degli Schiavoni with the Doge's Palace towards the East London (?), the late Lord Egerton of Tatton's Collection
Companion piece of no. 80. It is connected with a drawing at Windsor Castle (no. 7452) and with another in the Landesmuseum, Darmstadt, which bears the autograph inscription "View toward the castle, that is, of the *piazzetta*, March 1729, Venice" [Hadeln, 1930].

82 ▦ ◑ 73×123 / 1730? 目 ⋮

The Quay with the Doge's Palace towards the Church of the Salute Berlin,

Staatliche Museen-Gemäldegalerie.
A. The subject had already been painted about 1725 (no. 24, above). It is dated on the basis of style [Moschini, 1954].
B. A contemporary version (or slightly earlier?), companion piece of no. 72 D, is in the Museum of Art (Kress Collection), El Paso, Texas.

83 ▦ ◑ 44,5×75,5 / 1730* 目 ⋮

The Grand Canal from Palazzo Flangini towards San Marcuola London, Wallace Collection
A. A controversial work, like its companion piece (no. 71 B), doubtfully attributed to Bellotto. Constable re-attributed it to

77

79

80

81

83A

84A

85A

86A

87A   *87B*

88A   *88B*

89A   *91A*

Canaletto [1962].
B. Another version, very probably autograph and of fine quality, belongs to the Jones Collection, Minneapolis (60 × 92,5 cm.).

84

St Mark's Square towards the Basilica Woburn Abbey, Duke of Bedford's Collection
A. This is one of twenty-four views, all but two of which were of the same format, painted by Canaletto for the Duke of Bedford during the latter's tour of the continent before 1731–2 [Scharf, *Catalogue of ... Pictures at Woburn Abbey,* 1889]. The series is still owned by his descendants and unanimously dated about 1730–1 [Moschini, 1954; Brandi, 1960; Pallucchini, 1960; Constable, 1962, etc.]. Some were used by Visentini for the complete edition of his album (see no. 67, above), published in 1742 (and included in the 1735 edition). This subject was reproduced in 1742 as well.
B. A version (88,5 × 111,8 cm.) dated by Constable to some time after 1725–6 and so contemporary with no. 84 A, is in the Barlow Collection, Wendover (Buckinghamshire).
C. The version (61 × c 92,5

85 47 × 80 1730-31

St Mark's Square from the Basilica towards the Church of San Geminiano and the Procuratie Nuove Woburn Abbey, Duke of Bedford's Collection
A. For Visentini's engraving (1742, pl. XL) and other information, see no. 84 A, above. "Finished" drawings related to this painting are in Windsor Castle (no. 7433) and in the Louvre (no. 4794) [Hadeln, 1930; Parker, 1948].
B. The whereabouts are now unknown of a version (75 × 118 cm.) acquired by the second Duke of Newcastle (see the *post mortem* inventory, drawn up in 1794 [Constable, 1962]).

86 47 × 78,8 1730-31

The Piazzetta towards the Torre dell'Orologio Woburn

cm.) in the Cartwright Collection, Aynhoe Park (Northampton), is also probably contemporary; companion piece to no. 90 B.
D. Also probably contemporary, because of the impasto and the soft atmospheric tonality. This beautiful version (61 × 94 cm.) is in the Douglas-Pennant Collection, Penrhyn Castle, Wales.

the drawing was copied from the painting to serve as a basis for later versions.
B. Perhaps this is one of the later versions (79 × 124,5 cm.); considered autograph by Constable [1962]. It is in the Weitzner Collection, New York.
C. Another version, close in date, because of great similarity of style, in the Speelman Collection, London (80 × 127 cm.).
D. No comment can be made about this version (75 × 118 cm.), formerly the property of the second Duke of Newcastle (see no. 85 B) and now lost. It was, however, certainly earlier than 1755 [Constable, 1962].

87  47 × 80 1730-31

The Quay from the Harbour of St Mark's Woburn Abbey, Duke of Bedford's Collection
A. For its provenance and Visentini's engraving (1735; pl. XIV), see no. 84 A. above. It is also related to a "finished" drawing at Windsor Castle (no. 7451) which may have been used for his frequent portrayals of the arrival or departure of the Bucintoro on Ascension Day [Constable, 1962].
B. A more "open" version (because of a slight shift in angle of view), but certainly based on the Windsor drawing mentioned above; in the Uffizi, Florence (51 × 83 cm.). A fine work but hard to date, though certainly painted before 1755, when the third storey of the clock tower, not shown here, was completed. It belonged to the Medicis before 1796. Fritzsche erroneously attributed it to Bellotto [1836].
C. Another, larger (65 × 103 cm.) version, with some differences in detail; autograph. It is a little later than the Woburn Abbey prototype, and belongs to the Earl of Cadogan.
D. Another autograph version with very rich colours (68,5 × 113,5 cm.). In the Duke of Norfolk's Collection, at Arundel Castle.

Abbey, Duke of Bedford's Collection
A. For its provenance see no. 84 A, above. It is a variation of the subject already depicted in one of the six large Windsor Castle views (no. 52) and is related to a drawing at Windsor Castle and another in the Landesmuseum, Darmstadt, dated 1732 but highly controversial [Hadeln, 1930; Arslan, *AB*, 1949; etc.]. Probably

88  47 × 79 1730-31

Entrance to the Grand Canal with the Church of the Salute Woburn Abbey, Duke of Bedford's Collection
A. For the history and dating, see no. 84 A, above. This subject, which was dear to Canaletto's heart, was first painted in the Windsor Castle version (70 A).
B. This version (53 × 70,5 cm.), of controversial date, was engraved by Fletcher and printed by Baudin in 1739. It was in the possession of Rosenberg and Stiebel, New York, in 1956. The companion piece to no. 140 A, it is datable before 1735 because of style and outside evidence.

89  47 × 78,7 1730-31

The Grand Canal from Palazzo Cornaro to Palazzo Contarini dagli Scrigni Woburn Abbey, Duke of Bedford's Collection
A. Related to some sketches in the Accademia, Venice, as shown by Pignatti [1958] and Gioseffi [1959]. It was used again in the 1742 edition of Visentini's engraving (II, pl. X), perhaps after "finished" autograph drawings at Windsor Castle (nos. 7469 and 7470 [Parker, 1948]). See also no. 84 A, above.
B. A good version is in the Hampden Collection, Alton (Hampshire) (44,5 × 76 cm.), part of a series of four (see no. 110 A, below). Slightly later in date.

90 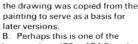 47 × 80 1730-31

The Grand Canal from Palazzo Contarini dagli Scrigni to Ca' Rezzonico Woburn Abbey, Duke of Bedford's Collection
A. For its provenance, see no. 84 A, above. It can be related to a drawing in Windsor Castle and to a series of six sketches in the sketchbook in the Accademia, Venice [Parker, 1948; Pignatti, 1958].
B. A fine version (61 × 92,5 cm.) was formerly in the Cartwright Collection, Aynhoe Park (Northampton); the companion piece of no. 84 C.

90A   *90B*

93A   *93D*

92

95

96

97 (Plate XXXVIII)

98

99B

91 The Grand Canal from Ca' Rezzonico to Palazzo Balbi
Woburn Abbey, Duke of Bedford's Collection

47×80
1730-31

A. For its provenance, see no. 84 A, above. Several sketches in the sketchbook at the Accademia, Venice, are preparatory for this work [Pignatti, 1958; Gioseffi, 1959], and there is a related "finished" drawing at Windsor Castle (no. 7468) [Parker, 1948].
B. The version in the Mills Collection, Hillborough, Thetford, is probably autograph (59,5 × 127 cm.).

92 The Grand Canal from Palazzo Corner Spinelli to the Rialto Bridge
Woburn Abbey, Duke of Bedford's Collection

47×80
1730-31

For its provenance, see no. 84 A, above. It is a variation on a theme already depicted in the youthful and more dramatically angled painting in Dresden (no. 17). Preliminary sketches have been identified in the sketchbook in the Accademia, Venice [Pignatti, 1958], and there is a "finished" drawing of it at Windsor Castle (no. 7471) [Parker, 1948].

93 The Grand Canal from Palazzo Balbi to the Rialto Bridge
Woburn Abbey, Duke of Bedford's Collection

47×80
1730-31

A. For general information, see no. 84 A, above. The subject, one of Canaletto's favourites, had already been treated in the earlier work in the Mario Crespi Collection, Milan (see no. 13). A preparatory sketch is in the Courtauld Institute, London [Constable, 1962].
B. A version mentioned by Constable [1962] as being the possession of the executors of Sir George Leon (85 × 139 cm.). Judging by photographs, it is of high quality.
C. Another good version (85 × 137 cm.), was mentioned in Dodsley's *London Guide* of

1761 as in the possession of Sir Sampson Gideon. It was shown at Agnew's, London, in 1955, and is related to the Leon version. The companion piece of no. 109 A.
D. Another autograph version (76 × 120 cm.) of the Leon painting, in the Mario Crespi Collection, Milan; companion piece to no. 109 B, in the same collection.

94 The Rialto Bridge from the South
Woburn Abbey, Duke of Bedford's Collection

47×80
1730-31

A. For its provenance, see no. 84 A, above. The composition follows the painting of a couple of years earlier, in the possession of the Earl of Leicester (no. 58). The subject was to be painted again. A drawing at Windsor Castle (no. 7466) has been related to this painting [Parker, 1948].
B. This version shows several variations. It is related to earlier or later versions as well. The authorship is controversial and the dating uncertain. In the Wallace Collection, London (58 × 92,5 cm.). The companion piece to no. 99 B, in the same collection.

95 The Grand Canal from Ca' Pesaro to the Fondaco dei Tedeschi
Woburn Abbey, Duke of Bedford's Collection

47×79
1730-31

For general information, see no. 84 A, above. Some sketches in the sketchbook in Venice, Accademia, are preparatory for this [Pignatti, 1958].

96 The Grand Canal from Palazzo Vendramin Calergi to Palazzo Fontana
Woburn Abbey, Duke of Bedford's Collection

47×80
1730-31

For the provenance of the painting, see no. 84 A, above. Its relationship to sketches in the sketchbook in the Accademia, Venice, have been

pointed out by Pignatti [1958] and Gioseffi [1959].

97 The Grand Canal from Palazzo Bembo to Palazzo Vendramin Calergi
Woburn Abbey, Duke of Bedford's Collection

47×80
1730-31

For the provenance of the painting, see no. 84 A, above. (See also Pallucchini [1960] and Zampetti [*CMV*, 1967].) Some drawings in the sketchbook in the Accademia, Venice, are certainly connected with this painting [Pignatti, 1958]. Visentini included the view in his series of engravings (1742, II, pl. IV).

98 The Grand Canal from the Church of Santa Croce to the Church of San Geremia
Woburn Abbey, Duke of Bedford's Collection

47×80
1730-31

For general information, see no. 84 A, above. A "finished" drawing at Windsor Castle (no. 7472) is related to the painting [Parker, 1948], as are some sketches in the sketchbook in the Accademia, Venice [Pignatti, 1958]. These sketches were also used for the slightly later version of the same subject (see no. 114, below).

99 The Santa Chiara Canal at the Fondamenta della Croce
Woburn Abbey, Duke of

47×80
1730-31

Bedford's Collection
A. For the provenance of the painting, see no. 84 A, above. A drawing at Windsor Castle (no. 7476) [Parker, 1948], is related to the painting, as are some sketches in the sketchbook in the Accademia, Venice [Pignatti, 1958].
B. A rather cold version, but very probably autograph, in the Wallace Collection, London (58 × 92 cm.). Derived from the drawings mentioned above, it is very similar to Visentini's engraving (1742, II, pl. I). Companion piece to no. 94 B, in the same collection.
C. Another version, difficult to date but almost certainly autograph, is in the Musée Cognacq-Jay, Paris (48,5 × 79 cm.). Constable [1962] dates it shortly after 1730.

94A

94B

100 (Plate XXXV)

102

101A (Plates XXXVI–XXXVII)

101B

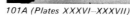

100 ⊞ ⊘ 47×78,8 ▤ ⦂
1730-31

The Arsenal Bridge Woburn
Abbey, Duke of Bedford's
Collection
For the history of the painting,
see no. 84 A, above. Related to
it are drawings at Windsor Castle
(no. 7477) and the Lugt
Collection, The Hague [Parker,

1948], as well as sketches in the
sketchbook in the Accademia,
Venice [Moschini, 1954;
Pignatti, 1958; Constable, 1962;
Zampetti, *CMV*, 1967].

101 ⊞ ⊘ 47×80 ▤ ⦂
1730-31

**Campo Santa Maria
Formosa** Woburn Abbey,
Duke of Bedford's Collection
A. For general information, see
no. 84 A, above. This is one of
the finest works, not only of the
Bedford series, but of all of
Canaletto's paintings [Zampetti,

CMV, 1967]. Two drawings at
Windsor Castle (nos. 7478 and
7479) [Parker, 1948] and
various sketches in the
sketchbook in the Accademia,
Venice are related to it [Pignatti,
1958].
B. A slightly different version
(92 × 150,5 cm.), based on the
Windsor Castle drawings
mentioned above. Of uncertain
date, but probably later than the
Woburn Abbey version. It
belongs to the Earl of Cadogan
[Constable, 1962].
C. Another version, very close
to Visentini's engraving (1742,
III, pl. VIII) and certainly
autograph, is in an Italian private
collection [Constable, 1962];
companion piece to no. 105 B,
in the same collection.

102 ⊞ ⊘ 47×80 ▤ ⦂
1730-31

Campo Santo Stefano
Woburn Abbey, Duke of
Bedford's Collection
For general information, see no.
84 A, above. Visentini engraved
the scene (1742, III, pl. VII). It is
related to a drawing at Windsor
Castle (no. 7480).

103 ⊞ ⊘ 47×80 ▤ ⦂
1730-31

Cannaregio Woburn Abbey,
Duke of Bedford's Collection
A. For general information, see
no. 84 A, above. A couple of
sketches in the sketchbook in
the Accademia, Venice, were
used for this view [Pignatti,
1958].
B. The version (57 × 87,5 cm.)
in the Bacon Collection, which
seems slightly later, is probably
autograph [Constable, 1962].

104 ⊞ ⊘ 47×79 ▤ ⦂
1730-31

**The Church of the
Redentore** Woburn Abbey,
Duke of Bedford's Collection
A. For general information, see
no. 84 A, above. There is a
corresponding drawing at
Windsor Castle (no. 7484)
[Parker, 1948].
B. Another version, which is
slightly different in angle of view,
but is close in style and date.
It is in the Leggatt Collection,
London [Constable, 1962];
companion piece to no. 108.

105 ⊞ ⊘ 47×80 ▤ ⦂
1730-31

The Scuola di San Rocco
Woburn Abbey, Duke of
Bedford's Collection
A. For general information, see
no. 84 A, above. It was depicted,
with some variation, in plate V
(III) of the 1742 edition of
Visentini's album.

B. Another version, perhaps
slightly later, is in an Italian
private collection (45,5 × 76
cm.); it is very closely followed
by the plate mentioned above in
V sentini [Constable, 1962];
companion piece to no. 101 C.

106 ⊞ ⊘ 115,5×194 ▤ ⦂
1730-31'

Regatta on the Grand Canal
Woburn Abbey, Duke of
Bedford's Collection
A. With its companion piece,
no. 107 A, below, this is the
largest painting in the Bedford
series (nos. 84 A–107 A). Levey
[*BM*, 1953] notes in the picture
the insignia of Alvise Pisani,
Doge from January 1735 to June
1741, and would date the work,
with its companion piece
(107 A), to that period.
Constable does not agree, and
though he believes the two
larger paintings were done at a
different time, he suggests a
date not much later than 1730–1
and before 1735. The subject
was depicted several times in
different periods.
B. A fine version (116 × 186,5
cm.), close in date to no. 106 A,
is in the National Gallery,
London [Levey, *BM*, 1953]. It
has also been studied by Longhi
[1946].

107 ⊞ ⊘ 115,5×194 ▤ ⦂
1730-31'

**The Bucintoro Leaving the
Quay on Ascension Day**
Woburn Abbey, Duke of
Bedford's Collection
A. For general information, see
no. 106 A, above. There is a
preparatory sketch at Windsor
Castle (no. 7453).
B. A version related to the
Windsor Castle drawing
mentioned above was the
property of the trustees of
Castle Howard, but it was
destroyed. It was imported to
England before 1745 and
perhaps just after 1734 [Finberg,
WS, 1920–1].

108 ⊞ ⊘ 47,5×79 ▤ ⦂
1730-31?

**The Church of San Giorgio
from the Harbour of St
Mark's** London, Private
collection
The style points to a date close
to the Bedford group (nos.
84 A–107 A). Companion piece
to no. 104 B.

109 ⊞ ⊘ 86,5×138,5 ▤ ⦀
1731-32

**The Bucintoro Returning to
the Quay on Ascension Day**
A Formerly in the Sampson
Gideon Collection. For reasons
of style, it can be dated close to

103A

104A

105A (Plates XXXIX–XL)

110B

112A

104B

105B

111

112D

113

114

115

116

117

118A

125

126

the similar painting in Woburn Abbey (no. 107 A). Companion piece to no. 93 C.
B. A probably contemporary version, in the Mario Crespi Collection, Milan (76 × 120 cm); companion piece to no. 93 D.

110 ▦ ◑ 46×76 1731-32
The Church of Santi Giovanni e Paolo and the Scuola di San Marco
London, Matthiesen Property (?)

A. Another treatment of the subject depicted in the Dresden (no. 18) and Montreal (no. 22 A) paintings. One of a group of four views, one of which was in the Hampden Collection (see no. 89 B). There is a preparatory drawing at Windsor Castle (no. 7481) [Constable, 1962].
B. A version that is probably slightly later (71 × 112 cm.) is in the National Gallery, Washington, and was formerly in the Widener Collection. A drawing by Bellotto, dated 8 December 1740, in the Landesmuseum, Darmstadt

(no. 2218 AE) [Parker, 1929], and derived from this painting establishes *a terminus ante quem.*

111 ▦ ◑ 47×77,5 1731-32
The Piazzetta with the Libreria towards the West
Alton, Hampshire, Viscount Hampden's Collection
The companion piece to no. 89 B (see also no. 110 A). Constable [1962] dates it shortly after 1730. The subject was depicted again about ten years later (no. 186).

112 ▦ ◑ 47,5×77,5 1731-35
The Grand Canal from Campo San Vio Milan, Private collection
A. Belongs to a series of twenty-one views purchased in Venice by the last Duke of Buckingham and Chandos and inherited by Sir Robert Grenville Harvey. The works were sold in 1957. Ten of them, including this view, are now in a private collection in Milan [*AC*, 1963; *CMV*, 1967]. The location of the other pieces is not known. Nine of the views were engraved by Visentini for the second, enlarged edition of his album (1742). This view is a variation on the Windsor Castle version of the same subject (no. 72 A), engraved by Visentini in the 1735 edition.
B. An autograph version, slightly different, in the Matarazzo Collection, São Paulo (48,5 × 80,3 cm.); companion piece to no. 132 A [Constable, 1962].
C. Another fine version, formerly at Langley Park, Norfolk, is in a private collection in London (46,5 × 78,5 cm.); companion piece to no. 132 B.
D. Another version in some ways related to no. 72 A at Windsor Castle, but much later. It is in the Pinacoteca di Brera, Milan (53 × 70 cm.). Companion piece to no. 132 C.

113 ▦ ◑ 47,5×77 1731-35
The Santa Chiara Canal at the Fondamenta Della Croce
For general information, see no. 112 A. A version of the similar scene at Woburn Abbey (no. 99). See no. 99, above, for information.

114 ▦ ◑ 47,5×77 1731-35
The Grand Canal from the Church of Santa Croce to the Church of San Geremia
For the provenance, see no. 112 A. A version of the similar view at Woburn Abbey (no. 98), it may be based on preparatory drawings used for no. 98.

Constable [1962] mentions several derivations, but none of them can be considered as certainly autograph.

115 ▦ ◑ 47,5×77 1731-35
The Grand Canal from Campo della Carità towards Palazzo Venier della Torresella
For general information, see no. 112 A. The use of optical devices in the preparation accounts for the unusual perspective distortion [Moschini, 1954].

116 ▦ ◑ 47,2×77,5 1731-35
The Grand Canal from Palazzo Tiepolo to Ca' Foscari Milan, Private collection
See no. 112 A.

117 ▦ ◑ 46,5×77,7 1731-35
The Grand Canal from the Rialto Bridge to Ca' Foscari
For its provenance, see no. 112 A, above. This composition was frequently repeated by Canaletto, beginning with the Windsor Castle version (no. 69 A).

118 ▦ ◑ 47,5×77,5 1731-35
The Grand Canal from Ca' da Mosto to the Rialto Bridge
A. See no. 112 A.
B. A very fine autograph version, in the Accademia Carrara, Bergamo (61 × 99 cm.).
C. Certainly later but somewhat doubtful is the version mentioned as being in the Wharton Collection, London (44,5 × 65,5 cm.) [Constable, 1962].

119 ▦ ◑ 47,5×77,5 1731-35
The Grand Canal from Palazzo Michiel dalle Colonne to the Fondaco dei Tedeschi
A. See no. 112 A, above.
B. Doubtful but probably partly

119A

120A

121

122

123

124

127

128 (Plates XLIX–LI)

129A

Two of three fragments formerly comprising the version of 129A listed at 129B.

130A

131 (Plates XLI–XLII)

132A

132C

133A

134A

135A

136A

137

138 (Plate XLIII)

autograph. Belongs to the Cini family, Venice (52,5 × 82 cm.).

120   46×77   1731-35

The Grand Canal from the Church of San Stae to the Fabbriche Nuove di Rialto
Milan, Private collection
A. See no. 112 A, above.
B. A fine version (47 × 78 cm.) that Constable [1962] is inclined to consider contemporary or slightly earlier. It was formerly in the Institute of Arts, Minneapolis, and later (1957) at Rosenberg and Stiebel in New York, but its present ownership is unknown.

121   46,5×77   1731-35

The Grand Canal from the Church of the Scalzi to Cannaregio   Milan, Private collection
See no. 112 A, above.

122   46,5×77,5   1731-35

Campo Sant'Angelo
For general information, see no. 112 A, above. Constable [1962] confirms that it is related to a drawing in the Museo Correr, Venice, executed by Visentini, however, and not by Canaletto. This is the only time Canaletto is known to have painted this subject.

123   46×76,5   1731-35

Campo San Geremia
For its provenance, see no. 112 A, above. This subject was never painted again by Canaletto. It is a very fine work, showing a lesser known part of Venice.

124   47×78   1731-35

Campo dei Gesuiti
Milan, Private collection
For general information, see no. 112 A, above. There was a drawing of a *Vue de la Place des Jésuites* (probably related to this painting) in the Mariette Collection, in whose catalogue it is mentioned in 1775. The drawing has been lost since 1866 [Constable, 1962]. The view was engraved by Visentini in the album that appeared in 1742 (III, pl. IX). Like nos. 123 and 124, this subject was also only treated once by the artist.

125   47,7×77,5   1731-35

Campo Santa Margherita
For its provenance, see no. 112 A, above. A drawing of the same subject in the Museo Correr, Venice, is the work of Visentini. Perhaps it was preparatory to an engraving that was never executed [Constable, 1962]. No autograph variants of the painting are known.

126   46,3×77   1731-35

Campo San Polo
For general information, see no. 112 A, above.
A. Engraved by Visentini (for

which there are studies in the Museo Correr, Venice, and the British Museum) for the 1742 edition of his album (III, pl. IV).

127   46,8×77,5   1731-35

Campo San Salvatore
For its provenance, see no. 112 A, above. The composition recalls the engraving (no. 40) in Carlevaris' *Fabbriche*. It was included by Visentini in the 1742 album (III, pl. III).

128   45×77,5   1731-35

Campo Santi Apostoli
Milan, Private collection
For general information, see no. 112 A, above. It was engraved with some differences by Visentini for the 1742 album (III, pl. X).

129   47,5×77,5   1731-35

Campo San Francesco della Vigna   Milan, Private collection
A. For its provenance, see no. 112 A, above. There is an autograph related drawing at Windsor Castle (no. 7494) [Parker, 1948].
B. A variant surviving only in three fragments and dispersed on the art market, has been lost from sight. Constable [1962] has made an ideal, partial recomposition of the three sections (37,5 × 23 cm.; 19 × 14 cm.; and 25 × 39 cm.).

130   47×78   1731-35

The Church of Santa Maria Zobenigo
A. For general information, see no. 112 A, above. Engraved by Visentini for the 1742 album (III, pl. VI).
B. Another version, very close in date and probably autograph, was formerly in the Jaffé Collection and sold in Berlin in 1931 as a work of Bellotto. It is now lost.

131   47,5×77,5   1731-35

The Church of San Nicolò di Castello   Milan, Private collection
For its provenance, see no. 112 A, above. Piece of a preparatory drawing, formerly in the Brass Collection, Venice, was part of the *carnet* reconstructed by Miotti [*AV*, 1966]. The view was engraved by Visentini for the 1742 album (III, pl. II). It is also important as a document illustrating an architectural environment that no longer exists. The church was demolished in 1807 along with neighbouring structures, to make room for the Napoleonic gardens [Zampetti, *CMV*, 1967].

132   48,5×80,5   1730-35?

The Quay from The Harbour of St Mark's   São Paulo, Matarazzo Collection
A. Another treatment of one of Canaletto's favourite views, first rendered in no. 87 A, and executed for the Duke of Norfolk (no. 87 D). The style is of the

period of the Bedford version. It is the companion piece of no. 112 B.

B. A fine version, formerly at Langley Park, Norfolk, was purchased by George Proctor with its companion piece (no. 112 C) during a trip to Italy. The date of the trip is not known [Constable, 1962]. Proctor acquired Langley Park in 1742, where the two paintings remained until 1946 at least. This view is now in a private collection, London (47 × 78,5 cm.).

C. Another version, the companion piece of no. 112 D, is in the Brera, Milan (53,5 × 71 cm.). Probably a bit later than no. 132 A. Constable [1962] relates it to a drawing at Windsor Castle (no. 7451), which also shows the Bucintoro and which was used for various versions.

133 ⊞ ◑ 134,5 × 233,5 / 1732-33 ▤ ⁝

St Mark's Square towards the Libreria between the Basilica and the Church of San Geminiano Hamstead Marshall, Berkshire, Craven Collection

A. Constable's [1962] date of shortly after 1730 for this painting may perhaps be fined down to about 1732-3 because of similarities to the Bedford paintings (nos. 84 A–107 A), and also to the Grenville Harvey series (nos. 112 A ff.). A variant drawing is at Windsor Castle (no. 7422) [Parker, 1948]. Companion piece to no. 134 A.

B. A version (57,5 × c 84 cm.) similar in style to the views in the Galleria Nazionale, Rome (no. 136 A) [Constable, 1962], is in the Samuel Collection, London (see also no. 136, below).

134 ⊞ ◑ 135,5 × 232,5 / 1732-33 ▤ ⁝

The Grand Canal with the Church of the Salute and the Customs House from Campo Santa Maria Zobenigo Hamstead Marshall, Berkshire, Craven Collection

A. Companion piece of no. 133 A (q.v.).

B. Another version (72 × 96,5 cm.), fairly close to it and almost certainly autograph, belongs to the Stewart Property, New York [Constable, 1962].

C. Another, wider view, of doubtful authorship, is in the Cincinnati Art Museum (57 × 95,5 cm.).

D. A third, from a different angle, in the Schwerin Staatliche Museum (71,5 × 110,5 cm.). Constable, perhaps too severely, attributes it to the workshop.

E. Still another version, probably later but very possibly by Canaletto, is in the Ca' Rezzonico Museum, Venice (51 × 71 cm.). Companion piece to no. 135 A.

135 ⊞ ◑ 51 × 71 / 1732-33*? ▤ ⁝

The Entrance to the Grand Canal with the Customs House and the Church of the Salute Venice, Ca' Rezzonico

A. Companion piece to no. 134 E (q.v., and for its attribution).

B. A very controversial variant, is in the Ashmolean Museum, Oxford (52 × 94 cm.).

136 ⊞ ◑ 68,5 × 93,5 / 1733-35 ▤ ⁝

St Mark's Square from the Basilica towards the Church of San Geminiano and the Procuratie Nuove Rome, Galleria Nazionale

A. Forms a group with three others (nos. 137–9) formerly ascribed to Bellotto [Fritzsche, 1936] and now generally attributed to Canaletto. Zampetti's [CMV, 1967] date of shortly after the Bedford group (nos. 84 A–107 A) seems convincing. This is a variation on no. 85 A.

B. A controversial version in the Wallace Collection, London (58 × 125 cm.). The present writer considers it autograph. Its date seems close to the Corsini group (nos. 136 A–139 A).

137 ⊞ ◑ 68,5 × 92 / 1733-35 ▤ ⁝

The Grand Canal with the Rialto Bridge from the South Rome, Galleria Nazionale

142A

142B

143A

144A (Plates LV–LVI)

145

146 (Plate LIV)

For general information, see no. 136 A. It is an earlier version of no. 242 (dated 1744).

138 ⊞ ◑ 58,7 × 93,3 / 1733-35 ▤ ⁝

The Grand Canal from the Rialto Bridge towards Ca' Foscari Rome, Galleria Nazionale

For general information, see no. 136 A, above. It repeats a subject already treated at Windsor Castle (no. 69 A) and (no. 69 B) in the Houston Museum of Fine Arts [Zampetti, CMV, 1967].

139 ⊞ ◑ 68,5 × 91,5 / 1733-35 ▤ ⁝

The Piazzetta towards the South Rome, Galleria Nazionale

A. For its provenance, see no. 136 A, above. One of Canaletto's favourite subjects, it was also depicted in the Windsor Castle painting (no. 48).

B. A variant (52,5 × 71 cm.) in the Speelman Collection, London. May be slightly earlier [Constable, 1962].

C. Another beautiful version, with a narrower view. It dates from about 1735. Formerly in the Liechtenstein Collection, it is now in the John Herron Art Museum, Indianapolis (55 × 73 cm.) [Constable, 1964].

140 ⊞ ◑ 53 × 70,5 / *1735* ▤ ⁝

St Mark's Square towards the Torre dell'Orologio Kansas City, William Rockhill Nelson Gallery of Art

A. The view was engraved by Fletcher and published by Baudin in 1739, which gives a terminus for the dating. (For the problem of the engravings, see Watson [BM, 1955].) The picture was in England when it was reproduced and the Gai gates, in the Loggetta, which were made between 1735 and 1737, are not shown, so one may assume that the view was painted some years earlier, according to Morassi [BM, 1955]. Constable did not agree [1962], and would date it simply to 1730–40 [1964]. It is a companion piece to no. 88 B.

B. A fine version, which was in the Bergstens Collection, Stockholm (57 × 48 cm.) [Constable, 1962].

141 ⊞ ◑ 114,2 × 153,5 / *1735* ▤ ⁝

St Mark's Basilica and the Doge's Palace from the Procuratie Vecchie Washington, National Gallery Bears the initials "A.C.F." Formerly the possession of the Howard family, who probably purchased it about 1734–5 [Finberg, WS, 1920–1; Constable, BM, 1929]. Its style would also suggest a date of about 1735. Related drawings have been identified at Windsor Castle (no. 7428) [Parker, 1948] and in the *carnet* formerly in the Brass Collection, Venice [Miotti, 1966]. Companion piece to no. 142 A.

142 ⊞ ◑ 114,5 × 153 / *1735* ▤ ⁝

The Entrance to the Grand Canal from the End of the Quay Washington, National Gallery

A. Companion piece to no. 141, bearing the initials "A.C.F."

B. A fine version, executed about the same time or slightly earlier, in Windsor Castle (46 × 77,5 cm.). George III bought it from Smith. The subject had been painted before (nos. 44 A and 44 B). It may be related to the Boitard engraving published by Baudin in London in 1736. Likewise, a drawing in the Ashmolean Museum, Oxford [Parker, 1948], may be connected with this painting.

C. Another version, of doubtful authorship, which Constable ascribes to the workshop. In the Wallace Collection, London (47,5 × 78 cm.).

139A

139B

140A

141

148A

150A

151

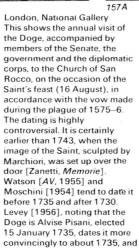

155A

157A

159

143 ⊞⊗ 110,5 × 185,5 *1735*

The Riva degli Schiavoni towards the East Rome, Albertini Collection
A. A superb treatment of the subject, one he painted often, published by Modigliani [*D*, 1924–5]. It has been recently restored; and was shown to be of extraordinarily high quality at the Venice exhibition of view painters (1967). Zampetti [*CMV*, 1967] correctly dates it not long after 1730. The prototype may be no. 59, and it was treated again (no. 156). Companion piece to no. 144 A.
B. This version, almost certainly autograph, is in the Railing Collection, London (47,5 × 77,5 cm.). It is also close in date. Companion piece to no. 144 C.

144 ⊞⊗ 110,5 × 185,5 *1735*

The Quay with the Libreria and the San Teodoro Column towards the west Rome, Albertini Collection
A. Companion piece to no. 143 A, above, and also published by Modigliani [*D*, 1924–5].
B. A fine version (62,5 × 101,5 cm.) in its atmospheric colour [Constable, 1962]; almost contemporary. It is in the Jenks Collection, Astbury Hall, Shropshire.
C. Another version, very probably autograph, in the Railing Collection, London (46,3 × 76,3 cm.); companion piece to no. 143 B.

145 ⊞⊗ 44,5 × 75 *1735*

The Loggetta of Sansovino Birmingham, Barber Institute of Fine Arts
Datable, because of the state of the Loggetta, to before 1735–7. Since the Loggetta is depicted in isolation, it is an "ideal" rather than a real view, even though the monument is painted with rigorous attention to its real features.

146 ⊞⊗ 147 × 199 *1735*

The Doge Visiting the Church of San Rocco

London, National Gallery
This shows the annual visit of the Doge, accompanied by members of the Senate, the government and the diplomatic corps, to the Church of San Rocco, on the occasion of the Saint's feast (16 August), in accordance with the vow made during the plague of 1575–6. The dating is highly controversial. It is certainly earlier than 1743, when the image of the Saint, sculpted by Marchiori, was set up over the door [Zanetti, *Memorie*]. Watson [*AV*, 1955] and Moschini [1954] tend to date it before 1735 and after 1730. Levey [1956], noting that the Doge is Alvise Pisani, elected 15 January 1735, dates it more convincingly to about 1735, and this theory has also been accepted by Moschini [*AV*, 1962].

147 ⊞⊗ 53,5 × 70,5 1735 *?

The Rialto Bridge from the South Hamstead Marshall, Berkshire, Craven Collection
A. Derived from the Bedford painting (no. 94 A), or rather, from the related drawings. Constable [1962] supposes there was some slight collaboration, perhaps that of Bellotto.
B. A version, whose interest is chiefly documentary because of the depiction of Giorgione's and Titian's frescoes on the Fondaco dei Tedeschi. In the Hoogendijk Collection, Amsterdam (88 × 144,5 cm.).
C. Another version, probably autograph (albeit with the same problem as no. 147 A). In the Stuart Collection, London (77,5 × 118 cm.).

148 ⊞⊗ 60,5 × 100 *1735-37

St Mark's Square from the Piazzetta towards the Procuratie Vecchie Milan, Borletti Collection
A. The dating is affected by the absence in it of the gates set up by Gai in 1735–7 in the Sansovino Loggetta [Arslan, *AB*, 1948]. However, these gates are not shown in the

Windsor Castle version (no. 235), which is dated 1744, either. But the earlier dating is also supported by stylistic evidence.
B. Another version, close in date, belonged (1939) [Constable, 1962] to D. Tziracopoulo, Berlin (127 × 148 cm.).

149 ⊞⊗ 132 × 165 *1735-37

St Mark's Square from the Libreria to the Loggetta Zurich?, Property of Brown, Boveri and Co.
This, together with the following three paintings (nos. 150–2), formed a group painted to decorate the dining room of the

residence of William Holbech at Farnborough Hall (Warwickshire). where the pictures remained until 1930, when they were sold [Constable, 1962]. Holbech was in Italy about 1730 and had returned to England by about 1745. Hence the paintings must have been done in that period. The fact that the Loggetta gates (erected in 1735–7) are not shown suggests an earlier date, which would be confirmed by the style of the painting. Constable [1964] has dated the works *c*. 1735.

150 ⊞⊗ 132 × 165 *1735-37

St Mark's Square with the Torre dell'Orologio Ottawa,

National Gallery
A. For general information, see no. 149, above. The clock tower is shown without the alterations made about 1755. A possible date is 1735–7 [Constable, 1962] (see no. 149). A related "finished" drawing is at Windsor Castle (no. 7425) [Parker, 1948]. Partial preparatory drawings are in the Kupferstichkabinett, Berlin, and elsewhere [Hadeln, *BM*, 1926; and 1930].
B. This view (20 × 41 cm.) is from a different angle; it is painted after the Windsor Castle drawing, in the Neave Collection, Astramont (Wexford).

152A

152B

160

163

161A (Plates XXXIII–XXXIV)

161B

151 ⊞ ⊘ 132×165 *1735-37 ▤ ⦂

The Entrance to the Grand Canal with the Church of the Salute London (?), Property of Arthur Tooth
See no. 149, above.

152 ⊞ ⊘ 132×165 *1735-37 ▤ ⦂

The Harbour of St Mark's from the Piazzetta London (?), Property of Arthur Tooth
A. See no. 149, above.
B. A smaller version (46 × 75 cm.), but with a wider and more distant view. It belongs to the Knoedler Property, New York. Constable [1962] considers it to be contemporary with the Bedford pictures (nos. 84 A–107 A).

153 ⊞ ⊘ 75×104 1735-40 ▤ ⦂

The Grand Canal with the Rialto Bridge from the North Milton Park, Peterborough, T. W. Fitzwilliam Collection
A. This is one of a group of eight pictures, all contemporary (nos. 154–9 and 161 B), that have long been the property of the Fitzwilliam family. External evidence (the Church of the Pietà is shown as it was before the 1745 remodelling) makes the group earlier than 1745 in date. All these works, in fact, seem to date to about or shortly after 1735. There is an earlier version of the same subject (no. 74).
B. A version in the Lyon Collection, Geneva, companion piece to no. 160, is autograph or largely autograph.

154 ⊞ ⊘ 75,5×106 1735-40 ▤ ⦂

The Quay with the Libreria towards the West Milton Park, Peterborough, T. W. Fitzwilliam Collection
See no. 153, above.

155 ⊞ ⊘ 75×106 1735-40 ▤ ⦂

St Mark's Square towards the Basilica Milton Park, Peterborough, T. W. Fitzwilliam Collection
A. See no. 153, above.
B. This version in the Speelman Collection, London (49 × 73 cm.) may be contemporary, but in composition it is related to the Bedford and Barlow versions (nos. 84 A and 84 B).

156 ⊞ ⊘ 73,5×104,5 1735-40 ▤ ⦂

The Riva degli Schiavoni towards the East Milton Park, Peterborough, T. W. Fitzwilliam Collection
See no. 153, above.

157 ⊞ ⊘ 73,8×104,5 1735-40 ▤ ⦂

St Mark's Square from the Basilica towards the Church of San Geminiano Milton Park, Peterborough, T. W. Fitzwilliam Collection
A. See no. 153, above.
B. A contemporary version in the Detroit Institute of Arts (76 × 114,5 cm.); it is a companion piece to no. 165 A.

158 ⊞ ⊘ 75×106 1735-40 ▤ ⦂

The Harbour of St Mark's from the Riva degli Schiavoni towards the West

168

169

170A

170B

Milton Park, Peterborough, T. W. Fitzwilliam Collection
See no. 153, above.

159 ⊞ ⊘ 73,7×104,5 1735-40 ▤ ⦂

St Mark's Square towards the Procuratie Nuove with a View of the Church of San Geminiano Milton Park, Peterborough, T. W. Fitzwilliam Collection
See no. 153, above.

160 ⊞ ⊘ 118×152 *1735-40* ▤ ⦂

The Entrance to the Grand Canal with the Church of the Salute Geneva, Lyon Collection
A much discussed version of the subject, larger but similar in composition to no. 73, above, at Windsor Castle. However, for stylistic reasons, it is certainly later in date. Companion piece to no. 153 B [Browning, AJ, 1905].

161 ⊞ ⊘ 125×204 1735-40 ▤ ⦂

The Harbour of St Mark's towards the East Boston, Museum of Fine Arts
A. This is one of Canaletto s masterpieces [Constable, BMFA, 1939], generally dated to the 1730s [Pallucchini, 1960]. The exhibition of view painters however confirmed [Zampetti, CMV, 1967] the date of Constable [1964], who tended to set it earlier in the decade.
B. An autograph version (75,5 × 105,5 cm.) with variations. The point of view is further back in the Giudecca Canal and the scene is narrower. It is in the Fitzwilliam Collection and is part of that group (see nos. 153 A and ff.), and so is probably contemporary.

162 ⊞ ⊘ 66×112 1735-40? ▤ ⦂

The Fonteghetto della Farina Venice, Giustiniani Collection
A. One of the most unusual of Canaletto's works. He only painted this subject in one other painting and some drawings (Windsor Castle, nos. 7462, 7463, 7464 and 7465), none of which are directly related to this one [Parker, 1948]. The dating above has been convincingly argued by Pallucchini [in CMV, 1967].
B. This slightly different version is in the Museum of Fine Arts, Boston (37 × 51 cm.). According to Constable [1962], it might be slightly earlier than the Giustiniani version, but the present author sees little to suggests that it is much different in date.

163 ⊞ ⊘ 127×188 1735-40? ▤ ⦂

The Harbour of St Mark's towards the East London, Wallace Collection
The flattened form of the top of the Campanile of San Giorgio provides a chronological limit. However, exact dating is difficult. The use of optical devices in preparing the architectural background [Watson, 1949] suggests a date before 1730, but the style seems later. Zampetti [CMV, 1967] suggests a date about the period of the Boston view (no. 161). Some reserves have been expressed concerning the authorship. Constable [1962] suggests that assistants might have been used, though there is no evidence in the picture itself.

164 ⊞ ⊘ 76×114,5 1735-40? ▤ ⦂

The Harbour of St Mark's from the Riva degli Schiavoni Companion piece to no. 163 (q.v.).

165 ⊞ ⊘ 76×114,5 1735-40? ▤ ⦂

St Mark's Square towards the Basilica Cambridge, Massachusetts, Fogg Art Museum
A. Companion piece to no. 157 B. A very fine view with notable width; seen from above.
B. This version is probably very close in date and style; it varies only slightly in the viewpoint. It belonged in 1939 to D. Tziracopoulo, Berlin [Constable, 1962].

166 ⊞ ⊘ 54,5×96,5 1735-40? ▤ ⦂

Campo Santo Stefanin Penrhyn Castle, Wales, Douglas-Pennant Collection
Sometimes attributed to Bellotto. It belongs to the period when Canaletto painted lesser-known views of Venice.

162A (Plates XLVII–XLVIII)

162B

164

167

165A (Plate XLVI)

165B

167 121×183 1735-41

The Bucintoro Leaving the Quay on Ascension Day
London, National Gallery
Levey (1956) dates this work to 1735–41, because of the appearance of the insignia of Alvise Pisani, who was Doge at that time. He gives the same date to its companion piece, no. 168.

168 121×183 1735-41

Regatta on the Grand Canal
London, National Gallery
Companion piece to no. 167 (q.v.). The subject was often treated by Canaletto. There is an earlier version in the National Gallery (no. 106 B), and another

fine version at Windsor Castle (no. 68 A). The insignia of Alvise Pisani appear on the structure set up in front of Ca' Foscari, on the left [Levey, *BM*, 1953].

169 94,5×145,5 1738*

The Grand Canal from the Church of San Simeone Piccolo to Cannaregio
London, Wallace Collection
A much discussed work, recently attributed by Constable [1962] entirely to the school. It is more likely to be by Canaletto because of the high quality of the work, though he may have had some help from assistants. It dates from after 1738, when the staircase of San Simeone was completed.

170 124×204 1738-40

The Grand Canal from the Church of the Scalzi towards the Fondamenta della Croce with the Church of San Simeone Piccolo
London, National Gallery.
A. Variation of a subject painted in 1729 and engraved by Visentini (see no. 77). The style of the work and the presence of the staircase of San Simeone suggest a dating after 1738 [Levey, 1956], though perhaps not by much.
B. This version presents some doubts about authorship. It is in a private collection in Turin (120,3 × 125,5 cm.), and was formerly the property of the Duke of Buccleuch (see no.

171) – which provenance tends to confirm its authenticity.

171 121×152 1738-42

The Entrance to the Grand Canal with the Customs House London, the late Sir Alexander Korda Collection
Constable [1962] re-examined the documentary sources, which confirm that Canaletto painted six views for the Buccleuchs, obviously at the same period. There is external as well as stylistic evidence for fixing this period as 1738–42. The works were in the possession of the Buccleuchs at Dalkeith Palace until they were sold about fifteen years ago.

172 120,5×151 1738-42

The Grand Canal from the Rialto Bridge to Ca' Foscari
Zurich, Bührle Collection
Formerly the property of the Buccleuch family (see no. 171, above).

173 121×151 1738-42

The Entrance to the Grand Canal with the Church of the Salute towards the East
Zurich, Bührle Collection
Formerly in the Buccleuch Collection (see no. 171). The slightly earlier version (no. 160) in the Lyon Collection, Geneva, is an almost exact replica.

174 120,5×157 1738-42

The Bucintoro at the Quay on Ascension Day Turin, Private collection
A. Formerly in the Buccleuch Collection (see no. 171). A fine treatment of one of Canaletto's favourite subjects.
B. A copy, with slight variations, perhaps contemporary. It belongs to the Earl of Leicester, Holkham Hall (106,5 × 106,5 cm.), and was documented as being in England in the possession of the same family in 1773 [Constable, 1962].

175 120,5×151 1738-42

Regatta on the Grand Canal
Great Britain, Private collection
Formerly in the Buccleuch Collection (see no. 171). Another treatment of a subject already depicted in the Bedford Collection (no. 106 A) and the National Gallery (no. 168). As in these, the insignia on the structure erected in front of Ca' Foscari are those of Doge Pisani (1735–41).

176 47×75 1738-42

The Entrance to Cannaregio with the Church of San Geremia London, National Gallery
A. A rather controversial work, sometimes attributed to the workshop [Levey, 1956; Constable, 1962], though Canaletto may well have had a hand in the execution. The dating is established by the absence of the balustrade and

statue in front of San Geremia. Companion piece of no. 177 A.
B. This version in the Bührle Collection, Zurich (120,5 × 151 cm.), seems close in date. Its authenticity is guaranteed by its provenance from the Duke of Buccleuch's Collection (see no. 171). Hence it is datable certainly to after 1738 and before 1742.

177 46,5×77 1738-42

The Church of San Pietro di Castello London, National Gallery
A. Companion piece to no. 176 A. Levey [1956] attributes it to the workshop, while Constable [1962] sees Canaletto's hand in its execution. A drawing at Windsor Castle (no. 7485) seems to be related.
B. This version in the Lindsay-Fynn Collection, London (67,3 × 113,5 cm.), is even harder to consider autograph even in part. Its date is uncertain.

178 60×94 *1740

The Grand Canal from Ca' Pesaro to the Church of San Marcuola Chilbolton, Hampshire, Parrington Collection
An inscription on the back reads "painted for Henry Duke of ..." The missing word is most likely "Kent". Since Henry Grey was Duke of Kent from 1710 until his death in 1740, a *terminus post quem* of 1740 is reasonable. Stylistic considerations suggest that it was not painted much before that year. It was engraved in Visentini's 1742 album (II, pl. VI). Companion piece to no. 179.

179 60×94 *1740

The Grand Canal from Campo Santa Sofia to the Church of San Marcuola
Companion piece to no. 178. In 1939 it belonged to the Matthiesen Collection, London [Constable, 1962].

180 61,5×108 *1740

The Quay and the Doge's Palace towards the West
London, Lord Lucas and Dingwall Collection
A. This was painted for Henry Grey, Duke of Kent and second Baron Lucas, and kept by his descendants. Since Kent died in 1740 (see no. 178), we have a *terminus post quem*. It is also likely that this picture, a variation of one of Canaletto's favourite subjects, was not painted much before 1740.
B. This version (179 × 265,5 cm.), formerly the property of the Duke of Newcastle, appeared on the market after 1948.
Constable [1962] mentions several other, non-autograph versions.

181 50,5×81 *1740*

The Piazzetta with a View of the Doge's Palace and the

174A

174B

176A

177A

178

181

184

183

186A

188

189A

189B

190A

192

193A

198

199

200

decade later. (Constable [1964] dates it *ca.* 1735.)
B. Another version, in the Soane Museum, London (53,5 × 110,5 cm.). It is perhaps by Canaletto, although Constable ascribes it to the school [1962]. Companion piece to no. 191 A.

191 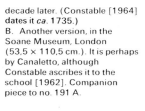 53,5×110,5
1740-45?

The Rialto Bridge from the North London, Sir John Soane's Museum
A. Companion piece to no. 190 B. The fairly consistent quality suggests it is by Canaletto, but it has been rejected by Constable [1962] and others.
B. This version in the Rijksmuseum, Amsterdam (60 × 80 cm.), among numerous versions generally not by Canaletto, might be autograph.

192  72,5×85,5
1740-46?

St Mark's Harbour towards the West London, Embiricos Collection
There is a drawing, which was perhaps used for no. 341 A as well, related to this view, at Windsor Castle (no. 7454) [Parker, 1948]. Some sketches in the sketchbook in the Accademia, Venice, were also used for it. Despite Constable's rejection [1962], the work seems to be totally autograph.

193  46×78
1741*

Campo Santi Giovanni e Paolo with the Colleoni Monument Windsor Castle, Royal Collections
A. This very beautiful view, once the property of Consul Joseph Smith, was reproduced in the 1742 edition of Visentini's engravings (III, pl. 1) and should date, then, from shortly before that year. Similarities of style to other works of that period make 1742 a likely date. Levey [1964], however, dates it between 1739 and 1740. Canaletto used four sketches in the sketchbook in the Accademia, Venice, for this painting [Pignatti, 1958].
B. This version (73,5 × 80 cm.), which also differs from Visentini's engraving, has been mentioned by Constable [1962] as being in the Norton Gallery, Palm Beach, Florida, and a work of the school. But Canaletto might have taken some part in its execution.

194  58,5×109
1741-42

View of Mestre Canada, Sangster Collection
A. The composition is very close to the autograph etching published in the 1744 album [Pallucchini and Guarnati, 1944, no. 5] and to a drawing at Windsor Castle (no. 7490) [Parker, 1948].
B. Another version (30,5 × 44,5 cm.), which was in the Norbury Collection, Malvern, until 1939 [Constable, 1962]; companion piece to no. 195 B.

Loggetta Allentown, Pennsylvania, Art Museum (Kress Collection)
Although rejected by Constable [1962], this painting is generally and justly considered autograph. The style and quality suggest the period about 1740.

182 99×129,5
1740?

The Campo dell'Arsenale London, Sabin Collection
Related to the view in the Ottawa National Gallery (no. 358), recently reattributed to Bellotto [Pignatti, *AV*, 1966]. This one, however, is stylistically very different. Perhaps Bellotto's was painted after this view.

183 57×101,5
1740?

St Mark's Square with View of the Basilica and the Doge's Palace, the Loggetta and the Campanile Bloomfield Hills, Michigan, Museum of Cranbrook Academy of Art
The date is that given by Constable [1964].

184 *20×40*
1740*

The Doge's Palace, Façade Artramont, Wexford, Neave Collection
A view of the palace, similar in its unusual composition and quality to no. 186.

185 23×40
1740*

St Mark's Square from the Basilica towards the Church of San Geminiano
A. A version of the same subject as no. 157 A. Companion piece to no. 186 B. The dating given is Constable's [1962].
B. This version appeared on the London market in 1956

(56 × 73,5 cm.) and is mentioned by Constable [1962].

186 *61×91*
1740*

The Piazzetta with the Libreria of St Mark's towards the West Artramont, Wexford, Neave Collection
A. A very beautiful version of no. 111. The dating has been rightly confirmed by Constable [1962].
B. Another version of no. 111, but close in time to no. 186 A, was in the Watney Collection, London (23 × 40 cm.); companion piece to no. 185 A.
C. Another version of the same period, formerly in the Eigenberger Collection, Vienna (58,5 × 66 cm.). It has been attributed on solid grounds to

Canaletto, though some ascribe it to Bellotto.

187 61×100,5
1740*

The Basilica of St Mark's and the Doge's Palace from the Procuratie Vecchie Bloomfield Hills, Michigan, Booth Collection
A variant of the subject of no. 141. At least five years later.

188 29×38
1740-45

The Piazzetta towards the Quay London, Private collection
A lovely small picture with warm colours, which seems to have been painted before the departure for England. Companion piece to no. 189 A.

189 29,2×38
1740-45

Customs House Point London, Private collection
A. Companion piece to no. 188.
B. A similar view, from the harbour of St Mark's, and perhaps belonging to the same period. It is the property of an English collector (28 × 21,5 cm.). As Constable [1962] acutely noted, it was probably part of a larger composition.

190 67×103
1740-45

St Mark's Square with View of the Basilica and the North-east Side Hartford, Conn., Wadsworth Atheneum
A. Variation of the theme of no. 133 A and executed about a

194A

195A

201A

202A

203

204

205

206

207

208

209A

210A

211

212

213

214

215

216

195 ⊞ ◕ 32×45 / 1741-42 ▤ ⁝

View of Dolo Venice, Brass Collection
A. Fairly similar to the autograph etching published in 1744 [Pallucchini and Guarnati, 1944, no. 4] and to a drawing in the Victoria and Albert Museum [Hadeln, 1930].
B. Another version (30,5 × 44,5 cm.), in the Norbury Collection, Malvern; companion piece to no. 194 B.

196 ⊞ ◕ 39×52,5 / 1741-42? ▤ ⁝

An Island of the Venetian Lagoon and Motifs from the Church of San Francesco della Vigna: a Capriccio
Leipzig, Museum der bildenden Künste
Fairly close in style to the works datable on the basis of the album of autograph etchings, published in 1744 [Constable, 1962]. Fritzsche's attribution [1936] to Bellotto, which was accepted by the museum, does not seem

convincing. Companion piece to no. 197.

197 ⊞ ◕ 39×52,5 / 1741-42? ▤ ⁝

An Island of the Venetian Lagoon and a Church: a Capriccio Leipzig, Museum der bildenden Künste
Companion piece to no. 196.

198 ⊞ ◕ 30,5×44,5 / 1741-42? ▤ ⁝

The Marghera Tower
Formerly in Berlin, in the Tziracopoulo Collection, and lost since 1939. Fairly close to the autograph etching of the same subject [Pallucchini and Guarnati, 1944, no. 8]. Probably based on a drawing also used for the etching. The style of the work suggests a dating slightly before that of the views and *capricci* dated between 1743 and 1744.

199 ⊞ ◕ 51×68,5 / 1741-44? ▤ ⁝

The Venetian Lagoon with an Arch and a Church: a Capriccio London, (?), Hall Collection
The seated figure on the left is similar to one in an etching by Canaletto [Pallucchini and Guarnati, 1944, no. 13b]. This might suggest a date just after 1740, which is also indicated by style. The door structure suggests that of San Giovanni in Padua. We know that this imaginary view was purchased, with its companion piece (no. 200), by Lord Boston during a stay in Italy, though the date of his visit is not known.

200 ⊞ ◕ 51×68,5 / 1741-44? ▤ ⁝

The Venetian Lagoon with a Church and a Column: a Capriccio London, (?), Hall Collection
Companion piece of no. 199. The church may be modelled after San Simeone Piccolo.

201 ⊞ ◕ 61×95 / *1742* ? ▤ ⁝

Ruins of the Roman Forum with the Capitol in the Background Windsor Castle, Royal Collections
A. This is related to a youthful drawing in the Roman series at the British Museum (no. 4 in Constable's list [1962]), but it is more likely that the painting was done in the 1740s. Companion piece to no. 202 A.
B. A good version, with variations. In the National Gallery of Victoria, Melbourne (82,5 × 145 cm.).

202 ⊞ ◕ 61×95 / *1742* ▤ ⁝

The Temple of Antoninus and Faustina in Rome
Windsor Castle, Royal Collections
A. Companion piece to no. 201 A, hence its dating. Related to one of the youthful drawings in the British Museum (no. 5 in Constable's list [1962]).
B. Autograph version belonging

to the Earl of Sandwich (62 × 98 cm.).

203 ⊞ ◕ 188×104 / 1742 ▤ ⁝

Ruins of the Roman Forum with the Capitol in the Background Windsor Castle, Royal Collections
This is one of five paintings (nos. 203–7) of Roman subjects signed and dated 1742 (this one reads: "ANT. CANAL FECIT ANNO MCCXLII" [sic]), all from the Joseph Smith Collection. The subjects have led some scholars to suppose that Canaletto visited Rome in 1742 or a little earlier. Pallucchini [1960] notes the advances made in these works when compared with his youthful versions of the same subjects, which were so deeply influenced by Ricci, and rightly says "The *mise en scène* tends to emphasise the monuments, as elements of the pictorial narration also, with a bright and warm light, a light … recaptured in his studio from a precise

217A

217B

218

sensation recorded by a careful visual sensitivity and recreated by the artist's imagination. ...
It is at this time that Pannini interested Canaletto and not earlier. It is possible that the modulated and slightly muddy colours of the artist from Piacenza made Canaletto's palette take on a denser, more vibrant and atmospheric quality".

204 🔲 ⊘ 181,5 × 103 / 1742 ▤ ⦂

The Arch of Constantine
Windsor Castle, Royal Collections
The inscription reads "*ANT. CANAL FECIT ANNO MDCCXLII*" (see no. 203, above). The picture is related to a drawing in the Petit Palais, Paris, which bears an autograph note and also to a sheet of the youthful series in the British Museum (no. 2 in Constable's list [1962]).

205 🔲 ⊘ 179 × 104 / 1742 ▤ ⦂

The Arch of Septimius Severus Windsor Castle, Royal Collections
Signed and dated: "*ANT. CANAL FECIT ANNO MDCCXLII*" (see no. 203, above).

206 🔲 ⊘ 190 × 104 / 1742 ▤ ⦂

The Arch of Titus Windsor Castle, Royal Collections
The inscription reads: "*ANT. CANAL FECIT / ANNO MDCCXLII*" (see no. 203, above).

207 🔲 ⊘ 179 × 106,5 / 1742 ▤ ⦂

The Pantheon Windsor Castle, Royal Collections
The inscription reads: "*ANT. CANAL FECIT / ANNO MDCCXLII*" (see no. 203, above).

208 🔲 ⊘ 49,5 × 83 / 1742 ▤ ⦂

View of the Brenta near Padua
London, Private collection
There are four drawings related to the painting ("one of the most inspired and moving landscapes

by Canaletto ... [whose] sweet atmosphere, almost overflowing with the languor and melancholy of autumn sunsets gives ... a new, highly poetic intimacy" [Pallucchini, 1960]): two at Windsor Castle (nos. 7497 and 7498), one in the Pierpont Morgan Library, New York, and one in the Fogg Art Museum, Cambridge (Mass.). This last drawing, signed 1742 by Canaletto, allows one to date the painting. It is fairly similar to one of the autograph etchings published in 1744 [Pallucchini and Guarnati, 1944, no. 9]. Constable [1964] however, thinks it precedes Canaletto's departure from Venice.

209 🔲 ⊘ 59,7 × 106,7 / 1742 ▤ ⦂

The Brenta at the Portello of Padua
A. Pallucchini connected this splendid work ("with a serenity worthy of Corot" [1960]) with no. 208. Formerly some scholars had attributed it to Bellotto. Its owner, F. F. Madan, London, put it on the American market, and in 1955 it was in the possession of D. Koetser, New York [Constable, 1962]. It is related to a drawing in the Albertina, Vienna (no. 1876).
B. A freer version (61,5 × 106,5 cm.), of doubtful authorship, which belongs to the Dunkels Collection, Sussex.

210 🔲 ⊘ 40 × 87,5 / 1742* ▤ ⦂

Prato della Valle, Padua, with the Churches of Santa Giustina and the Misericordia London, Lord Brownlow Collection
A. This is dated on the basis of similarities of style with the two preceding works, above; and it was used for two etchings in Canaletto's 1744 album [Pallucchini and Guarnati, 1944, nos. 6–7]. This may be the painting which was mentioned in an undated letter John Strange wrote to Sasso, published by Mauroner [*AV*, 1964]. The painting is also important as a document of the city of Padua.

B. Another version, sometimes ascribed to Bellotto but painted by Canaletto, is in the Museo Poldi Pezzoli, Milan (39 × 88 cm.).
C. Another autograph version, but very cold, is in the Friedenburg Collection, Venice (38 × 89 cm.) [Constable, 1962].

211 🔲 ⊘ 61 × 96,5 / 1742-45 ▤ ⦂

St John Lateran Square, Rome London, Clifford Curzon Collection

Canaletto's authorship is confirmed by the unmistakable quality of the work and its provenance (the painting was in the Lovelace family in the eighteenth century), as well as its connection with an autograph drawing at Windsor Castle (no. 7517) [Parker, 1948] and one of the British Museum drawings (no. 22) used by Brustolon.

212 🔲 ⊘ 82 × 122 / 1742-45 ▤ ⦂

The Arch of Constantine with the Colosseum London, Martin Collection
Signed "*ANT⁰ CANALETO FE*". This rather arbitary view is stylistically related to the Roman subjects, after Canaletto's presumed second visit to Rome (c. 1742).

213 🔲 ⊘ 52 × 70 / 1742-45 ▤ ⦂

The Arch of Septimius Severus and the Church of Santi Martina e Luca, Rome Cincinnati, Ohio, Art Museum
Although closely related to a drawing (no. 3 in Constable's [1962] listing of early drawings; London, British Museum) executed in Rome, the painting itself was undoubtedly done when he turned a second time to Roman subjects, shortly after 1742 [Constable, 1964].

214 🔲 ⊘ 39,5 × 68,5 / 1742-45? ▤ ⦂

The Quirinal Palace, Rome
Artramont, Wexford, Neave

Collection
This work, with its companion piece (no. 215), has been attributed to Bellotto, with some plausibility. But its long presence in the Neave family and the way in which figures and architecture are treated [Constable, 1962] lead one to prefer an attribution to Canaletto until other evidence is presented.

215 🔲 ⊘ 39,5 × 68,5 / 1742-45? ▤ ⦂

Piazza Navona, Rome
Artramont, Wexford, Neave Collection
Companion piece to no. 214.

216 🔲 ⊘ 26 × 35 / 1742-45? ▤ ⦂

The Colosseum Rome, Galleria Borghese
It is usually ascribed to Bellotto [*A*, 1913; Fritzsche, 1936; etc.], together with its companion piece (no. 217 B). This ascription is supported by the existence of a drawing by Bellotto (Rome, Gabinetto Nazionale delle Stampe) of the work. But the view is also related to a drawing of Canaletto's Roman series (British Museum) that was used by Brustolon (Constable's [1962] no. 15). Hence the question of attribution remains open. Constable [1962] is also uncertain of the authorship, though he had ascribed it to Bellotto.

219

220

221

222

223

224

217 ⊞ ◍ 150×109 / 1742-45? 📋 ⁝

The Roman Forum with the Basilica of Constantine and the Church of Santa Francesca Romana Milan, Campanini Bonomi Collection
A. Probably based on the drawing (Constable's [1962] no. 6; British Museum) used by Brustolon, and related, too, to a drawing at Windsor Castle (no. 7522) [Parker, 1948]. According to Morassi [AV, 1950], it can be dated before 1745.
B. A variant (26 × 35 cm.), in the Galleria Borghese, Rome, which is usually ascribed to Bellotto [Fritzsche, 1936, etc.]. The same considerations apply here as for no. 216, above.

218 ⊞ ◍ 109×287 / 1743 📋 ⁝

The Colosseum and the Arch of Constantine Hampton Court, Royal Collections
Signed and dated: "ANT. CANAL F. MDCCXLII".

219 ⊞ ◍ 60,5×95,5 / 1743 📋 ⁝

The Quay with the Doge's Palace and the Prisons towards the West Windsor Castle, Royal Collections
Signed and dated: "A. CANAL FECIT XXIV OCTOBRIS MDCCXLIII"; companion piece to no. 220.

220 ⊞ ◍ 58,5×94 / 1743 📋 ⁝

The Piazzetta towards the Torre dell'Orologio from the Libreria to the Doge's Palace Windsor Castle, Royal Collections
The inscription is identical with that of the companion piece (no. 219): "A. CANAL FECIT XXIV OCTOBRIS MDCCXLIII". The corresponding drawing is also at Windsor Castle (no. 7436).

221 ⊞ ◍ 108×129,5 / 1743? 📋 ⁝

The Horses of the Basilica of St Mark's in the Piazzetta: a Capriccio Windsor Castle, Royal Collections
Signed: "A. CANAL FE"; the

225

226

227

228A

229A

statues on the bridge by Tiziano Aspetti. (Actually, one is by Aspetti and the other by G. Campagna.) The two statues are now in the atrium of the Biblioteca Marciana. The buildings of the Mint, on the right, and, on the left, the Granaries are also shown in the painting. A "finished" drawing, which is in part related to the painting, is also at Windsor Castle (no. 7459) [Parker, 1948].

230A

232

following inscription is found on the first pedestal: "AB VRB. COND. MCCCXXXII / P. G[RI]MANI VEN. DVCE FOEL. REG". Since AD 421 is generally considered to be the foundation date of the city of Venice, the inscription date should allude to 1753, but this date does not fit the style of the work. Constable [1962] has suggested that Canaletto may have made an error by using one X too many. In that case the inscription on the pedestal would read MCCCXXII (1322 years after the foundation of Venice), referring to the year 1743, which would accord with the style of the painting. The work is one of thirteen painted as decorations to be put over doorways,

executed for Joseph Smith between ca. 1743 and 1744 (judging by dates inscribed in some of the paintings) (see 222 ff and 238 ff.). They were registered in the inventory at Windsor Castle, which still contains nine of the series [Levey, 1964].

222 ⊞ ◍ 102×129,5 / 1743-44 📋 ⁝

The Church of San Giorgio Maggiore: a Capriccio Windsor Castle, Royal Collections
Signed: "A. CANAL F.". It belongs to the series described in no. 221, above.

223 ⊞ ◍ 109×131 / 1743-44 ⁝

Motifs of the Quay and St Mark's Square: a Capriccio Windsor Castle, Royal Collections
Part of the group described in no. 221, above. In Joseph Smith's inventory, it is described (no. 7) as "the Piazzetta with three flag poles set up in front of the Church of St Mark".

224 ⊞ ◍ 84,5×129,5 / 1743-44 📋 ⁝

The Pescheria Bridge and Buildings on the Quay: a Capriccio Windsor Castle, Royal Collections
Another of the thirteen works belonging formerly to Joseph Smith (see no. 221, above). Smith's inventory mentions two

225 ⊞ ◍ 106×128 / 1743-44 📋 ⁝

The Convent of the Carità, Venice: a Capriccio London, Buckingham Palace
This was part of the group described under no. 221, above, and inventoried (no. 3) by Joseph Smith, who correctly identifies the architectural subject.

226 ⊞ ◍ 90×130 / 1743-44 📋 ⁝

The Rialto Bridge after Palladio's Design: a Capriccio Windsor Castle, Royal Collections
Signed: "A. CANAL F."
Another one of the same group (see no. 221, above) inventoried (no. 1) by Smith. The fountain in the painting is to be found [Watson, 1954] in Andrea Palladio's project, shown in the Quattro Libri dell'architettura, published in Venice, 1570, and certainly known to Canaletto. (Palladio's drawing, now in the Museo Civico, Vicenza, is different from the version printed in 1570.)

233

234

235

236

238

239

240

241

227 ⊞ ⊘ 101,5 × 129,5 / 1743-44 ⊟ ⦂

The Prisons of Venice: a Capriccio New York (?), Schaeffer Collection
Initialled "AC". Constable [1962] first thought this was a view of Villa Pisani, at Stra. But his later hypothesis [1964] that this is an imaginary composition based on the prisons of Venice is much more convincing. This hypothesis allows us to identify the painting as one of the doorpieces inventoried by Joseph Smith (no. 9). See no. 221, above.

228 ⊞ ⊘ 119 × 185 / 1743-44? ⊟ ⦂

The Grand Canal from Campo Santa Sofia to the Rialto Bridge Berlin, Gymnasium zum grauen Kloster
A. This work, together with three others (nos. 229–31), was donated as a group by Sigmund Streit to its present home (1763). The donor was in Italy for a long time, chiefly in Venice and Padua, so it is not possible to establish the date when he purchased the paintings. The dating is established solely on considerations of style. Voss's attempt [RKW, 1925] to ascribe the works to Moretti is unacceptable. Constable's detailed chronological ascription (given here) [SLV, 1956] seems totally acceptable. The composition is connected with sketches on a sheet formerly in the Viggiano Collection and now in the Miotti Collection, Udine [Miotti, AV, 1966].
B. Another version (98 × 131 cm.), perhaps entirely autograph, is in the Dulverton Collection, Batsford Park [Constable, SLV, 1956].

229 ⊞ ⊘ 119 × 185 / 1743-44? ⊟ ⦂

Campo di Rialto Berlin, Gymnasium zum grauen Kloster
A. Part of the group described in no. 228, above.
B. A fine replica (94 × 127,5 cm.), probably contemporary, belongs to the Ward Collection, London.
C. Another version (93 × 127 cm.), slightly later, which was in the Drury Lowe Collection, Locko Park [Constable, SLV, 1956].

230 ⊞ ⊘ 119 × 185 / 1743-44? ⊟ ⦂

Festival at Night at the Church of San Pietro di Castello Berlin, Gymnasium zum grauen Kloster
A. Part of the set of four discussed in no. 228, above. A print signed by G. B. Moretti "et Filii", engraved by Brustolon and included in the set of ten Venetian views published by Furlanetto (no. 10) is derived from this singular painting.
B. Another version (96,5 × 131 cm.) is mentioned by Constable [SLV, 1956] as being in the possession of a collector in Athens.

231 ⊞ ⊘ 119 × 185 / 1743-44? ⊟ ⦂

Festival at the Arzere di Santa Marta Berlin, Gymnasium zum grauen Kloster
For general information, see no. 228, above. Sketches related to the painting are on two sheets in (?) the Brass Collection, Venice [Miotti, AV, 1966], where the subject is mistakenly called Santa Maria. It was engraved by Brustolon and published by Furlanetto in the series of Venetian views (no. 9) described at no. 230, above.

232 ⊞ ⊘ 56 × 100,5 / 1743-44? ⊟ ⦂

The Bucintoro Returning to the Quay on Ascension Day London, Dulwich College Picture Gallery
A version of the subject painted by Canaletto in his youth in the splendid picture at Windsor Castle (no. 67 A). It is based on the same preparatory drawing, also at Windsor Castle (no. 7451) [Parker, 1948].

233 ⊞ ⊘ 28,5 × 37 / 1743-44? ⊟ ○○

The Church of San Salvatore, Venice
Seems stylistically very close to no. 246 A. It used to belong to the Hope family. From 1917 to 1923 (when it disappeared from view) it appeared frequently on the art market, sometimes incorrectly attributed to Bellotto.

234 ⊞ ⊘ 41 × 31 / 1743-44? ⊟ ⦂

The Scuola di San Teodoro London, Ward Collection
Constable [1962] has convincingly related this work to no. 233, above.

235 ⊞ ⊘ 77,5 × 119,5 / 1744 ⊟ ⦂

St Mark's Square from the Libreria to the Basilica towards the West London, Buckingham Palace
The inscription reads: "ANT. CANAL FECIT MDCCXLIV". Note that Gai's gates are not depicted in the Loggetta, although they were set up in 1735–7. The composition, with its "cropping" of the Campanile, is particularly daring. Companion piece to no. 236.

236 ⊞ ⊘ 76 × 119,5 / 1744 ⊟ ⦂

St Mark's Square with a View of the Basilica towards the South Windsor Castle, Royal Collections
Companion piece to no. 235. Signed and dated: "ANT. CANAL FECIT MDCCXLIV". The viewpoint seems to be the Torre dell'Orologio.
Two versions, mentioned by Constable [1962], have been lost.

237 ⊞ ⊘ 127 × 203 / 1744 ⊟ ⦂

The Entrance to the Grand Canal with the Church of the Salute Windsor Castle, Royal Collections
A. The inscription reads: "A. CANAL F. 1744". This view was often depicted, with slight variations in the angle of view.
B. Another version (98 × 113 cm.), very similar in composition and style, and hence datable about 1744, belonging to the Neave Collection, Artramont, Wexford; companion piece to no. 245 A.
C. Another version (47,5 × 79,5 cm.), also with variations, was in the possession of J. Weitzner, New York, in 1957 [Constable, 1962]. The dating is uncertain, but it may be fairly close to the Windsor Castle and Artramont versions listed above.

238 ⊞ ⊘ 108 × 129,5 / 1744 ⊟ ⦂

The Scala dei Giganti: a Capriccio Windsor Castle, Royal Collections
It is signed: "ANTO C. F. / MDCCXLIV". It appeared in the Smith inventory of the thirteen doorpieces described at no. 221, above.

239 ⊞ ⊘ 106,5 × 128,5 / 1744 ⊟ ⦂

The Libreria and other Venetian Buildings: a Capriccio Windsor Castle, Royal Collections
It is inscribed: "A. CANAL F. / 1744". One of the thirteen works inventoried by Smith (see no. 221, above). Smith described it as a "corner (with three arches) of the Library of St Mark's by Sansovino".

240 ⊞ ⊘ 107,5 × 129,5 / 1744 ⊟ ⦂

Roman Ruins and the Venetian Monument to Colleoni: a Capriccio Windsor Castle, Royal Collections
Inscribed: "ANTO C. F. / MDCCXLIV". It is difficult to find a corresponding description in Smith's inventory of the thirteen works mentioned in no. 221, above, but there seems to be no doubt [Constable, 1962] that this was one of the works.

241 ⊞ ⊘ 97 × 127 / 1744 ⊟ ○

The Church of San Francesco della Vigna: a Capriccio Milan, Private collection
It is signed: "A. CANAL F. / 1744". One of the thirteen decorative pieces (see no. 221, above), inventoried by Smith as the Church of San Francesco della Vigna by Palladio.

237A

237B

242A

244

245B

246A

246B

247A

248

249

250

242 · 47,5×77,5 / 1744

The Rialto Bridge from the South
A. It is inscribed: *"ANT. CANAL FECIT MDCCXLIV"*. Formerly (1930) in the Trotti Collection, Paris.
B. A variant, almost certainly contemporary, in the Bisgood Collection, London (46 × 76 cm.); companion piece to no. 243 A.
C. Another variant in the Musée Jacquemart-André, Paris (45 × 76 cm.); companion piece to no. 243 C.

243 · 46×76 / 1744

St Mark's Square towards the Basilica London, Bisgood Collection
A. The dating given above is based on that of its companion piece, no. 242 B.
B. This version (61 × 92,5 cm.), in the Price Collection, Wakehurst Place (Sussex), is probably of the same period; companion piece to no. 244.
C. This controversial version in the Musée Jacquemart-André, Paris (45 × 76 cm.), is rather late, but fairly close to the works above; companion piece to no. 242 C, above.

244 · 61×92,5 / 1744

The Harbour of St Mark's from the Giudecca Canal Wakehurst Place, Sussex, Price Collection
Companion piece to no. 243 B, and so datable to 1744. It should be noted that the façade of the Church of the Pietà appears as it was before its reconstruction in 1745.

245 · 98×113 / *1744*

The Quay with the Doge's Palace towards the West Artramont, Wexford, Neave Collection

A. The dating is that of its companion piece, no. 237 B.
B. Another version, in the Wallace Collection, London (59 × 93 cm.); companion piece of no. 247 A.

246 · 41,5×33,5 / 1744-45?

Campo Santi Giovanni e Paolo with the Colleoni Monument London, Lord Brownlow Collection
A. An inscription on the back says that the painting was acquired by Sir Abraham Hume, who gave it to Lord Alford. This does not, however, provide sufficient information for dating, nor does the probable reference to it in the correspondence between Sesso and John Strange [Mauroner, *AV*, 1947; Constable, 1962]. The hints of fantasy which are comparable to that of other works dated 1744, suggests a tentative dating to that year.
B. This lovely version is probably close to no. 246 A above in date. The variation is only slight. Formerly in the Mountbatten Collection, Broadlands (28 × 20,5 cm.).

247 · 59×93 / *1745

The Riva degli Schiavoni towards the East London, Wallace Collection
A. This version was painted before 1745, when the new façade of the Church of the Pietà was erected, as it is not shown here. But it is later than other versions such as the Egerton (no. 81) and Albertini (no. 143 A). Companion piece to no. 245 B.
B. Another version, with slight variations; it is probably very near in date and belongs to the Earl of Normanton (57 × 92,5 cm.); companion piece to no. 248.

248 · 57×92 / *1745

The Grand Canal from Palazzo Grimani to Ca' Foscari Ringwood, Earl of Normanton's Collection
Only slightly different from the Windsor Castle and former Harvey versions (nos. 69 A and 116). It is later, though before 1745, the date established by the companion piece, no. 247 B. Constable [1962] has noted the use of sketches in the sketchbook in the Accademia, Venice.

249 · 137×162,5 / 1745

The Bucintoro at the Quay on Ascension Day Philadelphia, Museum of Art, William L. Elkins Collection
The Campanile of St Mark's seems to be damaged. From a note written by Canaletto on the corresponding drawing, now at Windsor Castle (no. 7426) [Parker, 1948], we know that this was the result of lightning damage on 23 April 1745, which makes it possible to date this picture exactly.
At first Constable [1962] ascribed the picture to the workshop, but later [1964] attributed it to Canaletto.

250 · 69×94 / *1745-46*

The Quay from the Harbour of St Mark's Munich, Alte Pinakothek
A version of a subject already painted, for example, in the group for the Duke of Bedford (no. 87 A), and one he was to return to for the painting at Holland House (no. 274 A). It was a group of four (including nos. 251–3) that once belonged (1806) to Antonio Canova [Guattoni, *Memorie enciclopediche*, 1806–19]. Constable [1962], ascribes all four works to the workshop, at most under Canaletto's supervision, which is

259

unquestionably recognisable. The four have also been attributed to Bellotto.

251 · 69×94 / *1745-46*

The Entrance to the Grand Canal with the Church of the Salute towards the East Munich, Bayerische Staatsgemäldesammlungen
For general information, see no. 250, above. Another version, painted a few years earlier, is in the Lyon Collection, Geneva (no. 160).

252 · 69×94 / *1745-46*

The Grand Canal from Campo San Vio London, Joel Collection
For general information, see no. 250, above. The one formerly in the Harvey Collection (no. 112 A) is another version.

253 · 69×94 / 1745-46*

The Grand Canal from near the Rialto Bridge towards the North London, Joel Collection
For general information, see no. 250, above. It is a repetition of the Windsor Castle view (no. 75 A) and is not stylistically dissimilar from the other two paintings listed as nos. 75 B and 75 C, though it is later in date.

254 · 66×127 / 1745-46?

The Islands of San Cristoforo, San Michele and Murano from the Fondamenta Nuove Leningrad, Hermitage
The authorship was once challenged, but on insufficient grounds. The subject is the same as that in the controversial painting at Windsor Castle (no.

254

255

256

257

260

262

261

263

264A

265

365). Style would date it to probably just before Canaletto's departure for England. Companion piece to no. 255.

255 66 × 127 1745-46?
The Church of San Giovanni dei Battuti at Murano with Venice in the Background
Leningrad, Hermitage
Companion piece to no. 254. Parker [1948] and Constable relate it to a drawing at Windsor Castle (no. 7458). The subject had been previously misinterpreted by von Hadeln [1930]. This drawing is connected with a drawing in the Museum Boymans-van Beuningen, Rotterdam, and with a sketch in (?) the Brass Collection, Venice [Miotti, AV, 1966].

256 148,5 × 132,5 *1746?
The Bucintoro at the Quay on Ascension Day
Formerly in the Lovelace Collection, it was lost from sight after it appeared on the London market in 1937. It is different in style from the uniform group of six works that also once belonged to the Lovelace Collection and which date from about 1754 (see nos. 305 ff.). This painting was probably done just before Canaletto's departure for England. A very closely related drawing is at Windsor Castle (no. 7453), one that was also used for other versions of the same subject.

257 46 × 76 *1746*?
The Prisons London, Private collection
There is no external evidence for dating this singular work, which to judge from the style was probably painted just before Canaletto's departure for England. Companion piece to no. 258.

258 46 × 76 *1746*?
The Church of the Redentore
London, Private collection
Companion piece to no. 257. A version of the subject depicted in the Leggatt painting (no. 104 B), but a bit later.

259 35.5 × 28 1746?
Self-portrait Anglesea Abbey, Lord Fairhaven Collection
The following inscription is on the upper part of the simulated

oval frame: "*GIO. ANTONIO. DA CANALE ORIGINE. CIVIS. VENETVS*" and "*IL CELEBRE CANALETO*" is inscribed on the lower part. Published as an autograph work by Watson [BM, 1956]. (Haskell [AB, 1962] agrees, but Moschini [AV, 1962] seems doubtful.) Watson persuasively argues that the background is rendered in Canaletto's style. Examination of this part of the picture, in particular of the view of St Paul's Cathedral, so close to its depiction in the Richmond painting (no. 260; 1746), confirms the date of the work.

260 105 × 117,5 1746
London and the Thames from Richmond House
Goodwood, Duke of Richmond and Gordon's Collection
On the basis of Hill's letter (see *Outline biography*), this picture and its companion piece (no. 261) have been considered to be Canaletto's first works in England and are therefore dated 1746. Hayes [BM, 1958] has related the two works to a drawing in the Blofeld Collection, Hoveton House, Norfolk, which seems to date from 1747. Hayes therefore dates the paintings to 1747, and Constable [1962] partially agrees. "In some of his earlier Venetian paintings – for example ... The *Church of the Carità, from San Vitale*, in the National Gallery, London (no. 33) – Canaletto had already made use of the raised viewpoint: the view from above is no longer just a circumstance of the viewpoint that does not substantially modify the pictorial composition ... the great terrace which seems to continue right under the observer is the very manner of 'declaring' the sense of space with which the artist wants to invest the picture ... movement is stated in a way that could not be more explicit. The transverse cropping goes far beyond the limits of the frame, and is intended to make the observer take part 'existentially' in the painter's station point, to put the observer inside the painting". [Brandi, 1960].

261 109 × 119,5 1746
Whitehall and the Privy Garden from Richmond House Goodwood, Duke of Richmond and Gordon's Collection
Companion piece to no. 260.

266

268

273

274A

267

269

274B

262 118 × 238 1746-47
The Thames towards the City with St Paul's Cathedral in the Background Prague, Národni Galerie
It was acquired about 1752, together with its companion piece (no. 263), by Prince Lobkowicz. It belonged to his descendants until it was transferred to the Prague Gallery [Safarik, AV, 1964]. The dating is based on the condition of Westminster Bridge as depicted in the companion piece.

263 118 × 238 1746-47
The Thames with Westminster Bridge in the Background Prague, Národni Galerie
For provenance, see no. 262, above. The picture can be dated to 1746 from the condition of the bridge. Further, in the painting formerly in the Buccleuch Collection (no. 267), dated to 1747, the bridge is shown as completed. But it is also possible that Canaletto may have done both pictures expressly for Prince Lobkowicz about 1752 and used sketches

of 1746–7. However the style does not support this hypothesis.

264 48 × 81 1746-47
The Thames from York Water Gate towards Westminster Bridge
London (?), Wood Collection
A. Westminster Bridge appears as it must have before May 1746, when Canaletto reached Great Britain. The bridge is shown in the same stage of construction as here in a drawing rightly connected with the painting (London, property of Montagu Bernard) [Finberg, WS, 1920–1;

270

271

272

113

Hadeln, 1930]. This contradiction may be due to the fact that our information about the progress of the bridge is incomplete, being based chiefly on the evidence [1751] of the architect C. Labelye. The dating 1946–7 for both the picture and the drawing fits the style.

B. An autograph version (75,5 × 106,5 cm.) in which the bridge is shown as complete is consequently dated about 1750 [Constable, 1962], although it seems very close to the Wood version. The painting is in the Douglas-Pennant Collection, London (?).

265 ⊞ ◐ $\frac{57 \times 95}{1746\text{-}47}$ ▤ ⦂

Panorama of London seen through an Arch of Westminster Bridge
Great Britain, Duke of Northumberland's Collection
An engraving published in 1747 by J. Brindley is derived from this painting and provides a certain *terminus ante quem* for it. The work could not have been done before July 1746, judging from the report of the architect of the bridge, C. Labelye [1751]. There is a drawing at Windsor Castle (no. 7561) related to the painting [Constable, *OMD*, 1929]. The whereabouts of another drawing that was in the Monro Collection until 1833 [Finberg, *WS*, 1920–1] is unknown.

266 ⊞ ◐ $\frac{58,5 \times 95}{1746\text{-}47}$ ▤ ⦂

Westminster Bridge Being Built Great Britain, Duke of Northumberland's Collection
Another bold composition inspired by Westminster Bridge, which is depicted shortly before it was finished (25 October 1746), when the scaffolding had not yet been removed and finishing touches were still to be made; and repairs of defects that were soon discovered had not yet been started. Hence the picture must be dated between autumn 1746 and the beginning of 1747 [Constable, 1962].

267 ⊞ ◐ $\frac{96 \times 137,5}{1746\text{-}47}$ ▤ ⦂

Westminster Bridge from the North
Formerly in the Duke of Buccleuch's Collection. The date is assured by a print published in 1747, and is confirmed by the stage of construction of the bridge [Finberg, *WS*, 1920–1; Constable, 1962].

268 ⊞ ◐ $\frac{60,5 \times 95}{1746\text{-}47}$ ▤ ⦂

The Venetian Lagoon with an Oval Church: a Capriccio
New York, Fonda Collection
This enchanting picture may belong to the beginning of Canaletto's stay in England [Constable, 1962].

269 ⊞ ◐ $\frac{165 \times 114,5}{1746\text{-}50}$ ▤ ⦂

The Church of San Giorgio Maggiore and the Rialto Bridge: a Capriccio Raleigh, North Carolina, State Art Museum
Constable [1962 and 1964] observed that the format and manner of composition suggest that the painting belongs to a set similar to that painted for Farnborough Hall (nos. 149 ff.). He dates the work to Canaletto's English period; the present writer would date it to the beginning of the English period.

270 ⊞ ◐ $\frac{100,5 \times 146}{1746\text{-}55}$ ▤ ⦂

A Renaissance Palace and a Roman Arch: a Capriccio
Arundel Castle, Duke of Norfolk's Collection
The style of this work and its two companion pieces (nos. 271 and 272) date them to the English period, perhaps its second half, judging from the location of the pictures, although there is no certain documentation.

271 ⊞ ◐ $\frac{100,5 \times 128}{1746\text{-}55}$ ▤ ⦂

A Triumphal Arch from the Portico of a Palace: a Capriccio Arundel Castle, Duke of Norfolk's Collection
For general information, see no. 270, above. "Canaletto's bizarre mixture of styles ... presenting a

medieval pastiche which is already romantic in feeling, are painted with such elaboration that one ought to consider them apart from the broader *capricci*, however similar, that he painted before his departure for London" [Morassi, 1954].

272 ⊞ ◐ $\frac{100,5 \times 146}{1746\text{-}55}$ ▤ ⦂

Renaissance and Gothic Buildings and Church: a Capriccio Arundel Castle, Duke of Norfolk's Collection
See nos. 270 and 271, above.

273 ⊞ ◐ $\frac{84 \times 137}{1747}$ ▤ ⦂

Panorama of Windsor Castle
Great Britain, Duke of

Northumberland's Collection
An eighteenth-century inscription in English written on a sheet of paper attached to the back attributes the painting to "Mr. Canaletti" and dates the work 1747. It provides information that has been interpreted by Finberg [*WS*, 1920–1] and indicates that the view was painted for Sir Hugh Smithson, first Duke of Northumberland, who also commissioned other works of Canaletto that still belong to the family. It was painted in the years a little before and after Canaletto's stay in England.

274 ⊞ ◐ $\frac{85 \times 134,5}{1747\text{-}50}$ ▤ ⦂

The Quay from the Harbour of St Mark's
A. A version of a subject already painted as early as 1730–1, in the Bedford view (no. 87 A). It seems to have been done for Holland House, hence during Canaletto's stay in England, between 1747 and 1750. It was documented as early as 1767 [Constable, 1962]. In 1941 it was on the New York market.
B. A smaller version (44 × 59 cm.) belonged in 1939 to D. Tziracopoulo of Berlin, but it has since disappeared. It must belong to the period 1747–50.

275A

280

276A

277

283 (Plate LIX)

278

279

281 (Plate LXII)

282

284A

285A

287

288

275 ⊞ ◐ 66×112.5 / 1747-50 ▤ ⦂

Greenwich Hospital, London, from across the Thames London, National Maritime Museum
A. There is no external evidence to establish precise dating, but this beautiful view has the same style as the works Canaletto painted during the first part of his stay in England.
B. Another version (54,5 × 89 cm.) was noted by Finberg [WS, 1920–1] in the Burns Collection, London, where it was also examined by Constable [1962].

276 ⊞ ◐ 76×66 / 1747-50 ▤ ⦂

Henry VII's Chapel at Westminster Abbey: Interior Great Britain, Kleinworth Collection
A. It is supposed that this painting, with a possible companion piece (no. 277), belonged to S. Dickenson until 1774. It would seem to date to the first part of Canaletto's stay in England, judging from its relationship to no. 283 [Finberg, WS, 1920–1]. The quality of the painting, which is not particularly high, has raised some doubts about authorship.
B. A far more controversial version [Constable, 1962] is in the London Museum, London (71 × 60 cm.).

277 ⊞ ◐ 75,5×67,5 / 1747-50 ▤ ⦂

King's College Chapel, Cambridge: Interior
Probably the companion piece to no. 276 – hence also in the possession of S. Dickenson until 1774. The authorship has justifiably been questioned on many occasions, and Constable suggests that it may be an able copy. It is hard to solve the question, since the painting's whereabouts are unknown, though it did appear at the Canadian exhibition in 1964 [Constable, 1964].

278 ⊞ ◐ 86×122 / 1748 ▤ ⦂

Badminton House from the Park Badminton House, Gloucestershire, Duke of Beaufort's Collection
This picture was expressly painted, together with its companion piece (no. 279), for the third Duke of Beaufort, as reported by Vertue, who also provides information about the date [Constable, BM, 1929].

279 ⊞ ◐ 86×122 / 1748 ▤ ⦂

Badminton Park from the House Badminton House, Gloucestershire, Duke of Beaufort's Collection
Companion piece to no. 278, above. "Canaletto ... immediately understood the charm of the English landscape ..." and here reveals "a singular sense of landscape in its panoramic grandeur, carrying our view as far as the horizon, which is marked by a line of trees. The gradation of the green of the fields is very subtle, with the cows grazing, the carriages drawn by three pairs of horses,

and tiny bits of undergrowth: a diffused and bland luminosity, full of atmosphere, dominates the grand scene" [Pallucchini, 1960].

280 ⊞ ◐ 45,5×76 / 1749 ▤ ⦂

The Old Horse Guards and the Banqueting Hall, London, from St James's Park Great Britain, Trustees of the late Sir Arthur Wilmot
The most convincing date, suggested by Watson [BM, 1950], was before autumn 1749. The old Horse Guards was demolished in 1749–50, and the trees in the park are in summer bloom. Two preparatory sketches, formerly in the Viggiano Collection, where Watson and Constable [1962] saw them, have gone to the Accademia, Venice [Miotti, 1965].

281 ⊞ ◐ 122×249 / 1749 ▤ ⦂

The Old Horse Guards from St James's Park Basingstoke, (?), Earl of Malmesbury's Collection
The date of the work, which was mentioned in 1756 in the possession of the Earl of Radnor, can be established with certainty, not only because of the demolition of the building in 1749–50 but because of the announcement that Canaletto published in the Daily Advertiser (reported by Vertue on 26 July 1749, but printed on 25 July) inviting anyone interested to see the view of St James's Park in his studio in Silver Street (see Outline biography). A drawing related to the painting is in the British Museum (no. 1863–3–28–305) [Constable, 1927; Hadeln, 1930].

282 ⊞ ◐ 84×137 / 1749 ▤ ⦂

View of Syon House, Middlesex Great Britain, Duke of Northumberland's Collection
This was painted for Hugh Smithson, first Duke of Northumberland, who wrote from Syon to the Duchess of Somerset on 2 July 1749 saying that the painting had been begun and that he expected it to be an important work [Constable, 1962].

283 ⊞ ◐ 99×101,5 / 1749 ▤ ⦂

Westminster Abbey with the Procession of the Knights of the Order of the Bath London, Westminster Abbey
This shows the Knights of the Order of the Bath in the Chapel of Henry VII in the Abbey on 26 June 1749. Thus the painting may be dated just after that event. It was painted for Joseph Wilcocks, dean of Westminster and Bishop of Rochester [Finberg, WS, 1920–1]. We may note "the bizarre humour ... which is more emphatic in its expressive characterisation" [Moschini, 1954] that marks the figures. It is quite different from the handling of figures in his Venetian paintings and also unlike other works he painted during his English visit.

284 ⊞ ◐ 45,5×76 / 1750? ▤ ⦂

Westminster Bridge with Lambeth Palace in the Background from the North London, (?), Earl of Strathcona's Collection
A. The bridge looks as it did after the repairs carried out of defects found in 1750. However considerations of style suggest that it is not later than 1750. Related drawings are at Windsor Castle (no. 7558) [Parker, 1948], the British Museum (no. 1868–3–28–305) [Hadeln, 1930] and the National Trust, Stourhead [Watson, BM, 1950].
B. A contemporary version by Canaletto (45,5 × 76 cm.) is in

the Vestey Collection (Stowell Park); companion piece to no. 285 B.

285 ⊞ ◐ 105,5×186,5 / 1750-51 ▤ ⦂

The Thames with the City in the Background from the Terrace of Somerset House Windsor Castle, Royal Collections
A. This view originally belonged to Joseph Smith, and this has led scholars to construct two different hypotheses about its date. Finberg [WS, 1920–1] and others think that Canaletto received the commission from Smith just before his brief trip to Venice between 1750 and 1751

(see Outline biography), when he might have brought the painting and its companion piece (no. 286 A) to him. Constable [1962], more convincingly, thinks that Canaletto painted both pictures during that stay, on the basis of drawings he had already done in England. These drawings would be a "finished" drawing at Windsor Castle (no. 7560) [Parker, 1948] and another in the Seilern Collection, London [Constable, BM, 1927; Hadeln, 1930]. Levey [1964], however, dates the work to before 1750.
B. A small autograph version (46 × 76 cm.), perhaps slightly earlier, in the Vestey Collection;

286A

286B (Plates LII–LIII)

289

290A (Plates LVII–LVIII)

290B

291A

291B

292

293

294A

294B

295

296A

297

298

299A

299B

companion piece to no. 248 B.
Many other non-autograph versions are listed by Constable [1962].

286 ⊞ ⊘ 40,5 × 70,5 / 1750-51

The Thames with Westminster Bridge in the Background from the Terrace of Somerset House Windsor Castle, Royal Collections
A. Companion piece to no. 285 A. A preparatory drawing is at Windsor Castle (no. 7559).
B. Another version (106,5 × 185,5 cm.) belongs to the Duke of Hamilton and Brandon at Haddington. The date is hard to determine, but it has been ascribed to the last part of Canaletto's stay in England [Zampetti, CMV, 1967].
Constable [1962] mentions various non-autograph copies.

287 ⊞ ⊘ 50,8 × 76,8 / 1751?

The Grand Walk, Vauxhall Gardens, London Brynkinallt, Denbighshire, Lord Trevor Collection
An engraving published by R.

Sayer and H. Overton on 2 December 1751 makes dating to that year plausible [Constable, 1927]. The inscription on the print "CANALETI DELIN." however, refers to a drawing and not to a painting by Canaletto [Constable, 1962 and 1964].

288 ⊞ ⊘ 118,5 × 273,5 / 1751

Whitehall and the Privy Garden towards the North Bowhill, Duke of Buccleuch's Collection
This was painted for the Duke of Montagu [Finberg, WS, 1920–1]. The Duke died on 5 July 1749, but the architecture shown is later than 1749. Hence it has been supposed that the painting had not been finished when the Duke died and was only completed a couple of years later [Hayes, BM, 1958]. The style of the picture would fit in with this hypothesis.

289 ⊞ ⊘ 95,5 × 233,5 / 1751

Chelsea College with Ranelagh House and the Rotunda Great Britain, National Trust; and Havana,

Private collection or Museo Nacional
The dimensions given above are hypothetical and the picture may originally have been larger.

This broad view was cut in two at an unknown date. The left part (86,5 × 106,5 cm.) belongs to the National Trust; the other (95,5 × 127 cm.) is in Cuba. It was in a private collection and may now be in the possession of the state. Canaletto painted it in 1751 and showed it in his studio in Silver Street, according to the announcement that appeared in the *Daily Advertiser* on 31 July [Constable, 1962] (see also *Outline biography*). The Ranelagh Rotunda, a masterpiece begun *ca.* 1740 after plans by W. Jones, particularly struck Canaletto's fancy. Chelsea College (now Chelsea Hospital) had been begun in 1682 after plans by Christopher Wren. The Cuban half of the picture was published by Simonson [BM, 1922]; the English half was in the *Canaletto in England* Exhibition (1959).

290 ⊞ ⊘ 42 × 71 / *1751*

South Front of Warwick Castle Warwick Castle, Earl of Warwick's Collection
A. One of a set of splendid views of Warwick Castle, which vary in size but were painted at the same period. All except one (no. 290 C) were most probably painted for Francis Greville, who became Earl of Warwick in 1759, and are in the possession of his descendants. Pallucchini [1960] dates them a few years after Canaletto's arrival in England; they probably date from just after his return from his short trip to Venice (1750–1). A drawing related to this view is in the same collection, and was acquired in the nineteenth century.
B. Another version (75 × 120,5 cm.), varied by a closer viewpoint, also in the possession of the Earl of Warwick.
C. A version of no. 290 A, almost certainly painted after the drawing mentioned at no. 290 A above [Constable, 1962], in the Collection of Lord Astor of Hever, London (72,5 × 120,5 cm.). The only differences are in the arrangement and depiction of figures.

291 ⊞ ⊘ 73 × 122 / *1751*

East Front of Warwick Castle Warwick Castle, Earl of Warwick's Collection
A. Companion piece of no. 291 B (for other information, see no. 290 A, above). A preparatory drawing is in the Lehman Collection, New York [Constable, 1962].
B. Another version (75 × 122 cm.), also painted for Greville, still at Warwick Castle. It is painted from a different angle and is the companion piece to no. 291 A.

292 ⊞ ⊘ 79,5 × 118 / 1751 ?

Old Somerset House from the Thames Minneapolis, Institute of Arts
This work is of great documentary interest. Old Somerset House, built in 1549, had been a royal residence and was later used for foreign ambassadors. It seems to have been occupied in 1763 by an envoy of the Venetian Republic. The building was demolished (and replaced by Chambers' Somerset House), from 1766 onwards. There is no external evidence for the date of the painting, but it must have been done in the second half of Canaletto's stay in England. A related drawing is in the Du Cane Collection, London [Hadeln, 1930].

293 ⊞ ⊘ 113,5 × 139,5 / 1751-52

View of Alnwick Castle in Northumberland Albury Park, Duke of Northumberland's Collection
A. One of the most evocative works of Canaletto's period in England. It shows the castle before the restoration by Robert Adam (1752–3). There is a copy of the painting by S. Scott and dated 1752.
B. Another version, identical in size (133,5 × 139,5 cm.), also in the possession of the Duke of Northumberland, at Alnwick Castle [Constable, 1962].

301

302

303A (Plates LX–LXI)

313

294 ⊞◐ 81,5×115,5 / 1751-55? ▤ ⦂

Motifs of Vicenza and Rome: a Capriccio Italy, Private collection
A. Signed: "ANT CANALETTO FE". In the middle there is a singular juxtaposition of Palladio's Rotunda at Vicenza with what seem to be the remains of the Temple of Saturn in the Roman Forum on the right. Stylistic evidence suggests that it dates from the second part of Canaletto's English period.
B. Another version, almost identical in size (81 × 115 cm.) and only slightly different (the addition of the figure of a man drawing in the foreground, perhaps Canaletto himself) [Zampetti, CMV, 1967]). This is in the Albertini Collection, Rome and is certainly contemporary.

295 ⊞◐ 174×136,5 / 1751-56? ▤ ⦂

St Mark's Square from the Libreria to the Loggetta Alnwick Castle, Duke of Northumberland's Collection
A variant of no. 149, above. It may have been painted in the last years of Canaletto's stay in England or immediately after.

296 ⊞◐ 56×109 / 1752-53 ▤ ⦂

The New Horse Guards from St James's Park Hampshire, Buxton Collection
A. This building, erected to replace the old Horse Guards, demolished in 1749–50 (see no. 281, above, in which the same angle of vision is used), is depicted here almost completed. Graphic sources identified by Finberg [WS, 1920–1] – an etching published on 2 November 1753, showing the finished structure, and an earlier version, published on 2 November 1752, in which the dome of the building is missing, both executed at the expense of R. Sayer – allow us to date the picture between 1752 and 1753, perhaps to the beginning of 1753.
B. Another version, with the new Horse Guards finished (59 × 110,5 cm.), and hence later in date (perhaps late 1753 or 1754). It is in the Drury-Lowe Collection.

297 ⊞◐ 84×137 / 1752-53 ▤ ⦂

Northumberland House, London Alnwick Castle, Duke of Northumberland's Collection
This can be dated on the basis of an engraving inscribed "CANALETI PINX ET DELIN", executed by Bowles and published by Sayer in 1753 [Finberg, WS, 1920–1]. A drawing related to the painting but not preparatory (from a different viewpoint) is in the Institute of Arts, Minneapolis.
The subject was painted in several versions, some of which have been occasionally ascribed to Canaletto. They have been recorded by Finberg and Constable [1962], though the latter rightly rejects all attributions to Canaletto.

305

306

307

308

310A

310B

311

309

312

314C

298 ⊞◐ 44×71,5 / 1752-56? ▤ ⦂

A Round Domed Church: a Capriccio Worcester, Massachusetts, Art Museum
An imaginary view that is hard to date. It might have been painted at the end of his English period or just after his return to Venice. A drawing of the same subject, in the Fogg Art Museum, Cambridge, Mass., is closely related to sketches executed in England, and this would suggest the earlier dating. The painting was reproduced in an etching by Bellotto, and this has erroneously led some scholars to attribute it to that artist. Constable [1964] says it was painted before Canaletto's return to Venice.

299 ⊞◐ 52×61 / 1754 ▤ ⦂

The Capitol Square and the Cordonata, Rome Mexico City, Gavito Collection
A. This view is derived from an engraving by A. Specchi, dated 1692. On the back of the painting there is a fragmentary inscription that guarantees its authenticity [Finberg, A, 1926]. The incomplete inscription has been restored on the basis of those on similar paintings (see

300 ⊞◐ 51×61 / 1754 ▤ ⦂

St Paul's Cathedral, London USA, Mellon Collection (?)
A view of Christopher Wren's masterpiece, a printed derivation

no. 303 A, in particular): "FATTO NEL AN … GNI MA. GIOR ATTEN … CAVALIER … ANTONIO C …" ("Done in the year … in London with every care, at the request of Mr Hollis, my very esteemed patron Antonio Canal, known as Canaletto" [Finberg]). One can, therefore, establish that the painting was one of six painted in 1754 for Thomas Hollis. This is also confirmed by other evidence from its provenance. There is some doubt of its order in the series [see Constable, 1962].
B. A fine version (86,5 × 136 cm.), in the Neave Collection, Artramont, Wexford, which is even closer to the original engraving by Specchi. The date is hard to determine, but it must be close to that of the Gavito version.
C. Another version (84 × 136 cm.), closely related in style to no. 299 B, belongs to the Marquis of Crewe [Constable, 1962].

of which is mentioned by Cicogna as having been done by Fambrini. The work belonged to James Wadsworth before it appeared on the American market. It was executed for Thomas Hollis (see no. 299 A, above).

301 ⊞◐ 52×61 / 1754 ▤ ⦂

London Architectural Motifs: a Capriccio New Jersey, USA, Rionda Braga Collection
Painted for Thomas Hollis (see no. 299 A, above). The architectural features shown are the Banqueting Hall, the wall of the Privy Garden, Richmond House, and the equestrian monument to Charles I, etc. [Finberg, WS, 1920–1].

302 ⊞◐ 46,5×75 / 1754 ▤ ⦂

Old Walton Bridge London, Dulwich College Picture Gallery
Painted for Thomas Hollis (see no. 299 A, above). On the back is an inscription which repeats, with slight differences, the text of that on the back of no. 303 A.

303 ⊞◐ 46×75,5 / 1754 ▤ ⦂

The Ranelagh Rotunda: Interior London, National Gallery
A. Painted for Thomas Hollis (see no. 299 A, above). On the back is the inscription: "Done in the year 1754 in London for the first [and] last time with every care [at the] request of Mr Hollis my very esteemed patron. Antonio del Canal, known as Canaletto …" Constable rightly draws attention to a print of the same subject published by Sayer on 2 December 1751, which is marked: "CANALETI DELIN." This shows that Canaletto had done a drawing of this evocative subject as early as 1751.
B. Another version (50,8 × 76,2 cm.), with a different viewpoint, in the collection of Lord Trevor, Brynkinallt, Denbighshire. Sewter [BM, 1949] notes that the statement "done … for the first [and] last time" on the back of no. 303 A must inevitably raise problems and, of course, appears contradictory. Since there is no doubt about the authorship of the Trevor version or its close connection with the Hollis version, it seems that the artist considered this version as a

free and independent work [Constable, 1962]. The work seems chronologically close to the Hollis version, and it seems unlikely that Canaletto might have painted it later in Venice, when he considered he was no longer bound to his agreement with Hollis.

304 ⊞ ⊗ 1754 目 ⦂

Westminster Bridge
One of the paintings done for Thomas Hollis (see no. 299 A, above). It went from the Disney Collection to the London market. It was auctioned at Christie's on 3 May 1884 [Constable, 1962] and has not been seen since.

305 ⊞ ⊗ 81,5 × 115,5 1754 目 ⦂

A River with Eton College Chapel: a Capriccio London, Collection of the Princess Royal
It is signed: "*A.C. / 1754*". It belonged, with five other works (nos. 306–10), to the Lovelace family until a sale in 1937. Finberg [*BM*, 1938] has shown with good reason that Canaletto painted the six paintings for Peter King (who died in 1754) and his brother William. The dating of the set is based on the date on this painting. An autograph drawing, derived from this painting and perhaps intended for an engraving (the composition is executed in reverse) belongs to the Städelsches Kunstinstitut, Frankfurt.

306 ⊞ ⊗ 75 × 123 1754 目 ⦂

The Island of San Michele with Venice in the Background Sussex, Clarke Collection
For general information, see no. 305, above. Constable [1962] identified the subject, but notes the addition of some imaginary elements. Finberg [*BM*, 1938] thought it was a *capriccio* of Murano. It is related to drawings (which Hadeln [1930] considers to be of Murano) in the Ashmolean Museum, Oxford, the Museum Boymans-van Beuningen, Rotterdam (lost during the war), and in the Ten Cate Collection, Holland. The first of these drawings was engraved by Wagner in the series of *Six Country Villages*, with the note: "*Quanto più bello appare presso la terra il mare*". A date for

the prints of 1742 has been suggested by Finberg, but has been rightly rejected by Constable.

307 ⊞ ⊗ 132 × 106,5 1754 目 ⦂

English Landscape and Architectural Motifs: a Capriccio Great Britain, Bryant Collection
For general information, see no. 305, above. It is the companion piece to no. 308. Finberg [*BM*, 1938] has tried to identify the buildings, which seem to be pastiches, but in the manner of English buildings. Finberg has pointed out that the "exotic" boat on the right reflects the great popularity of the taste for chinoiserie in English society in the middle of the eighteenth century.

308 ⊞ ⊗ 132 × 104 1754 目 ⦂

Motifs of Roman Antiquity and English Landscape: a Capriccio Great Britain, Bryant Collection
This is one of the set that formerly belonged to the Lovelace family (see no. 305, above) and is companion piece to no. 307. The individual structures cannot be identified with certainty.

309 ⊞ ⊗ 152,5 × 137 1754 目 ⦂

A Ruined Church and the Venetian Monument to Colleoni: a Capriccio
For general information, see no. 305, above. None of the architectural features has been identified, except for the famous equestrian monument. Companion piece to no. 310.

310 ⊞ ⊗ 150 × 134,5 1754 目 ⦂

A Palace and a Bridge and an Obelisk in the Background: a Capriccio
A. Another figurative picture. On the right is a portal with a statue on top and on the left is another building, Renaissance in style, with spires. For general information, see no. 305, above. Companion piece to no. 309. A drawing related to this painting and to no. 310 B is in the Cleveland Museum of Art.
B. Another version (46 × 61 cm.), with the same compositional elements, in the possession of the Earl of Cadogan, Snaigow (Perthshire). It is very close in

315

316A

321

322

date to the other version. For a related drawing, see above. The drawing was engraved by Berardi and published by Wagner with the note: ("*Anto. Canaletto. inten. Berardi scul*'. The caption reads: "*L'età che non divora, Se strugge i sassi ancora*". Companion piece to no. 311.

311 ⊞ ⊗ 46 × 61 1754 目 ⦂

A Villa, a Church and a Column Bearing a Statue: a Capriccio Snaigow, Perthshire, Earl of Cadogan's Collection
Companion piece to no. 310 B.

312 ⊞ ⊗ 51 × 85 1754 目 ⦂

The Venetian Lagoon with Classical Ruins: a Capriccio

New York, Brandt Collection
On the back is an inscription that is believed to have been copied for the original canvas (rebacked): "*1754 Io Antonio Canaleto Pinx v. invenzione*". This date would fit the style of the work.

313 ⊞ ⊗ 61,5 × 107 '1754' 目 ⦂

Eton College Chapel, Windsor London, National Gallery
Finberg [*WS*, 1920–1] notes stylistic similarities to no. 273 and dated this work to 1747. Levey's more convincing analysis has related it to no. 303 and dated it about 1754. Constable's cautious suggestion [1962] that the painting may have been executed after

Canaletto's return to Venice is not convincing. A related drawing was in the Harmsworth Collection, Mereworth Castle [Levey].

314 ⊞ ⊗ 137 × 126 '1754' 目 ⦂

The Venetian Lagoon with Classical Ruins: a Capriccio Chicago, Epstein Collection
A. Another version of the subject in the left half of no. 312, above, with which it is certainly contemporary [Constable, *BM*, 1923, and 1962].
B. A good variant (105,5 × 104 cm.), although not universally attributed to Canaletto, in the Baltimore Museum of Art [Constable, 1964].
C. A third, fine version 83,2 × 95,2 cm.), which was in the Davies Collection, Elmley Castle (Gloucestershire). Its present location is not known.

315 ⊞ ⊗ 46 × 123 1755 目 ⦂

Old Walton Bridge London, Skrine Collection
Another version of the subject already painted the year before for Thomas Hollis (no. 302), with variations, that are chiefly due to a more distant viewpoint. Canaletto himself must have considered this an independent composition, to judge from the inscription on the back: "Done in 1755 in London / For the first and last time with all care, at the request of Mr Dickers / My very esteemed patron / Antonio Canal, known as Canaleto" (see *Outline biography*). The authenticity of the inscription is confirmed by an autograph note on a drawing derived from the painting, now in the Mellon Collection, Washington.

316 ⊞ ⊗ 86,5 × 134,5 '1755' ? 目 ⦂

Motifs of the Scuola di San Marco and of the Church of Santi Giovanni e Paolo: a Capriccio Artramont, Wexford, Neave Collection
A. This may have been painted just before Canaletto's return to Venice or at the very end of his stay in England.
B. A fine version (47 × 77 cm.), in the Brian Mountain Collection (London ?) [Constable, 1962].

320A

324A

325

326

327

328

329

330

335

331

332

333

317 64 × 46,5 1755*?

A Staircase and Triumphal Arch from a Loggia: a Capriccio Rome, Accademia di San Luca
This is a unique piece in Canaletto's repertory and was given to the Accademia by the painter Domenico Pellegrini. Hence the dating and authenticity of the work are problematic. It might have been painted after the return to Venice.

318 45 × 35 1755*

St Mark's Square towards the Basilica from the South-west Corner London, National Gallery

The viewpoint is set with dramatic effect from within the portico of the Procuratie Nuove. Scholars are almost unanimous in dating the work and its companion piece (no. 319) after Canaletto's return to Venice; the present writer would say immediately after. Three drawings have been linked to it: one at Windsor Castle (no. 7427) [Parker, 1948], one in the Wallraf Collection [Hadeln, 1930], and one formerly in the Reveley Collection [Levey, 1956]. All drawings include the Clock Tower without its last floor, however, which was added in 1755, so that they probably antedate the canvas.

319 46,5 × 39 1755*

St Mark's Square towards the Basilica from the North-west Corner London, National Gallery
Companion piece to no. 318, above. "One might say that the stylised manner of the later Canaletto here seems marked by a certain wit. This is not because too much importance has been given to the figures of the worldly clients of Florian's, which are enchanting ... but because the painting is light, the tones are delicate, and the touch is freer." [Moschini, 1954].

320 44,5 × 60 1755-56*

The Venetian Lagoon with a Tomb: a Capriccio Florence, Uffizi
A. For the attribution, see no. 324 A. Engraved by Berardi for Wagner, it is marked "Anto. Canaletto", and bears the caption: "Propizio al pescator di luna il lume" ("Moonlight is lucky for the fisherman"). A related drawing has been noted by Constable [1962] in the Melbourne National Gallery.
B. See no. 324 B, below. A small painting (29,5 × 38 cm.), formerly in the Korda Collection; in 1955 it belonged to A. Grassi, New York.

321 35,2 × 32,7 1755-56

St Mark's Basilica: Interior Windsor Castle, Royal Collections
According to Smith's inventory, Canaletto shows here the Good Friday service. But Parker [1948] argues — not altogether convincingly — that Smith, who attributed to this subject painted in the "nocturne" at Windsor Castle (no. 353, below), was mistaken. Gallo [AIS, 1956-7] has dated the picture on external evidence to Canaletto's youth — 1722. But this must be rejected on stylistic grounds. Constable's theory [1962] is much more plausible. He thinks that the inscription "Verona Fidelis" may refer to the

honours that the Venetian Senate had decided to pay (15 March 1755) to Scipione Maffei, at the request of Verona.

322 ⊞ ◔ 42×29 1755-56 ▤ ⁝
St Mark's Basilica: Interior
Montreal, Museum of Fine Arts
A variation of the famous Windsor Castle painting (no. 321), to which it is close in style and probably also in date. A preparatory sketch is in the Scholz Collection, New York [Miotti, *AV*, 1966]. Companion piece to no. 323 A.

323 ⊞ ◔ 42×29 1755-56 ▤ ⁝
The Scala dei Giganti in the Doge's Palace Mexico City, Pagliai Collection
A. Companion piece to no. 322.
B. A fine version (174 × 136,5 cm.), perhaps contemporary, in the possession of the Duke of Northumberland, at Alnwick Castle.
C. A version of no. 323 B, formerly in the Paget Collection, Great Britain (83,8 × 61 cm.). It is considered autograph by Constable [1962] and Zampetti [CMV, 1967].

324 ⊞ ◔ 44,5×60 1755-56? ▤ ⁝
The Venetian Lagoon with a House, a Church and a Bell Tower: a Capriccio
Florence, Uffizi
A. Some scholars [Ferrari, 1914, etc.] have ascribed this to Bellotto, but Constable [1962], firmly attributes it to Canaletto, pointing out the decisive importance of the print Berardi did of it, published by Wagner with the declaration "*Anto. Canaletto Pinx.*" and the caption "Bread acquired by the sweat of the brow is sweet". A related drawing, certainly autograph, is in the Metropolitan Museum, New York. Companion piece to no. 320 A.
B. A version with slight differences (29,5 × 38 cm.) belonged to the Korda Collection, London (see no. 320 B, above).

325 ⊞ ◔ 31×43 1755-56 ▤ ⁝
Classical Ruins and a Gothic Building: a Capriccio
London, William Hallsborough Property
Companion piece to no. 326. Engraved by Berardi in a print published by Wagner with the inscription "*Ant° Canaletto Pinx*" and the caption "Man works and suffers to live".

336A

337A

337C

338

339

344

348B

326 ⊞ ◔ 31×43 1755-56 ▤ ⁝
The Venetian Lagoon with Triumphal Arch and a Gothic Building: a Capriccio
London, William Hallsborough Property
The authenticity is guaranteed by the inscription "*Ant Canaletto Pinx.*", which appears in an engraving published by Berardi with the caption "Proud eminence, I ignore you and pass by". Since the Gothic structure shown here and in the companion piece (no. 325) is a pastiche of King's College Chapel, Cambridge, and Eton College Chapel, the painting must have been painted after his final return to Venice, even if only shortly after. (Finberg [*BM*, 1938] does not agree with this.) A drawing in the Albertina, Vienna [Hadeln, 1930], which may have been done after the painting, may have been prepared by Canaletto for the engraving by Berardi.

327 ⊞ ◔ 29×41,5 1755-56 ▤ ⁝
The Venetian Lagoon with a Castle on a Bridge: a Capriccio London, Speelman Collection
The obvious similarities to no. 326 suggest the same dating. Despite earlier ascriptions to Bellotto, the work is certainly by Canaletto.

328 ⊞ ◔ 14,5×19 1755-56*? ▤ ⁝
A Farm, a Portal and Washing Pool: a Capriccio Springfield, Museum of Fine Arts
Together with the companion piece (no. 329), it is close to the *capricci* painted in 1755–6, though it also resembles, in its grey tones, the views painted about 1760. Constable [1964] considers that the two works should be dated before 1746.

329 ⊞ ◔ 14,5×19 1755-56*? ▤ ⁝
A River with a Palace, a Church and Ruins: a

Capriccio Springfield, Museum of Fine Arts
Companion piece to no. 328, above.

330 ⊞ ◔ 56×79 1755-59 ▤ ⁝
The Rialto Bridge after Palladio's Design, St Mark's Basilica and a View of Palazzo Chiericati at Vicenza: a Capriccio
Milan, Conti Collection (?)
Identified by Arslan [*AB*, 1948] as the painting mentioned by Algarotti in a letter to P. Pesci, 28 September 1759 [*Opere*, 1792]. Constable has raised difficulties [1962], pointing out that a version of the same subject now in the Galleria Nazionale, Parma (56 × 79 cm.), together with a companion piece correctly attributed by Fritzsche [1936] to Bellotto, is mentioned by Cicogna as once having been in Algarotti's picture collection. Nevertheless the present writer considers Arslan's argument more convincing.

331 ⊞ ◔ 40×47 1756*? ▤ ⁝
Palazzo Corner della Ca' Grande Euston Hall, Lord O'Neill Collection
Occasionally mistakenly attributed, with the following three works (nos. 332–4), to Bellotto. But in fact it is typical of Canaletto's development after his return to Venice, although it is rather cold in brushstroke.

332 ⊞ ◔ 30×39 1756*? ▤ ⁝
Palazzo Grimani London, National Gallery
For the attribution, see no. 331, above. Levey's assignment [Catalogue, 1956] of the work to the period after Canaletto's return to Venice is convincing, but his attribution to the workshop is not. Constable [1962] dates the work to the eve of Canaletto's departure for England.

333 ⊞ ◔ 38,5×48 1756*? ▤ ⁝
Ca' Pesaro London, Private collection
See nos. 331 and 332, above.

334 ⊞ ◔ 59,5×48 1756*? ▤ ⁝
Palazzo Vendramin Calergi
Lockinge, Berkshire, Lloyd Collection
See nos. 331 and 332, above.

335 ⊞ ◔ 29×43 1756*? ▤ ⁝
The Fondamenta Nuove and the Church of Santa Maria del Pianto
Engraved by Brustolon for the set of twenty-four prints published by Furlanetto and marked "*Antonio Canal Pinxit*". The dating has not been established, but the painting may have been done just after Canaletto's return to Venice.

340A   *341A*   *346*

336 ⊞ ◐ 116×166 / 1756*? 目 :

Motifs of Padua: a Capriccio
Hamburg, Kunsthalle
A. Stylistic evidence suggests a chronological connection with the two Windsor Castle paintings, nos. 338 (of which this can be considered a variant) and 339.
Of the many variations mentioned by Constable [1962], only the following two may – with some reservations – be attributed to Canaletto.
B. A canvas (96 × 85 cm.) in the possession of Lady Dupree, London (?).
C. Another (64 × 77 cm.) deposited by the Italian government at the Accademia, Venice [Pallucchini, *AV*, 1949], together with its companion piece (no. 337 B).

337 ⊞ ◐ 87,5×120,5 / 1756*? 目 :

Classical Motifs, a Capriccio
Milan, Museo Poldi Pezzoli
A. This may be a version of a companion piece to no. 336 A. Constable's suggestion [1962] that a collaborator was involved should be rejected.
B. A good derivation (63 × 77 cm.), companion piece to no. 336 C, in the Accademia, Venice, deposited there by the government and published by Pallucchini [*AV*, 1949], who also mentions a version in a private collection, Venice.
C. Another good version (124,5 × 108 cm.), in the Saumarez Collection, Great Britain.

338 ⊞ ◐ 52×65 / 1756*? 目 :

Classical Ruins and Paduan Motifs: a Capriccio Windsor Castle, Royal Collections
Part of a group which is difficult to date [Constable, 1962, etc.]. One piece of external evidence, of doubtful importance, is provided by the presence of Gothic elements, a style enjoying a revival in England at the time. This would suggest that the painting is related to Canaletto's English experience. In the case of this painting and its companion piece (no. 339), the fact that they were in the possession of Joseph Smith ought to indicate that they were painted after Canaletto's return to Venice. The style seems to corroborate this.

339 ⊞ ◐ 52×65 / 1756*? 目 :

Motifs of Padua: a Capriccio
Windsor Castle, Royal Collections
Companion piece to no. 338, above.

340 ⊞ ◐ 45×76 / 1756-57 目 :

St Mark's Square with the Doge's Palace and the Procuratie Nuove Dublin, National Gallery of Ireland
A. Constable [1962] rightly refers this to the period after Canaletto's return from England; the present writer would suggest just after his return to Venice.
B. A contemporary autograph version (101,5 × 152,5 cm.) appeared on the London market in 1938: now lost [Constable, 1962].

341 ⊞ ◐ 56,5×102 / 1756-60 目 :

The Harbour of St Mark's towards the West from the Riva degli Schiavoni New York, Erlanger Collection
A. Stylistic evidence links this painting to the works done shortly after his return to Italy [Constable, 1962]. Also the façade of the Church of the Pietà is depicted in a state after the restorations begun in 1745. Constable suggests that this may be that *Vue de Venise* which once belonged to Algarotti, according to a *post mortem* inventory (1776).

342 ⊞ ◐ 37×28 / 1758-60? 目 :

St Mark's Square from Campo San Basso Sarasota, Ringling Museum of Art
This bold imaginative view, pervaded by cold light, belongs to Canaletto's last period. Companion piece to no. 343. A drawing probably related to it is in the Musée Condé, Chantilly, and is also attributed to Bellotto [Constable, 1964].
Constable [1962] mentions several derivations, all of uncertain authorship or not by Canaletto.

B. Constable notes a version formerly in the Guernsey Curran Collection (56,5 × 101,5 cm.) and now lost.

343 ⊞ ◐ 37×28 / 1758-60? 目 :

The Riva degli Schiavoni towards the East Sarasota, Ringling Museum of Art
Companion piece to no. 342, above. Version of a subject previously painted (nos. 143, 156, 247), but this time the view is bolder.

344 ⊞ ◐ 118,7×129 / *1757* 目 :

Campo San Giacometto
Ottawa, National Gallery
A replica of no. 62 and certainly much later [Borenius, *BM*, 1941]. Constable [1962 and 1964] dates it to c 1746; Moschini [1954] dates it after the return from England. A related drawing is in the Seilern Collection, London.

345 ⊞ ◐ 68,5×106 / *1760 目 :

The Quay with the Libreria and the San Teodoro Column towards the West
Titsey Park, Surrey, Leveson-Gower Collection
A. This work was almost certainly painted by 1760 [Constable, 1962], but the present writer would say only shortly before that year. It is another version of the subject of the beautiful Albertini painting (no. 144 A) and forms a set with three other views in the same collection (nos. 346–8).
B. The version in the Alvan Fuller Collection, Boston (62,5 × c 94 cm.), does not seem totally autograph. Companion piece to no. 349. Related to the engraving (II, pl. XII) in Visentini's 1742 album.

342

343

354

353

355A (Plate LXIII)

356A

357

350A

351

352

346 ⊞ ◉ 68.5 × 106.5 *1760

The Entrance to the Grand Canal towards the West
Titsey Park, Surrey, Leveson-Gower Collection
The subject, which Canaletto painted many times, is here treated in the manner of the Bedford version (no. 88 A). (See also no. 345.)

347 ⊞ ◉ 68.5 × 106.5 *1760

The Entrance to the Grand Canal towards the East
Titsey Park, Surrey, Leveson-Gower Collection
A. For general information, see no. 345, above. A return to the subject of the youthful Windsor Castle painting (no. 47 A).
B. A fine version, formerly in the Pierpont Morgan Collection, which reappeared at the 1964 exhibition in Canada (Setterlee Ingalls Collection: 71 × 112 cm.). Constable [1964] dates it to c. 1735.

348 ⊞ ◉ 68.5 × 106 *1760

The Rialto Bridge from the North Titsey Park, Surrey, Leveson-Gower Collection
A. See no. 345, above.
B. Another version, in the Johnson Collection, Philadelphia (37 × 59,5 cm.). It is not universally considered autograph.

349 ⊞ ◉ 60 × 91,5 *1760

The Grand Canal from the Rialto Bridge to Ca' Foscari
Boston, Fuller Collection
The authorship is controversial, but it is very probably by Canaletto. A late treatment of a subject painted in his youth (no. 69 A). Companion piece to no. 345 B.

350 ⊞ ◉ 45,5 × 37 *1760

St Mark's Square from the Portico of the Torre dell'Orologio Cambridge, Fitzwilliam Museum
A. Long ascribed to the school, but Constable has rightly attributed it to Canaletto's late period [1962]. Companion piece to no. 351.
B. A contemporary version (74,3 × 57,8 cm.), in the Musée Smidt van Gelder, Antwerp.

351 ⊞ ◉ 46 × 37 *1760

The Doge's Palace: the Courtyard from the First Floor Loggia Cambridge, Fitzwilliam Museum
Companion piece to no. 350 A with the same unusual and effective framing of the view.

352 ⊞ ◉ 69 × 60,5 *1760

St Mark's Square towards the Basilica from the South-west Corner Halswell Park, Somerset, Lord Wharton Collection
The stylistic evidence points to the period after Canaletto's return to Venice. This is corroborated by a closely related drawing formerly in the Dodds-Crewe Collection [Hadeln, 1930], which can be dated to 1760. The drawing belonged to J. Crewe, who visited Venice in 1760 (see Outline biography). Another drawing, even more closely related from the Heseltine 'Collection was on the market in 1936 [Constable, 1962].

353 ⊞ ◉ 28 × 19 1760

St Mark's Basilica at Night: Interior Windsor Castle, Royal Collections
This is a splendid and unique view of the basilica down the north transept. There has been great disagreement over its date and occasion. Parker [1948] thinks that it represents the Good Friday service mentioned in Smith's inventory under the entry for another Interior of St Mark's, also at Windsor Castle (no. 321); more precisely, he suggests it is the service (as in the drawing at Windsor Castle [no. 7430]) performed on 7 February 1733 in honour of the relics of the Doge San Pietro Orseolo. Hence he dates it to Canaletto's youth, along with other scholars, like Watson [BM, 1948], who considers it a funeral service, and Zampetti [CMV, 1967]. Pallucchini's theory [1960] is more convincing. He believes it was painted after Canaletto's return to Venice and says, "It is an attempt unusual for its time, to create a night scene ... The whirling brushstrokes divide the light and create almost theatrical contrasts. The groups of figures and the statues on the iconostasis of St Mark's, which are rendered with such energy, create a great sense of living movement that brilliantly reverberates in that gloomy nocturnal space under the arches and domes of St Mark's. Canaletto still had the strength to break with the patterns imposed by his times ... His lesson was not to be lost, even if it was a dead letter in Venice."

354 ⊞ ◉ 99 × 145 *1761

Bull Fight in St Mark's Square Italy, Private collection
This was mentioned as early as 1761 as belonging to Bourchier Cleeve, Foots Cray Place, in Dodsley's Guide. Dodsley refers it to "Canaletti and Chimaroli" [G. B. Cimaroli], and because of his authority (his guide was published in Canaletto's lifetime), the collaboration has never been questioned, although it seems impossible to recognise two hands in the painting Watson, BM, 1953]. It is, however, possible that Canaletto only did the drawing two or three years before 1761, the year in which the work was already in England [Constable, 1962].

355 ⊞ ◉ 131 × 93 1765

A Colonnade and Courtyard: a Capriccio Venice, Gallerie dell'Accademia
A. It is marked: "Anton ... 1765". Canaletto presented it to the Venetian Academy of painting and sculpture on his admission (see Outline biography). A preparatory drawing [Modigliani, D, 1924–5] is in the Albertini Collection, Rome.
B. A fine version (129 × 93,5 cm.), in the Národni Galerie,

359

360

361

358

362

366

363

364

365

Prague, was shown at the recent exhibition of the Venetian eighteenth century in Czechoslovakia [Safarik, *AV*, 1964].

C. Another version (56 × 42 cm.), in the National Loan Collection Trust, London.

D. This version (65 × 47 cm.), in the Wallraf-Richartz-Museum, Cologne, is of doubtful authenticity.

Constable [1962] mentions other derivations, which are either lost, not authentic, or unavailable for examination.

356  51×66 1760-66

The Harbour of St Mark's towards the West Princeton, Princeton University

A. The painting was done after the restoration of the façade of the Church of the Pietà, begun in 1745. This may be one of Canaletto's last paintings, left unfinished after his illness and death.

B. Another unfinished version, but of uncertain authorship, in the Johnson Collection, Philadelphia (33,5 × 49 cm.).

357  63,5×100,5

Seaport with a Volcano Erupting

Signed "*Giuseppe Guerra / A.C.*" (see *Workshop*). Canaletto's contribution seems to have been limited to the figures and boats [Constable, 1962]. But the painting is very problematic because of the question of the collaboration with Guerra, who signed the painting, and because this may be the *View of Corfu* that Canaletto painted in 1726 (see *Outline biography*). [Haskell, *BM*, 1956], in which case Guerra's signature is inexplicable.

Other works attributed to Canaletto

There have been many more paintings attributed to Canaletto, particularly in the years following the Second World War, when eighteenth-century art, and Venetian view painting in particular, enjoyed a boom on the art market. Listed below are works that have been discussed by scholars and connoisseurs but whose attribution still remains an open question. We have not included many works that have been sold as Canalettos on the authority of reputable scholars, unless they have published arguments for their attributions.

358 151×122

The Campo dell'Arsenale Ottawa, National Gallery

This painting was ascribed to Canaletto until the Montreal Exhibition in 1965. Together with the three following works (nos. 359–61), which were also ascribed to Canaletto, Pignatti [*AV*, 1966] now attributes it to the early career of Bellotto (1740–2), after a close stylistic examination. Pignatti's attribution was confirmed at the Venetian Exhibition of View Painters (1967).

359 151×122

The Piazzetta towards the Torre dell'Orologio Ottawa, National Gallery

For general information, see no. 358, above. It is reminiscent of Canaletto's painting at Windsor Castle, dated 1743 (no. 220).

360 150×122

The Piazzetta towards the South Ringwood, Hampshire, Mills Collection

For general information, see no. 358, above. It was considered apart from the two preceding works (nos. 358 and 359) and was attributed [Constable, *BM*, 1929; until 1962] to *c* 1730 from its relation to the view at Windsor Castle (no. 48). A sketch, which is certainly by Canaletto, is in the Ashmolean Museum, Oxford [Constable, *OMD*, 1938; Byam Shaw and Parker, 1958], and is also connected with it. It may have been used by Bellotto.

361 150×122

The Entrance to the Grand Canal from the Piazzetta Ringwood, Mills Collection

See nos. 358 and 360, above.

362 77×97

The Harbour of St Mark's towards the West from the Riva degli Schiavoni

Frankfurt, Städelsches Kunstinstitut

In the past there was much

doubt as to whether it should be attributed to Bellotto [Fritzsche, 1936, etc.] or Canaletto. Constable gives it to Canaletto and dates it 1730–40 [1962]. But Pallucchini [*Vedute del Bellotto*, 1961] convincingly ascribes it to Bellotto, and says he probably painted it about 1742.

363 39×49

The Venetian Lagoon with Triumphal Arch: a Capriccio Asolo, Museo Civico

The current attribution of this to Bellotto, about 1742, which was corroborated by the Exhibition of Masterpieces in Venetian Museums [Pallucchini, 1946], has been rejected by Constable [1962], who still ascribes it to Canaletto. But his attribution, which also covers the companion piece (no. 364), seems untenable. The Venetian Exhibition of View Painters [*CMV*, 1967] tends to confirm Bellotto's authorship.

364 39×49

The Venetian Lagoon with Classical Ruins and a Statue: a Capriccio Asolo, Museo Civico

Companion piece to no. 363, above.

365 122,5×129,5

The Islands of San Cristoforo, San Michele and Murano from the Fondamenta Nuove Windsor Castle, Royal Collections

This painting has almost unanimously been considered a youthful masterpiece of Canaletto and dated 1725–30. Watson [*AV*, 1955], especially attempted to reconstruct its provenance, since it did not arrive to Windsor Castle with Joseph Smith's Collection. He thinks it is a companion piece to no. 366 with part of the top cut off, and dates it about 1725. Constable [1962] does not reject the attribution but considers the two works independent. Levey [1964], who has considered the work's provenance and analysed its stylistic qualities, is doubtful about its authenticity and suggests that it is a copy of a lost original or, more probably, a pastiche by an imitator of the view of Murano now in the Hermitage (no. 254). This hypothesis has been vigorously rejected by Morassi [*AV*, 1966].

366 146×136,5

The Grand Canal towards the Church of the Salute Windsor Castle, Royal Collections

As no. 364 (q.v.), Levey [1964] rejects the attribution to Canaletto, but Morassi [*AV*, 1966] disagrees.

Indexes

Listed here are the names of the places and chief monuments which are traditionally given as the titles of Canaletto's paintings. The same places and monuments inevitably are depicted in more than one painting. The various versions can easily be found in the following list.

Index of subjects and titles

Arch of Constantine 2, 204; with the Colosseum 212
Arch of Septimius Severus 1, 205; with the Church of Santi Martina e Lucca, Rome 213
Arch of Titus 206
Arsenal Bridge 100

Bacino di San Marco, *see* Harbour of St Mark's
Badminton House from the Park 278
Badminton Park from the House 279
Basilica of St Mark's, *see* St Mark's Basilica
Brenta at the Portello of Padua 209 A, 209 B
Bucintoro at the Quay on Ascension Day 174 A, 174 B, 249, 256
Bucintoro Leaving the Quay on Ascension Day 107 A, 107 B, 167
Bucintoro Returning to the Quay on Ascension Day 32, 67 A, 67 B, 67 C, 67 D, 109 A, 109 B, 232
Bull Fight in St Mark's Square 354

Campo dei Gesuiti 124
Campo dell'Arsenale 182, 358
Campo di Rialto 229 A, 229 B, 229 C
Campo San Francesco della Vigna 129 A, 129 B
Campo San Geremia 123
Campo San Giacometto 62, 344
Campo San Polo 126
Campo San Salvatore 127
Campo Santa Margherita 125
Campo Santa Maria Formosa 101 A, 101 B, 101 C
Campo Sant'Angelo 122
Campo Santi Apostoli 128
Campo Santi Giovanni e Paolo, with the Colleoni Monument 193 A, 193 B, 246 A, 246 B
Campo Santo Stefanin 166
Campo Santo Stefano 102
Canals, *see under* their names
Cannaregio 103 A, 103 B
Ca' Pesaro 333
Capitol Square and the Cordonata, Rome 299
Capricci: Church of San Francesco della Vigna, Venice 241; Church of San Giorgio Maggiore 222; Church of San Giorgio Maggiore and the Rialto Bridge 269; Church, Round Domed 298; Church, Ruined, and the Colleoni Monument 309; Classical Motifs 337 A, 337 B, 337 C; Classical Ruins, 4, 5, 15; Classical Ruins and a Gothic Building 325; Classical Ruins and Paduan Motifs 338; Colonnade and

Courtyard 355 A, 355 B, 355 C, 355 D; Convent of the Carità, Venice 225; English Landscape and Architectural Motifs 307; Horses of St Mark's 221; Farm, Portal and Washing Pool 328; Island of the Venetian Lagoon and a Church 197; Island of the Venetian Lagoon and Motifs from the Church of San Francesco della Vigna, 196; Libreria and other Buildings, Venice 239; London Architectural Motifs 301; Padua, Motifs of 336 A, 336 B, 336 C, 339; Palace, Bridge and Obelisk in the Background 310 A, 310 B; Pescheria Bridge and Buildings on the Quay 224; Prisons of Venice 227; Quay and St Mark's Square, Motifs of 223; Renaissance and Gothic Buildings and Church 272; Renaissance Palace and Roman Arch 270; Rialto Bridge after Palladio's Design 226; Rialto Bridge after Palladio's Design with St Mark's Basilica and a view of Palazzo Chiericati, Vicenza 330; River with Eton College Chapel 305; River with Palace, Church and Ruins 329; Roman Antiquity and English Landscape, Motifs of 308; Roman Ruins and the Colleoni Monument, Venice 240; Rome with the Colleoni Monument, Venice 16; Scala dei Giganti 238; Scuola di San Marco and the Church of Santi Giovanni e Paolo, Motifs of 316 A, 316 B; Staircase and Triumphal Arch from a Loggia 317; Triumphal Arch from the Portico of a Palace 271; Venetian Lagoon with Arch and a Church 199; Venetian Lagoon with Castle on a Bridge 327; Venetian Lagoon with Church and Column 200; Venetian Lagoon with Classical Ruins 314 A, 314 A, 314 B, 314 C; Venetian Lagoon with Classical Ruins and Statue 364; Venetian Lagoon with House, Church and Bell Tower 324 A, 324 B; Venetian Lagoon with Oval Church 268; Venetian Lagoon with Tomb 320 A, 320 B; Venetian Lagoon with Triumphal Arch 363; Venetian Lagoon with Triumphal Arch and Gothic Building 326; Vicenza and Rome, Motifs of 294 A, 294 B; Villa, Church and Column with a Statue 311
Chelsea College with Ranelagh House and the Rotunda 289
Church of the Redentore 104 A, 104 B, 258
Church of the Salute and Customs House from near Palazzo Cornaro 54
Church of Santi Giovanni e Paolo with the Scuola di San Marco 18, 22 A, 22 B, 110 A, 110 B
Church of San Geremia and the Entrance to Cannaregio 64 A, 64 B, 64 C
Church of San Giorgio: from the Harbour of St Mark's 108; from the Giudecca Canal 40

Church of San Giovanni dei Battuti, Murano, with Venice in the Background 255
Church of San Nicolò di Castello 131
Church of San Pietro di Castello 177 A, 177 B
Church of San Salvatore, Venice 233
Church of Santa Maria Zobenigo 130 A, 130 B
Church and School of the Carità from the Marble Workshop of San Vitale 33
Colosseum 216; with the Arch of Constantine 218
Customs House and the Giudecca Canal 37
Customs House Point 38, 189 A, 189 B

Dogana, *see* Customs House
Doge Visiting the Church of San Rocco 146
Doge's Palace, Façade 184
Doge's Palace: Courtyard from the First Floor Loggia 351
Dolo Locks 60 A, 60 B

Entrance to Cannaregio with the Church of San Geremia 79, 176 A, 176 B
Entrance to the Grand Canal: from the Piazzetta 47 A, 47 B, 47 C, 361; from the Quay, End of 142 A, 142 B, 142 C; towards the East 347 A, 347 B; towards the West 346; with the Church of the Salute 23 A, 23 B, 73, 88 A, 88 B, 151, 160, 237 A, 237 B, 237 C; with the Church of the Salute towards the East 173, 251; with the Customs House 171; with the Customs House and the Church of the Salute 44 A, 44 B, 70 A, 70 B, 70 C, 70 D, 135 A, 135 B
Eton College Chapel, Windsor 313

Festival at the Arzere di Santa Marta 231
Festival at Night at the Church of San Pietro di Castello 230 A, 230 B
Fish Market 47 B
Fondamenta Nuove and the Church of Santa Maria del Pianto 335
Fonteghetto della Farina 162 A, 162 B
French Ambassador Being Received at the Doge's Palace 31

Grand Canal: at Santa Chiara towards the Lagoon 78 A, 78 B; from Ca' Foscari towards the Church of the Carità 71 A, 71 B, 71 C; from Ca' da Mosto to the Rialto Bridge 118 A, 118 B, 118 C; from Campo della Carità towards Palazzo Venier della Torresella 115; from Campo Santa Sofia to the Rialto Bridge 228 A, 228 B; from Campo Santa Sofia to the Church of San Marcuola 179; from Campo San Vio 12 A, 12 B, 112 A, 112 B, 112 C, 112 D, 252; from Campo San Vio near the Rialto Bridge 13; from Campo San Vio towards the Church of the Salute 72 A, 72 B, 72 C, 72 D; from Campo San Vio towards the East 57; from Ca' Pesaro to the Church of San Marcuola 178; from Ca'

Pesaro to the Fondaco dei Tedeschi 95; from Ca' Rezzonico to Palazzo Balbi 91 A, 91 B; from the Church of San Simeone Piccolo to Cannaregio 169; from the Church of San Stae to the Fabbriche Nuove di Rialto 120 A, 120 B; from the Church of Santa Croce to the Church of San Geremia 98, 114; from the Church of the Scalzi to Cannaregio 121; from the Church of the Scalzi towards the Fondamenta della Croce with the Church of San Simeone Piccolo 170 A, 170 B; from Palazzo Balbi 42 A, 42 B, 42 C, 42 D; from Palazzo Balbi to the Rialto Bridge 93 A, 93 B, 93 C, 93 D; from Palazzo Bembo to Palazzo Vendramin Calergi 97; from Palazzo Contarini dagli Scrigni to Ca' Rezzonico 90 A, 90 B; from Palazzo Cornaro to Palazzo Contarini dagli Scrigni 89 A, 89 B; from Palazzo Corner Spinelli to the Rialto Bridge 92; from Palazzo Flangini towards San Marcuola 83 A, 83 B; from Palazzo Grimani to Ca' Foscari 248; from Palazzo Michiel dalle Colonne to the Fondaco dei Tedeschi 119 A, 119 B; from Palazzo Tiepolo to Ca' Foscari 116; from Palazzo Vendramin Calergi to Palazzo Fontana 96; from Palazzo Vendramin Calergi to Palazzo Michiel dalle Colonne 46 A, 46 B; from Palazzo Vendramin Calergi towards San Geremia 76; from the Rialto Bridge to Ca' Foscari 69 A, 69 B, 69 C, 69 D, 117, 172, 349; from the Rialto Bridge towards Ca' Foscari 138; from near the Rialto Bridge towards the North 55, 75 A, 75 B, 75 C, 253; towards the Church of the Salute 366; with the Church of San Simeone Piccolo towards the Fondamenta della Croce 77; with the Church of the Carità towards the Harbour of St Mark's 21, 41 A, 41 B; with the Church of the Salute and the Customs House from Campo Santa Maria Zobenigo 134 A, 134 B, 134 C, 134 D, 134 E; with the Fabbriche Nuove from near the Rialto Bridge 19 A, 19 B, 19 C; with the Rialto Bridge from the North 56, 74, 153 A, 153 B; with the Rialto Bridge from Palazzo Corner Spinelli 17; with the Rialto Bridge from the South 137
Grand Walk, Vauxhall Gardens, London 287
Greenwich Hospital, London, from across the Thames 275 A, 275 B

Harbour of St Mark's: from the Giudecca Canal 244; from the Piazzetta 152 A, 152 B; from the Riva degli Schiavoni 164; from the Riva degli Schiavoni towards the West 158, 341 A, 341 B, 362; towards the East 161 A, 161 B, 163; towards the West 192,

356 A, 356 B; with the Customs House from the Giudecca Point 36 A, 36 B, 36 C; with the Island of San Giorgio from the Piazzetta 26 A, 26 B, 34 A, 34 B
Henry VII's Chapel, Westminster Abbey: Interior 276 A, 276 B

Imaginary Funerary Monument: for Archbishop Tillotson 10; for Lord Somers 9
Imperial Ambassador Being Received at the Doge's Palace 61
Island of San Giorgio with the Customs House from the Entrance to the Grand Canal 43
Island of San Michele with Venice in the Background 306
Islands of San Cristoforo, San Michele and Murano from the Fondamenta Nuove 254, 365

King's College Chapel, Cambridge: Interior 277

Landscape with Ruins and a Renaissance Building 6
Loggetta of Sansovino 145
London through an Arch of Westminster Bridge 265
London and the Thames from Richmond House 260

Marghera Tower 198
Molo, *see* Quay (of St Mark's)

New Horse Guards from St James's Park 296 A, 296 B
Northumberland House, London 297

Old Horse Guards from St James's Park 281
Old Horse Guards and the Banqueting Hall, London, from St James's Park 280
Old Somerset House from the Thames 292
Old Walton Bridge 302, 315

Palazzo Corner della Ca' Grande 331
Palazzo Grimani 332
Palazzo Vendramin Calergi 334
Pantheon 207
Piazza Navona, Rome 215
Piazzetta: towards the Island of San Giorgio 45, 48; towards the Island of San Giorgio with View of the Basilica and the Doge's Palace 65; towards the Quay, 188; towards the South 139 A, 139 B, 139 C, 360; towards the Torre dell'Orologio 52, 86 A, 86 B, 86 C, 86 D, 359; towards the Torre dell'Orologio from the Libreria to the Doge's Palace 220; with the Doge's Palace and the Loggetta, View of 181; with the Libreria of St Mark's towards the West 111, 186 A, 186 B, 186 C
Prato della Valle, Padua, with the Churches of Santa Giustina and the Misericordia 210 A, 210 B, 210 C
Prisons 257
Punta della Dogana, *see* Customs House Point

Quay of St Mark's: and the Riva degli Schiavoni from the Harbour of St Mark's 35; from the Harbour of St

Mark's 87 A, 87 B, 87 C, 87 D, 132 A, 132 B, 132 C, 250, 274 A, 274 B; with the Doge's Palace and the Paglia Bridge 27; with the Doge's Palace and the Prisons towards the West 219; with the Doge's Palace, Right Side of 24, 66; with the Doge's Palace towards the Church of the Salute 82 A, 82 B; with the Doge's Palace towards the West 180 A, 180 B, 245 A, 245 B; with the Libreria and the San Teodoro Column towards the West 144 A, 144 B, 144 C, 345 A, 345 B; with the Libreria on the Right and the Church of the Salute towards the Left 80; with the Libreria towards the West 154

Quirinal Palace, Rome 214

Riva degli Schiavoni 25; towards the East 143 A, 143 B, 156, 247 A, 247 B, 343; towards St Mark's 39 A, 39 B; towards the West, 59; with the Doge's Palace towards the East 81

Rialto Bridge: from the Fondamenta del Vin 53; from the North 191 A, 191 B, 348 A, 348 B; from the South 58, 94 A, 94 B, 147 A, 147 B, 147 C, 242 A, 242 B, 242 C; with Palazzo dei Camerlenghi 20

Rio dei Mendicanti 14 A, 14 B, 14 C

Roman Forum with the Basilica of Constantine and the Church of Santa Francesca Romana 217 A, 217 B

Rotunda, Ranelagh: Interior 303A, 303 B

Roman Forum, Ruins of, with the Capitol in the Background 201 A, 201 B, 203

St John Lateran Square, Rome 211

St Mark's Basilica: and the Doge's Palace from the Procuratie Vecchie 141, 187; Interior 321, 322; Interior at Night 353; and a View of Palazzo Chiericati, Vicenza 330

St Mark's Square: from the Basilica towards the Church of San Geminiano 157 A, 157 B, 185 A, 185 B; from the Basilica towards the Church of San Geminiano and the Procuratie Nuove 85 A, 85 B, 136 A, 136 B; from Campo San Basso 342; from the Libreria to the Basilica towards the West 235; from the Libreria to the Loggetta 149, 295; from the Piazzetta towards the Procuratie Vecchie 148 A, 148 B; from the Portico of the Torre dell'Orologio 350 A, 350 B; towards the Basilica 63, 84 A, 84 B, 84 C, 84 D, 155 A, 155 B, 165 A, 165 B, 243 A, 243 B, 243 C; towards the Basilica from the North-west Corner 319; towards the Basilica from the Procuratie Nuove 49 A, 49 B; towards the Basilica from the South-west Corner 318, 352; towards the Church of San Geminiano from the Piazzetta 50; towards the Libreria between the

Basilica and the Church of San Geminiano 133 A, 133 B; towards the Procuratie Nuove with a View of the Church of San Geminiano 159; towards the Procuratie Vecchie from the Basilica 51; towards the Torre dell'Orologio 140 A, 140 B; with the Basilica 11 A, 11 B; with the Basilica, the Doge's Palace, the Loggetta and the Campanile, Views of 183; with the Basilica, view of, and the North-east Side 190 A, 190 B; with the Basilica, view of, towards the South 236; with the Doge's Palace and the Procuratie Nuove 340 A, 340 B; with the Torre dell'Orologio 150 A, 150 B

St Paul's Cathedral, London 300

Santa Chiara Canal at the Fondamenta della Croce 99A, 99 B, 99 C, 113

Scala dei Giganti in the Doge's Palace 323 A, 323 B, 323 C

Scuola di San Rocco 105 A, 105 B

Scuola di San Teodoro 234

Seaport with a Volcano Erupting 357

Self-portrait 259

Capitol Square, Rome 299 A, 299 B, 299 C

Study of Figures 28, 29, 30

Temple of Antoninus and Faustina, Rome 202 A, 202 B

Thames, the: from the Terrace of Somerset House with the City in the Background 285 A, 285 B; from the Terrace of Somerset House with Westminster Bridge in the Background 286 A, 286 B; from York Water Gate towards Westminster Bridge 264 A, 264 B; towards the City with St Paul's Cathedral in the Background 262; with Westminster Bridge in the Background 263

Tower of Marghera, see Marghera Tower

View: of the Brenta near Padua 208; of Alnwick Castle, Northumberland 293 A, 293 B; of Dolo 195 A, 195 B; of Mestre 194 A, 194 B; of Syon House, Middlesex 282; of Rome 7; Roman, imaginary 3, 8

Warwick Castle, East Front 291 A, 291 B

Warwick Castle, South Front 290 A, 290 B, 290 C

Westminster Abbey with the Procession of the Knights of the Order of the Bath 283

Westminster Bridge 304; with Lambeth Palace in the Background from the North 284 A, 284 B; from the North 267; Being Built 266

Whitehall and the Privy Garden: from Richmond House 261; towards the North 288

Windsor Castle, Panorama 273

Topographical index

ALBURY PARK (SURREY)
Duke of Northumberland's Collection
View of Alnwick Castle, Northumberland 293 A

ALLENTOWN (PENNSYLVANIA)
Art Museum
Piazzetta, with a View of the Doge's Palace and the Loggetta 181

ALNWICK CASTLE (NORTHUMBERLAND)
Duke of Northumberland's Collection
Northumberland House, London 297
St Mark's Square from the Libreria to the Loggetta 295
The Scala dei Giganti in the Doge's Palace 323 B
View of Alnwick Castle, Northumberland 293 B

ALTON (HAMPSHIRE)
Viscount Hampden's Collection
The Grand Canal from Palazzo Cornaro to Palazzo Contarini dagli Scrigni 89 B
Piazzetta with the Liberería towards the West 111

AMSTERDAM
Rijksmuseum
Rialto Bridge from the North 191 B

ANGLESEA ABBEY (CAMBRIDGE)
Lord Fairhaven Collection
Self-portrait 259

ANTWERP
Musée Smidt van Gelder
St Mark's Square from the Portico of the Torre dell'Orologio 350 B

ARTRAMONT (WEXFORD)
Neave Collection
Motifs of the Scuola di San Marco and the Church of Santi Giovanni e Paolo: a Capriccio 316 A
Entrance to the Grand Canal with the Church of the Salute 237 B
The Quay with the Doge's Palace towards the West 245 A
The Quirinal Palace, Rome 214
The Doge's Palace, Façade 184
Capitol Square and the Cordonata 299 B
Piazza Navona, Rome 215
St Mark's Square with the Torre dell'Orologio 150 B
The Piazzetta with the Libreria of St Mark's towards the West 186 A

ARUNDEL CASTLE (SUSSEX)
Duke of Norfolk's Collection
Triumphal Arch from the Portico of a Palace: a Capriccio 271
Renaissance and Gothic Buildings and Church: a Capriccio 272
The Quay from the Harbour of St Mark's 87 D
Renaissance Palace and Roman Arch: a capriccio 270

ASOLO
Museo Civico
Venetian Lagoon with Classical Ruins and a Statue: a Capriccio 364
Venetian Lagoon with Triumphal Arch: a Capriccio 363

ASTBURY HALL (SHROPSHIRE)
Jenks Collection
The Quay with the Libreria and the San Teodoro Column towards the West 144 B

ATHENS
Private collection
Festival at Night at the Church of San Pietro di Castello 230 B

BADMINTON HOUSE (GLOUCESTERSHIRE)
Duke of Beaufort's Collection
Badminton House from the Park 278
Badminton Park from the House 279

BALTIMORE (MARYLAND)
Museum of Art
The Venetian Lagoon with Classical Ruins: a Capriccio 314 B

BASINGSTOKE (HAMPSHIRE) (?)
Earl of Malmesbury's Collection
Old Horse Guards from St James's Park 281

BATSFORD PARK
Dulverton Collection
Grand Canal from Campo Santa Sofia to the Rialto Bridge 228 B

BERGAMO
Galleria dell'Accademia Carrara
Grand Canal from Ca' da Mosto to the Rialto Bridge 118 B
Grand Canal from Palazzo Balbi 42 B

Private collection
Arch of Septimius Severus 1

BERLIN
Gymnasium zum grauen Kloster
Campo di Rialto 229 A
Grand Canal from Campo Santa Sofia to the Rialto Bridge 228 A
Festival at the Arzere of Santa Marta 231
Festival at Night at the Church of San Pietro di Castello 230 A

Staatliche Museen – Gemäldegalerie – Dahlem
Church of the Salute and the Customs House near Palazzo Cornaro 54
The Quay with the Doge's Palace towards the Church of the Salute 82 A

BIRMINGHAM (ALABAMA)
Museum of Art
Grand Canal from Palazzo Vendramin Calergi to Palazzo Michiel dalle Colonne 46 A

BIRMINGHAM (WARWICKSHIRE)
Barber Institute of Fine Arts
Loggetta of Sansovino 145

BLOOMFIELD HILLS (MICHIGAN)
Booth Collection
St Mark's Basilica and the Doge's Palace from the Procuratie Vecchie 187

Museum of Cranbrook Academy of Art
St Mark's Square with Views of the Basilica and the Doge's Palace, the Loggetta and the Campanile 183

BOSTON (MASSACHUSETTS)
Alvan Fuller Collection
Grand Canal from the Rialto Bridge to Ca' Foscari 349
The Quay with the Libreria and the San Teodoro Column towards the West 345 B

Museum of Fine Arts
Fonteghetto della Farina 162 B
Harbour of St Mark's towards the East 161 A

BOWHILL (SELKIRK)
Duke of Buccleuch's Collection
Whitehall and the Privy Garden towards the North 288

BRYNKINALLT (DENBIGHSHIRE)
Lord Trevor Collection
Grand Walk, Vauxhall Gardens, London 287
The Ranelagh Rotunda: Interior 303 B

CAMBRIDGE
Fitzwilliam Museum
The Doge's Palace: Courtyard from the First Floor Loggia 351
St Mark's Square from the Portico of the Torre dell'Orologio 350 A

CAMBRIDGE (MASSACHUSETTS)
Fogg Art Museum
St Mark's Square towards the Basilica 165 A

... (CANADA)
Setterlee Ingalls Collection
Entrance to the Grand Canal towards the East 347 A

Sangster Collection
View of Mestre 194 A

CARDIFF (WALES)
National Museum of Wales
Harbour of St Mark's with the Customs House from the Giudecca Point 36 A

CASTAGNOLA (LUGANO)
Thyssen Foundation
Grand Canal from Campo San Vio 12 A
St Mark's Square with the Basilica 11 A

CHICAGO (ILLINOIS)
Epstein Collection
Venetian Lagoon with Classical Ruins: a Capriccio 314 A

CHILBOLTON (HAMPSHIRE)
Parrington Collection
Grand Canal from Ca' Pesaro to the Church of San Marcuola 178

CINCINNATI (OHIO)
Art Museum
Arch of Septimius Severus with the Church of Santi Martina e Luca, Rome 213
Grand Canal with the Church of the Salute and the Customs House from Campo Santa Maria Zobenigo 134 C

COLOGNE
Wallraf-Richartz-Museum
Colonnade and Courtyard: a Capriccio 355 D

DETROIT (MICHIGAN)
Institute of Arts
St Mark's Square from the Basilica towards the Church of San Geminiano 157 B

DRESDEN
Gemäldegalerie
Campo San Giacometto 62
Church of SS. Giovanni e Paolo with the Scuola di San Marco 18
Entrance to the Grand Canal with the Church of the Salute 23 A
Grand Canal from Campo San Vio 12 B
Grand Canal with the Rialto Bridge from Palazzo Corner Spinelli 17

DUBLIN
National Gallery of Ireland
St Mark's Square with the

Doge's Palace and the
    Procuratie Nuove 340 A

EL PASO (CALIFORNIA)
Museum of Art
*The Quay with the Doge's
    Palace towards the Church of
    the Salute 82 B*

EUSTON HALL
Lord O'Neill Collection
*Palazzo Corner della Ca' Grande
    331*

FLORENCE
Galleria degli Uffizi
*Grand Canal from Palazzo Balbi
    42 C*
*Venetian Lagoon with a House,
    Church and Bell Tower: a
    Capriccio 324 A*
*Venetian Lagoon with a Tomb:
    a Capriccio 320 A*
*The Quay from the Harbour of
    St Mark's 87 B*

FRANKFURT
Städelsches Kunstinstitut
*Harbour of St Mark's towards the
    West from the Riva degli
    Schiavoni 362*

GENEVA
Lyon Collection
*Entrance to the Grand Canal
    with the Church of the Salute
    160*
*Grand Canal with the Rialto
    Bridge from the North 153 B*

GOODWOOD (SUSSEX)
**Duke of Richmond and
Gordon's Collection**
*Grand Canal from near the
    Rialto Bridge towards the
    North 55*
*Grand Canal with the Rialto
    Bridge from the North 56*
*London and the Thames from
    Richmond House 260*
*Whitehall and the Privy Garden
    from Richmond House 261*

**GREAT BRITAIN
(VARIOUS LOCATIONS)**
Bacon Collection
Cannaregio 103 B
Bryant Collection
*Motifs of Roman Antiquity and
    English Landscape: a Capriccio
    308*
*English Landscape and
    Architectural Motifs: a
    Capriccio 307*

**Chatsworth Settlement and
the Devonshire Collection,
Trustees of**
*Entrance to the Grand Canal
    from the Piazzetta 47 C*
*Riva degli Schiavoni towards the
    West 59*

Kleinworth Collection
*Henry VII's Chapel, Westminster
    Abbey: Interior 276 A*

National Trust
*Chelsea College with Ranelagh
    House and the Rotunda 289*

**Duke of Northumberland's
Collection**
*Panorama of London through an
    Arch of Westminster Bridge
    265*
Panorama of Windsor Castle 273
*View of Syon House, Middlesex
    282*
*Westminster Bridge Being Built
    266*

Private collections
*Grand Canal from the Rialto
    Bridge to Ca' Foscari 69 D*
*Grand Canal toward the Church
    of the Salute from Campo San
    Vio 72 B; 72 C*

Church of San Geremia and the
    Entrance to Cannaregio 64 B
Imaginary Funerary Monument
    to Archbishop Tillotson 10
Customs House Point 189 B
Boat Race on the Grand Canal
    68 B, 175
The Bucintoro Returns to the
    Quay on Ascension Day 67 C

Earl of Sandwich's Collection
*Temple of Antoninus and
    Faustina, Rome 202 B*

Saumarez Collection
Classical Motifs: a Capriccio 337 C

Wilmot, Arthur, Trustees of
*Old Horse Guards and the
    Banqueting Hall, London,
    from St James's Park 280*

GRENOBLE
**Musée de Peinture et de
Sculpture**
*Entrance to the Grand Canal
    with the Customs House and
    the Church of the Salute 44 A*

HADDINGTON
**Duke of Hamilton and
Brandon's Collection**
*The Thames with Westminster
    Bridge in the Background,
    from the Terrace of Somerset
    House 286 B*

THE HAGUE
Thurkow Collection
*Harbour of St Mark's with the
    Island of San Giorgio from the
    Piazzetta 26 A*

HAMBURG
Kunsthalle
Motifs of Padua: a Capriccio 336 A

**HALSWELL PARK
(SOMERSET)**
Lord Wharton Collection
*St Mark's Square towards the
    Basilica from the South-west
    Corner 352*

HAMPSHIRE
Buxton Collection
*New Horse Guards from St
    James's Park 296 A*

**HAMPTON COURT
(MIDDLESEX)**
Royal Collections
*Colosseum with the Arch of
    Constantine 218*

**HAMSTEAD MARSHALL
(BERKSHIRE)**
Craven Collection
*Grand Canal with the Church of
    the Salute and the Customs
    House from Campo Santa
    Maria Zobenigo 134 A*
*St Mark's Square towards the
    Libreria between the Basilica
    and the Church of San
    Geminiano 133 A*
Rialto Bridge from the South 147 A

**HARTFORD
(CONNECTICUT)**
Wadsworth Atheneum
*Landscape with Ruins and a
    Renaissance Building 6*
*St Mark's Square with View of
    the Basilica and the North-east
    Side 190 A*

HAVANA (CUBA)
**Museo Nacional (or Private
collection)**
*Chelsea College with Ranelagh
    House and the Rotunda 289*

HERON COURT
**Earl of Malmesbury's
Collection**
*Harbour of St Mark's with the
    Customs House from the
    Giudecca Point 36 C*

**HILLBOROUGH
(THETFORD)**
Mills Collection
*Grand Canal from Ca' Rezzonico
    to Palazzo Balbi 91 B*
*Grand Canal from the Rialto
    Bridge to Ca' Foscari 69 C*

**HOLKHAM HALL
(NORFOLK)**
Earl of Leicester's Collection
*Bucintoro at the Quay on
    Ascension Day 174 B*
*Grand Canal from Campo San
    Vio towards the East 57*
Rialto Bridge from the South 58

HOUSTON (TEXAS)
Museum of Fine Arts
*Grand Canal from the Rialto
    Bridge to Ca' Foscari 69 B*
*Entrance to the Grand Canal
    with the Customs House and
    the Church of the Salute 70 B*

INDIANAPOLIS
John Herron Art Museum
*The Piazzetta towards the South
    139 C*

ITALY
Private collections
Bull Fight in St Mark's Square 354
*Campo Santa Maria Formosa
    101 C*
*Church of San Geremia and the
    Entrance to Cannaregio 64 C*
*Motifs of Vicenza and Rome: a
    Capriccio 294 A*
Scuola di San Rocco 105 B

KANSAS CITY
**William Rockhill Nelson
Gallery of Art**
*St Mark's Square towards the
    Torre dell'Orologio 140 A*

LEIPZIG
**Museum der bildenden
Künste**
*Island of the Venetian Lagoon
    and Motifs of the Church of
    San Francesco della Vigna: a
    Capriccio 196*
*Island of the Venetian Lagoon
    and a Church: a Capriccio 197*

LENINGRAD
Hermitage
*Church of San Giovanni dei
    Battuti, Murano, with Venice
    in the Background 255*
*French Ambassador Being
    Received at the Doge's
    Palace 31*
*Islands of San Cristoforo, San
    Michele and Murano from the
    Fondamenta Nuove 254*
*Rialto Bridge from the
    Fondamenta del Vin 53*

LOCKINGE (BERKSHIRE)
Lloyd Collection
Palazzo Vendramin Calergi 334

LONDON
**Lord Astor of Hever
Collection**
*South Front of Warwick Castle
    290 C*

Bisgood Collection
*Rialto Bridge from the South
    242 B*
*St Mark's Square towards the
    Basilica 243 A*

Lord Brownlow Collection
*Campo Santi Giovanni e Paolo
    with the Colleoni Monument
    246 A*
*Prato della Valle, Padua, with
    the Churches of Santa
    Giustina and the Misericordia
    210 A*

Burns Collection
*Greenwich Hospital, London,
    from across the Thames 275 B*

Clifford Curzon Collection
St John Lateran Square, Rome 211

**Dulwich College Picture
Gallery**
*Bucintoro Returning to the Quay
    on Ascension Day 232*
Old Walton Bridge 302

Embiricos Collection
*Harbour of St Mark's towards
    the West 192*

**Property of William
Hallsborough**
*Classical Ruins and a Gothic
    Building: a Capriccio 325*
*Venetian Lagoon with Triumphal
    Arch and a Gothic Building:
    a Capriccio 326*

Joel Collection
*Grand Canal from Campo San
    Vio 252*
*Grand Canal from near the
    Rialto Bridge towards the
    North 253*

Leggatt Collection
Church of the Redentore 104 B

**George Leon Collection
(Executors)**
*Grand Canal from Palazzo Balbi
    to the Rialto Bridge 93 B*

Lindsay-Fynn Collection
*Church of San Pietro di Castello
    177 B*

London Museum
*Henry VII's Chapel, Westminster
    Abbey: Interior 276 B*

**Lord Lucas and Dingwall
Collection**
*The Quay with the Doge's
    Palace towards the West 180 A*

Lyons Collection
*Church of Santi Giovanni e Paolo
    with the Scuola di San Marco
    22 B*
*Grand Canal with the Fabbriche
    Nuove from the Vicinity of the
    Rialto Bridge 19 B*

Martin Collection
*Arch of Constantine with the
    Colosseum 212*

Matthiesen Property (?)
*Church of Santi Giovanni e Paolo
    with the Scuola di San Marco
    110 A*

National Gallery
*Bucintoro Leaving the Quay on
    Ascension Day 167*
*Church of San Pietro di Castello
    177 A*
*Church and School of the Carità
    from the Marble Workshop of
    San Vitale 33*
*Doge Visiting the Church of San
    Rocco 146*
*Entrance to Cannaregio with the
    Church of San Geremia 176 A*
Eton College Chapel, Windsor 313
*Grand Canal from the Church of
    the Scalzi toward the
    Fondamenta della Croce with
    the Church of San Simeone
    Piccolo 170 A*
*Ranelagh Rotunda: Interior
    303 A*
Palazzo Grimani 332
*Regatta on the Grand Canal
    106 B, 168*
*St Mark's Square towards the
    Basilica from the North-west
    Corner 319*
*St Mark's Square towards the
    Basilica from the South-west
    Corner 318*

**National Loan Collection
Trust**
*Colonnade and Courtyard: a
    Capriccio 355 C*

National Maritime Museum
*Greenwich Hospital, London,
    from across the Thames 275 A*

**Collection of the Princess
Royal**
*River with Eton College Chapel:
    a Capriccio 305*

Private collections
Ca' Pesaro 333
Church of the Redentore 258
*Church of San Giorgio from the
    Harbour of St Mark's 108*
Customs House Point 189 A
*Grand Canal from Campo San
    Vio 112 C*
The Piazzetta towards the Quay 188
Prisons 257
*The Quay from the Harbour of St
    Mark's 132 B*
Study of figures 28, 29, 30
View of the Brenta near Padua 208

**Queen's Gallery,
Buckingham Palace**
*Convent of the Carità, Venice:
    a Capriccio 225*
*St Mark's Square from the
    Libreria to the Basilica
    towards the West 235*

Railing Collection
*The Quay with the Libreria and
    San Teodoro Column towards
    the West 144 C*
*Riva delgi Schiavoni towards the
    East 143 B*

Sabin Collection
Campo dell'Arsenale 182

Samuel Collection
*St Mark's Square towards the
    Libreria between the Basilica
    and the Church of San
    Geminiano 133 B*

Skrine Collection
Old Walton Bridge 315

Soane Museum
*Rialto Bridge from the North
    191 A*
*Riva degli Schiavoni towards St
    Mark's 39 B*
*St Mark's Square with View of
    the Basilica and the North-east
    Side 190 B*

Speelman Collection
*The Piazzetta towards the South
    139 B*
*The Piazzetta towards the Torre
    dell'Orologio 86 C*
*St Mark's Square towards the
    Basilica 155 B*
*Venetian Lagoon with a Castle
    on a Bridge: a Capriccio 327*

Stuart Collection
*Rialto Bridge from the South
    147 C*

Wallace Collection
*Entrance to the Grand Canal
    from the End of the Quay
    142 C*
*Grand Canal towards the Church
    of the Carita from Ca' Foscari
    71 B*
*Grand Canal from the Church of
    San Simeone Piccolo to
    Cannaregio 169*
*Grand Canal from Palazzo
    Flangini towards San
    Marcuola 83 A*
*Harbour of St Mark's towards the
    East 163*
*Harbour of St Mark's from the
    Riva degli Schiavoni 164*
*The Quay with the Doge's
    Palace towards the West 245 B*
*Rialto Bridge from the South
    94 B*
*Riva degli Schiavoni towards the
    East 247 A*
*St Mark's Square from the
    Basilica towards the Church of
    San Geminiano and the
    Procuratie Nuove 136 B*
*Santa Chiara Canal at the
    Fondamenta della Croce 99 B*

Ward Collection
Campo di Rialto 229 B
Scuola di San Teodoro 234

Warde Collection
Grand Canal from Palazzo Balbi 42 D

Westminster Abbey
Westminster Abbey with the Procession of the Knights of the Order of the Bath 283

Wharton Collection
Grand Canal from Ca' da Mosto to the Rialto Bridge 118 C

LONDON (?)
Douglas-Pennant Collection
The Thames from York Water Gate towards Westminster Bridge 264 B

Lady Dupree Collection
Motifs of Padua: a Capriccio 336 B

Lord Egerton of Tatton's Collection
The Quay with the Libreria on the Right and the Church of the Salute towards the Left 80
Riva degli Schiavoni with the Doge's Palace towards the East 81

Hall Collection
Venetian Lagoon with an Arch and a Church: a Capriccio 199
Venetian Lagoon with a Church and a Column: a Capriccio 200

Korda Collection
Entrance to the Grand Canal with the Customs House 171

Brian Mountain Collection
Motifs of the Scuola di San Marco and the Church of Santi Giovanni e Paolo: a Capriccio 316 B

Earl of Strathcona's Collection
Westminster Bridge with Lambeth Palace in the Background, from the North 284 A

Arthur Tooth, Property of
Entrance to the Grand Canal with the Church of the Salute 1
Harbour of St Mark's from the Piazzetta 152 A

Wood Collection
The Thames from York Water Gate towards Westminster Bridge 264 A

MELBOURNE
National Gallery of Victoria
Ruins of the Roman Forum with the Capitol in the Background 201 B

MEMPHIS (TENNESSEE)
Brooks Memorial Art Gallery
Grand Canal from Campo San Vio towards the Church of the Salute 72 D

MEXICO CITY
Gavito Collection
Capitol Square and the Cordonata, Rome 299 A

Pagliai Collection
Scala dei Giganti in the Doge's Palace 323 A

MILAN
Campanini Bonomi Collection
Roman Forum with the Basilica of Constantine and the Church of Santa Francesca Romana 217 A

Borletti Collection
Grand Canal from Palazzo

Vendramin Calergi to Palazzo Michiel dalle Colonne 46 B
St Mark's Square from the Piazzetta towards the Procuratie Vecchie 148 A

Conti Collection (?)
Rialto Bridge after Palladio's Design, the Basilica of St Mark's and a View of Palazzo Chiericati, Vicenza: a Capriccio 330

Aldo Crespi Collection
Bucintoro Returning to the Quay on Ascension Day 67 B
Imperial Ambassador being Received at the Doge's Palace 61

Mario Crespi Collection
Bucintoro returning to the Quay on Ascension Day 109 B
Customs House and the Giudecca Canal 37
Grand Canal from Campo San Vio near the Rialto Bridge 13
Grand Canal from Palazzo Balbi to the Rialto Bridge 93 D
Grand Canal at Santa Chiara towards the Lagoon 78 B
Harbour of St Mark's with the Island of San Giorgio from the Piazzetta 34 A
Rio dei Mendicanti 14 A

Museo Poldi Pezzoli
Classical Motifs: a Capriccio 337 A
Prato della Valle, Padua, with the Churches of Santa Giustina and the Misericordia 210 B

Pinacoteca di Brera
Grand Canal from Campo San Vio 112 D
The Quay from the Harbour of St Mark's 132 C

Private collections
Bucintoro returning to the Quay on Ascension Day 67 D
Campo Santi Apostoli 128
Campo San Francesco della Vigna 129 A
Campo dei Gesuiti 124
Church of San Francesco della Vigna, Venice: a Capriccio 241
Church of San Niccolò di Castello 131
Classical Ruins: a Capriccio 15
Grand Canal from Campo San Vio 112 A
Grand Canal from the Church of San Stae to the Fabbriche Nuove di Rialto 120 A
Grand Canal from the Church of the Scalzi to Cannaregio 121
Grand Canal from Palazzo Tiepolo to Ca' Foscari 116

Rasini Collection
Harbour of St Mark's with the Island of San Giorgio from the Piazzetta 26 B

MILTON PARK (PETERBOROUGH)
Fitzwilliam Collection
Grand Canal with the Rialto Bridge from the North 153 A
Harbour of St Mark's from the Riva degli Schievoni towards the West 158
Harbour of St Mark's towards the East 161 B
The Quay with the Libreria towards the West 154
Riva degli Schiavoni towards East 156
St Mark's Square from the Basilica towards the Church of San Geminiano 157 A
St Mark's Square towards the Basilica 155 A
St Mark's Square towards the Procuratie Nuove with a View

of the Church of San Geminiano 159

MINNEAPOLIS
Institute of Arts
Old Somerset House from the Thames 292

Jones Collection
Grand Canal from Palazzo Flangini towards San Marcuola 83 B

MONTREAL
Pillow Collection
Church of Santi Giovanni e Paolo with the Scuola di San Marco 22 A
Grand Canal with the Church of the Carità towards the Harbour of St Mark's 21
Grand Canal with the Fabbriche Nuove near the Rialto Bridge 19 A
Rialto Bridge with Palazzo dei Camerlenghi 20

Museum of Fine Arts
St Mark's Basilica: Interior 322

MOSCOW
Pushkin Museum
Bucintoro Returns to the Quay on Ascension Day 32

MUNICH
Alte Pinakothek
The Quay from the Harbour of St Mark's 250

Bayerische Staatsgemäldesammlungen
Entrance to the Grand Canal with the Church of the Salute towards the East 251
St Mark's Square with the Basilica 11 B

NEW JERSEY
Rionda Braga Collection
London Architectural Motifs: a Capriccio 301

NEW YORK
Bracaglia Collection (?)
Arch of Constantine 2

Brandt Collection
Venetian Lagoon with Classical Ruins: a Capriccio 312

Erlanger Collection
Harbour of St Mark's towards the West from the Riva degli Schiavoni 341 A

Fonda Collection
Venetian Lagoon with an Oval Church: a Capriccio 268

Knoedler Property
Harbour of St Mark's from the Piazzetta 152 B

Metropolitan Museum of Art
Entrance to the Grand Canal from the Piazzetta 47 B

Rosenberg and Stiebel Collection
Entrance to the Grand Canal with the Church of the Salute 88 D

Stewart Property
Grand Canal with the Church of the Salute and the Customs House from Campo Santa Maria Zobenigo 134 B

Weitzner Collection
The Piazzetta towards the Torre dell'Orologio 86 B

NEW YORK (?)
Schaeffer Property
Prisons of Venice: a Capriccio 227

NOVARA
Poss Collection
Entrance to the Grand Canal

with the Customs House and the Church of the Salute 70 C
Grand Canal from near the Rialto Bridge towards the North 75 C

OAKLY PARK (SHROPSHIRE)
Earl of Plymouth Collection
Imaginary Funerary Monument for Lord Somers 9

OTTAWA
National Gallery of Canada
Campo dell'Arsenale 358
Campo San Giacometto 344
The Piazzetta towards the Torre dell'Orologio 359
St Mark's Square with the Torre dell'Orologio 150 A

OXFORD
Ashmolean Museum
Dolo Locks 60 A
Entrance to the Grand Canal with the Customs House and the Church of the Salute 135 B

PALM BEACH (FLORIDA)
Norton Gallery
Campo Santi Giovanni e Paolo with the Colleoni Monument 193 B

PARIS
Musée Cognacq-Jay
Grand Canal from near the Rialto Bridge towards the North 75 B
Santa Chiara Canal at the Fondamenta della Croce 99 C

Musée Jacquemart-André
Rialto Bridge from the South 242 C
St Mark's Square towards the Basilica 243 C

Musée National du Louvre
Entrance to the Grand Canal with the Church of the Salute 23 B

PENRHYN CASTLE (WALES)
Douglas-Pennant Collection
Campo Santo Stefanin 166
St Mark's Square towards the Basilica 84 D

PHILADELPHIA
J. Johnson Art Collection
Harbour of St Mark's towards the West 356 B
Rialto Bridge from the North 348 B

Museum of Art
Bucintoro at the Quay on Ascension Day 249

PILLNITZ (DRESDEN)
Castle
Grand Canal with the Fabbrich Nuove from the Vicinity of the Rialto Bridge 19 C
Grand Canal from Palazzo Balbi 42 A

PRAGUE
Nàrodni Galerie
Colonnade and Courtyard: a Capriccio 355 B
The Thames with Westminster Bridge in the Background 263
The Thames towards the City with St Paul's Cathedral in the Background 262

PRINCETON (NEW JERSEY)
University
Harbour of St Mark's towards the West 356 A

RALEIGH (NORTH CAROLINA)
State Art Museum
Church of San Giorgio Maggiore and the Rialto Bridge: a Capriccio 269

RINGWOOD (HAMPSHIRE)
Mills Collection
Entrance to the Grand Canal from the Piazzetta 361
The Piazzetta towards the South 360

Earl of Normanton's Collection
Grand Canal from Palazzo Grimani to Ca' Foscari 248
Riva degli Schiavoni towards the East 247 B

ROME
Accademia di San Luca
Staircase and Triumphal Arch from a Loggia: a Capriccio 317

Albertini Collection
Motifs of Vicenza and Rome: a Capriccio 294 B
The Quay with the Libreria and the San Teodoro Column towards the West 144 A
Riva degli Schiavoni towards the East 143 A

Galleria Borghese
Colosseum 216
Roman Forum with the Basilica of Constantine and the Church of Santa Francesca Romana 217 B

Galleria Nazionale
Grand Canal with the Rialto Bridge from the South 137
Grand Canal from the Rialto Bridge toward Ca' Foscari 138
The Piazzetta towards the South 139 A
St Mark's Square from the Basilica towards the Church of San Geminiano and the Procuratie Nuove 136 A

Rocchetti Collection
Entrance to the Grand Canal with the Customs House and the Church of the Salute 70 D

SÃO PAULO
Matarazzo Collection
Grand Canal from Campo San Vio 112 B
The Quay from the Harbour of St Mark's 132 A

SARASOTA (FLORIDA)
Ringling Museum of Art
Riva degli Schiavoni towards the East 343
St Mark's Square from Campo San Basso 342

SCHWERIN
Staatliche Museum
Grand Canal with the Church of the Salute and the Customs House from Campo Santa Maria Zobenigo 134 D

SNAIGOW (PERTHSHIRE)
Earl of Cadogan's Collection
Campo Santa Maria Formosa 101 B
Palace, Bridge and Obelisk in the Background: a Capriccio 310 B
The Quay from the Harbour of St Mark's 87 C
Villa, Church and a Column with a Statue: a Capriccio 311

SPRINGFIELD (MASSACHUSETTS)
Museum of Fine Arts
Farm, Portal and Washing Pool: a Capriccio 328
River with Palace, Church, and Ruins: a Capriccio 329

STOCKHOLM
National Museum
Grand Canal from Ca' Foscari towards the Church of the Carità 71 C

STOWELL PARK (GLOUCESTERSHIRE)
Vestey Collection
The Thames with the City in the Background from the Terrace of Somerset House 285 B
Westminster Bridge with Lambeth Palace in the Background from the North 284

STRASBOURG
Kauffman Collection
Entrance to the Grand Canal with the Customs House and the Church of the Salute 44 B

SUSSEX
Dunkels Collection
Brenta Canal at the Portello of Padua 209 B
Dolo Locks 60 B

Clarke Collection
Island of San Michele with Venice in the Background 306

TISSINGTON HALL (DERBYSHIRE)
Fitzherbert Collection
Church of San Geremia and the Entrance to Cannaregio 64 A

TITSEY PARK (SURREY)
Leveson-Gower Collection
Entrance to the Grand Canal towards the East 347 A
Entrance to the Grand Canal towards the West 346
The Quay with the Libreria and the San Teodoro Column towards the West 345 A
Rialto Bridge from the North 348 A

TOLEDO (OHIO)
Museum of Art
The Quay and the Riva degli Schiavoni from the Harbour of St Mark's 35

TORONTO
Art Gallery
Harbour of St Mark's with the Island of San Giorgio from the Piazzetta 34 B

TURIN
Galleria Sabauda
The Quay with the Doge's Palace and the Paglia Bridge 27

Private Collections
Bucintoro at the Quay on Ascension Day 174 A
Grand Canal from the Church of the Scalzi toward the Fondamenta della Croce with the Church of San Simeone Piccolo 170 B

UPTON HOUSE (WARWICKSHIRE)
National Trust
Harbour of St Mark's with the Customs House from the Giudecca Point 36 B

USA
Mellon Collection (?)
St Paul's Cathedral, London 300

Private Collections
Grand Canal with the Church of the Carità towards the Harbour of St. Mark's 41 A
The Piazzetta towards the Island of San Giorgio with the Basilica and the Doge's Palace 65
The Quay with Right Side of the Doge's Palace 66

VAN WULFFTEN PALTHE (OLDENZAAL)
Ten Cate Collection
The Piazzetta towards the Island of San Giorgio 45
St Mark's Square towards the Basilica from the Procuratie Nuove 49 B

VENICE
Brass Collection
View of Dolo 195 A

Ca' Rezzonico
Entrance to the Grand Canal with the Customs House and the Church of the Salute 135 A
Grand Canal with the Church of the Salute and the Customs House from Campo Santa Maria Zobenigo 134 E

Cini Collection
Classical Ruins: a Capriccio 4, 5
Grand Canal from Palazzo Michiel dalle Colonne to the Fondaco dei Tedeschi 119 B

Friedenburg Collection
Prato della Valle, Padua, with the Churches of Santa Giustina and the Misericordia 210 C

Gallerie dell'Accademia
Colonnade and a Courtyard: a Capriccio 355 A
Classical Motifs: a Capriccio 337 B
Motifs of Padua: a Capriccio 336

Giustiniani Collection
Fonteghetto della Farina 162 A

VIENNA
Kunsthistorisches Museum
Customs House Point 38
Riva degli Schiavoni towards St Mark's 39 A

WAKEHURST PLACE (SUSSEX)
Price Collection
Harbour of St Mark's from the Giudecca Canal 244
St Mark's Square towards the Basilica 243 B

WARWICK CASTLE (WARWICKSHIRE)
Earl of Warwick's Collection
East Front of Warwick Castle 291 A, 291 B
South Front of Warwick Castle 290 A, 290 B

WASHINGTON
National Gallery of Arts
Church of Santi Giovanni e Paolo with the Scuola di San Marco 110 B
Entrance to the Grand Canal from the End of the Quay 142 A
St Mark's Basilica and the Doge's Palace from the Procuratie Vecchie 141

WENDOVER (BUCKINGHAMSHIRE)
Barlow Collection
St Mark's Square towards the Basilica 84 B

WINDSOR CASTLE (BERKSHIRE)
Royal Collections
The Arch of Constantine 204
The Arch of Septimius Severus 205
The Arch of Titus 206
Bucintoro returning to the Quay on Ascension Day 67 A
Campo Santi Giovanni e Paolo with the Colleoni Monument 193 A
Grand Canal at Santa Chiara towards the Lagoon 78 A
Grand Canal with the Rialto Bridge from the North 74
Grand Canal with the Church of the Carità towards the Harbour of St Mark's 41 B
Grand Canal with the Church of San Simeone Piccolo towards the Fondamenta della Croce 77
Grand Canal from the Rialto Bridge to Ca' Foscari 69 A
Grand Canal from Ca' Foscari towards the Church of the Carità 71 A
Grand Canal towards the Church of the Salute 366
Grand Canal from Campo San Vio towards the Church of the Salute 72 A
Grand Canal from near the Rialto Bridge towards the North 75 A
Grand Canal from Palazzo Vendramin Calergi towards San Geremia 76
Rialto Bridge after Palladio's Design: a Capriccio 226
Horses of St Mark's: a Capriccio 221
Pescheria Bridge and Buildings on the Quay: a Capriccio 224
Church of San Giorgio Maggiore: a Capriccio 222
Libreria and other Venetian Buildings: a Capriccio 239
Scala dei Giganti: a Capriccio 238
Motifs of the Quay and St Mark's Square: a Capriccio 223
Motifs of Padua 339
Classical Ruins and Paduan Motifs: a Capriccio 338
Roman Ruins and the Venetian Monument to Colleoni: a Capriccio 240
Entrance to Cannaregio with the Church of San Geremia 79
Entrance to the Grand Canal with the Church of the Salute 73, 237 A
Entrance to the Grand Canal with the Customs House and the Church of the Salute 70 A
Entrance to the Grand Canal from the End of the Quay 142 B
Entrance to the Grand Canal from the Piazzetta 47 A
Island of San Giorgio with the Customs House from the Entrance to the Grand Canal 43
Islands of San Cristoforo, San Michele, and Murano from the Fondamenta Nuove 365
The Quay with the Doge's Palace and the Prisons towards the West 219
Pantheon 207
St Mark's Basilica: Interior 321
St Mark's Basilica at Night: Interior 353
St Mark's Square towards the Basilica from the Procuratie Nuove 49 A
St Mark's Square towards the Church of San Geminiano from the Piazzetta 50
St Mark's Square towards the Procuratie Vecchie from the Basilica 51
St Mark's Square with a view of the Basilica towards the South 236
The Piazzetta towards the Island of San Giorgio 48
The Piazzetta towards the Torre dell'Orologio 52
The Piazzetta towards the Torre dell'Orologio from the Libreria to the Doge's Palace 220
The Piazzetta towards the Island of San Giorgio 48
Regatta on the Grand Canal 68 A
Bucintoro returning to the Quay on Ascension Day 67 A
Ruins of the Roman Forum with the Capitol in the Background 201 A, 203
Temple of Antoninus and Faustina, Rome 202 A
The Thames with the City in the Background from the Terrace of Somerset House 285 A
The Thames with Westminster Bridge in the Background from the Terrace of Somerset House 286 A

WOBURN ABBEY (BEDFORDSHIRE)
Duke of Bedford's Collection
Arsenal Bridge 100
Bucintoro leaving the Quay on Ascension Day 107 A
Campo Santa Maria Formosa 101 A

Campo Santo Stefano 102
Cannaregio 103 A
Church of the Rendentore 104 A
Grand Canal from Ca' Pesaro to the Fondaco dei Tedeschi 95
Grand Canal from Ca' Rezzonico to Palazzo Balbi 91 A
Grand Canal from the Church of Santa Croce to the Church of San Geremia 98
Grand Canal from Palazzo Balbi to the Rialto Bridge 93 A
Grand Canal from Palazzo Bembo to Palazzo Vendramin Calergi 97
Grand Canal from Palazzo Contarini dagli Scrigni to Ca Rezzonico 90 A
Grand Canal from Palazzo Cornaro to Palazzo Contarini dagli Scrigni 89 A
Grand Canal from Palazzo Corner Spinelli to the Rialto Bridge 92
Grand Canal from Palazzo Vendramin Calergi to Palazzo Fontana 96
Entrance to the Grand Canal with the Church of the Salute 88 A
The Piazzetta towards the Torre dell'Orologio 86 A
Arsenale Bridge 100
The Quay from the Harbour of St Mark's 87 A
Regatta on the Grand Canal 106 A
Rialto Bridge from the South 94 A
St Mark's Square from the Basilica towards the Church of San Geminiano and the Procuratie Nuove 85 A
St Mark's Square towards the Basilica 84 A
Santa Chiara Canal at the Fondamenta della Croce 99 A
Scuola di San Rocco 105 A

WORCESTER (MASSACHUSETTS)
Art Museum
Round Domed Church: a Capriccio 298

ZURICH
Bührle Collection
Grand Canal from the Rialto Bridge to Ca' Foscari 172
Entrance to Cannaregio with the Church of San Geremia 176 B
Entrance to the Grand Canal with the Church of the Salute towards the East 173

ZURICH (?)
Property of Brown, Boveri and Co.
St Mark's Square from the Libreria to the Loggetta 149

DESTROYED WORK
Bucintoro Leaving the Quay on Ascension Day 107 B

WHEREABOUTS UNKNOWN
Brenta Canal at the Portello of Padua 209 A
Bucintoro at the Quay on Ascension Day 256
Bucintoro returning to the Quay on Ascension Day 109 A
Campo di Rialto 229 C
Campo San Francesco della Vigna 129 B
Campo San Geremia 123
Campo San Polo 126
Campo San Salvatore 127
Campo Santa Margherita 125
Campo Sant'Angelo 122
Campo Santi Giovanni e Paolo with the Colleoni Monument 246 B
Capitol Square, Rome 299 C
Church of San Giorgio from the Giudecca Canal 40
Church of San Salvatore, Venice 233
Church of Santa Maria Zobenigo 130 A, 130 B
Church, Ruined and the Venetian Monument to Colleoni: a Capriccio 309
Dolo, View of 195 B
Entrance to the Grand Canal with the Church of the Salute 237 C
Fondamenta Nuove and the Church of Santa Maria del Pianto 335
Grand Canal from Ca' da Mosto to the Rialto Bridge 118 A
Grand Canal from Campo della Carità toward Palazzo Venier della Torresella 115
Grand Canal from Campo Santa Sofia to the Church of San Marcuola 179
Grand Canal from the Church of San Stae to the Fabbriche Nuove di Rialto 120 B
Grand Canal from the Church of Santa Croce to the Church of San Geremia 114
Grand Canal from Palazzo Balbi to the Rialto Bridge 93 C
Grand Canal from Palazzo Contarini dagli Scrigni to Ca' Rezzonico 90 B
Grand Canal from Palazzo Michiel dalle Colonne to the Fondaco dei Tedeschi 119 A
Grand Canal from the Rialto Bridge to Ca' Foscari 117
Harbour of St Mark's towards the West from the Rivà degli Schiavoni 341 A
King's College Chapel, Cambridge: Interior 277
Marghera Tower 198
Mestie, View of 194 B
New Horse Guards from St James's Park 296 A
Palace, Bridge and Obelisk in the Background: a Capriccio 310 A
The Piazzetta towards the Torre dell'Orologio 86 D
The Piazzetta with the Libreria towards the West 186 B, 186 C
The Quay with the Right Side of the Doge's Palace 24
The Quay with the Doge's Palace, towards the West 180 B
The Quay from the Harbour of St Mark's 274 A, 274 A
Rialto Bridge from the South 147 B, 242 A
Rio dei Mendicanti 14 B, 14 C
Riva degli Schiavoni 25
Rome, View of 7
Rome, Imaginary View of 3, 8
Rome, View of, with the Venetian Monument to Colleoni: a Capriccio 16
St Mark's Square from the Basilica towards the Church of San Geminiano 185 A, 185 B
St Mark's Square from the Basilica towards the Church of San Geminiano and the Procuratie Nuove 85 B
St Mark's Square towards the Piazzetta towards the Procuratie Vecchie 148 B
St Mark's Square towards the Basilica 63, 84 C, 165 B
St Mark's Square towards the Torre dell'Orologio 140 B
St Mark's Square with the Doge's Palace and the Procuratie Nuove 240 B
Santa Chiara Canal at the Fondamenta della Croce 113
Scala dei Giganti in the Doge's Palace 323 C
Seaport with a Volcano Erupting 357
Venetian Lagoon with a House, Church and Bell Tower: a Capriccio 324 B
Venetian Lagoon with Classical Ruins: a Capriccio 314 C
Venetian Lagoon with Tomb: a Capriccio 320 B
Westminster Bridge 304
Westminster Bridge from the North 267